The Collapse of the Soviet Union

Other Books in the Turning Points Series:

Turning|Points

IN WORLD HISTORY

The Collapse of the Soviet Union

David L. Bender, *Publisher*
Bruno Leone, *Executive Editor*
Bonnie Szumski, *Series Editor*
Paul A. Winters, *Book Editor*

Greenhaven Press, Inc., San Diego, California

Every effort has been made to trace the owners of copyrighted material. The articles in this volume may have been edited for content, length, and/or reading level. The titles have been changed to enhance the editorial purpose.

Library of Congress Cataloging-in-Publication Data

The collapse of the Soviet Union / Paul A. Winters, book editor.
    p.   cm. — (Turning points in world history)
  Includes bibliographical references and index.
  ISBN 1-56510-997-X (lib. : alk. paper). — ISBN 1-56510-996-1
(pbk. : alk. paper)
  1. Soviet Union—Politics and government—1953–1985.
2. Soviet Union—Politics and government—1985–1991. 3. Russia
(Federation)—Politics and government—1991–   I. Winters, Paul
A., 1965–   . II. Series: Turning points in world history
(Greenhaven Press)
DK274.C59   1999
947.085—dc21   98-17506
                                                                         CIP

Cover photo: Reuters/Corbis-Bettmann

©1999 by Greenhaven Press, Inc.
P.O. Box 289009, San Diego, CA 92198-9009

Printed in the U.S.A.

Contents

Communist regimes in Eastern Europe and the Soviet Union. The Russian republic elections of July 1991 brought to power democratic politicians, including Boris Yeltsin, whose stated goal was the end of Soviet rule.

Chapter 4: Collapse of the Union

Chapter 5: Strife in the Former Union

of ethnic refugees. As an independent state, Azerbaijan is experiencing difficulty assimilating these refugees.

Foreword

Certain past events stand out as pivotal, as having effects and outcomes that change the course of history. These events are often referred to as turning points. Historian Louis L. Snyder provides this useful definition:

> A turning point in history is an event, happening, or stage which thrusts the course of historical development into a different direction. By definition a turning point is a great event, but it is even more—a great event with the explosive impact of altering the trend of man's life on the planet.

History's turning points have taken many forms. Some were single, brief, and shattering events with immediate and obvious impact. The invasion of Britain by William the Conqueror in 1066, for example, swiftly transformed that land's political and social institutions and paved the way for the rise of the modern English nation. By contrast, other single events were deemed of minor significance when they occurred, only later recognized as turning points. The assassination of a little-known European nobleman, Archduke Franz Ferdinand, on June 28, 1914, in the Bosnian town of Sarajevo was such an event; only after it touched off a chain reaction of political-military crises that escalated into the global conflict known as World War I did the murder's true significance become evident.

Other crucial turning points occurred not in terms of a few hours, days, months, or even years, but instead as evolutionary developments spanning decades or even centuries. One of the most pivotal turning points in human history, for instance—the development of agriculture, which replaced nomadic hunter-gatherer societies with more permanent settlements—occurred over the course of many generations. Still other great turning points were neither events nor developments, but rather revolutionary new inventions and innovations that significantly altered social customs and ideas, military tactics, home life, the spread of knowledge, and the human condition in general. The developments of writing, gunpowder, the printing press, antibiotics, the electric light, atomic energy, television, and the computer, the last two of which have recently ushered in the world-altering information age, represent only some of these innovative turning points.

Each anthology in the Greenhaven Turning Points in World History series presents a group of essays chosen for their accessibility. The anthology's structure also enhances this accessibility. First, an introductory essay provides a general overview of the principal events and figures involved, placing the topic in its historical context. The essays that follow explore various aspects in more detail, some targeting political trends and consequences, others social, literary, cultural, and/or technological ramifications, and still others pivotal leaders and other influential figures. To aid the reader in choosing the material of immediate interest or need, each essay is introduced by a concise summary of the contributing writer's main themes and insights.

In addition, each volume contains extensive research tools, including a collection of excerpts from primary source documents pertaining to the historical events and figures under discussion. In the anthology on the French Revolution, for example, readers can examine the works of Rousseau, Voltaire, and other writers and thinkers whose championing of human rights helped fuel the French people's growing desire for liberty; the French *Declaration of the Rights of Man and Citizen*, presented to King Louis XVI by the French National Assembly on October 2, 1789; and eyewitness accounts of the attack on the royal palace and the horrors of the Reign of Terror. To guide students interested in pursuing further research on the subject, each volume features an extensive bibliography, which for easy access has been divided into separate sections by topic. Finally, a comprehensive index allows readers to scan and locate content efficiently. Each of the anthologies in the Greenhaven Turning Points in World History series provides students with a complete, detailed, and enlightening examination of a crucial historical watershed.

Introduction

The seventy-four-year history of the Soviet Union is a paradox of accomplishment and failure. As a superpower, the Soviet Union built an extensive military and a vast nuclear arsenal, spread its political and ideological influence across the globe, and imposed a totalitarian system on its own people and on neighboring populations. Yet the Communist economic system to which the Soviet government clung could not provide sufficient food or modern consumer items to citizens. Considering the failures, it may be surprising that the Soviet Union lasted more than seventy years; however, equally surprising is the rapidity with which this country's government collapsed in 1991. In the analysis of librarian James H. Billington of the Library of Congress, "Considering the colossal economic failure and human cruelty of the Soviet system, the *nomenklatura*'s [Soviet bureaucratic elite's] ability to retain power must be recognized as one of the great, sinister political accomplishments of the 20th century." But it is perhaps a greater accomplishment that the people of the Soviet Union wrested control from such a powerful dictatorship.

The collapse of the Soviet Union occurred primarily because the leaders and dissidents of the constituent republics could no longer abide the Communist Party's inept central command of the economy and heavy-handed control of political power and privilege. Only a small percentage of average Soviet citizens joined in the demonstrations and protests that first rocked the party's authority; however, nearly all exercised the right to vote when the opportunity arose, and they voted the party out of power.

To some observers, the importance of the collapse of the Soviet dictatorship lay in the triumph of the worldwide spread of democracy—the power of citizens to control their governments. To others, the significance lay in the end of the cold war and the removal of the threat of nuclear war. To yet others, the importance of the Soviet Union's downfall was in the political and economic freedom that it brought to a substantial portion of the world's population.

Turning Points in World History: The Collapse of the Soviet Union traces the rapid demise of the Soviet Communist system from the death of Leonid Brezhnev, to the reforms implemented by Mikhail Gorbachev, to the reactionary coup against these reforms, and beyond to the aftermath of the union's breakup. The articles in this volume, selected for readability and content, analyze both the historical unfolding and the underlying causes of the collapse. They present a variety of views on the forces behind the Soviet system's fall from power and provide readers a thorough portrait of the events in this momentous historical time.

Like other titles in the Turning Points series, this volume has many features helpful to the student of history. Each book begins with a historical overview of the subject, and each selection begins with an introduction that summarizes the arguments of the author and explains the historical context of the article. A detailed chronology lists the most significant events, and a selection of primary source documents presents additional observations, statements, and other relevant excerpts.

Young readers may have no direct memory of the existence of the Soviet Union as a superpower or of the cold war between the Communist East and the democratic West. The readings presented here are intended to give insight into the end of the system that helped define the twentieth century.

A Brief History of the Soviet Union

Leonid Brezhnev, general secretary of the Communist Party of the Soviet Union (CPSU) since 1964, died in office on November 10, 1982. He was the last Soviet ruler to effectively wield authoritarian power as leader of the CPSU.

The post of Party general secretary was by tradition the seat of power in the Soviet system of government. The general secretary headed the Secretariat, which conducted the day-to-day business of the party. He also chaired the Politburo, which made all policy decisions in the country. Numbering two dozen or so, the Politburo members directed the economy and government of the entire Soviet Union. Members of these groups were chosen from the Party's Central Committee, a group of approximately five hundred Soviet Communists who met occasionally to ratify the decisions of the Politburo. The membership of the Central Committee was in turn chosen by the All-Union CPSU Congress, a gathering of some twenty-five hundred Party members that occurred every five years. The offices of the executive and legislative branches of the Soviet government were filled from the ranks of these Party organizations and were subordinate to the Party leaders.

The power of the Communist Party stemmed from its domination of all aspects of Soviet society. The Party controlled the appointments not only of government officials but also of managers of factories and other economic enterprises, scientists in high-tech industries, professors in universities, editors of newspapers, announcers at television stations, and on and on. Through a system of patronage known as *nomenklatura*, high-ranking Communist Party officials granted positions of privilege and influence to their personal supporters. Central control of the economy also allowed the leaders of the Party to distribute economic benefits to their supporters. Party bosses directed funds to factories and farms, universities and research institutes. With such control, they invariably reserved any available luxuries for loyal supporters within the Party.

Corruption and Stagnation

In his early years of leadership as general secretary, Brezhnev consolidated a tremendous amount of political power. But after eighteen years in office, his command of the country had slipped. By the end of his tenure, central control of the economy was badly mismanaged by Party officials whose only concern seemed to be obtaining personal privilege. With no interest in reforming the system and little idea how to revive the deteriorating economy, Brezhnev and the aging leaders of the Party who surrounded him essentially stood by and watched the economic deterioration of the Soviet Union.

The central Soviet government was inefficient at directing the economy. Every five years, the central government would adopt a plan that would outline goals for development. These five-year plans would establish targets for everything, including the quantities of crops to be grown, the amount of electrical energy to be generated, the numbers of factories and houses to be built, and the output of consumer goods of all kinds (from nails to ladies' shoes) to be produced. Managers of factories and supervisors of farms were given economic incentives to meet the goals; however, they were protected within the *nomenklatura* from repercussions if they failed to achieve them. Managers therefore had no reason to produce quality goods to meet their goals and little incentive to cooperate with others to meet greater goals. They could fulfill the centrally set goals by producing the required number of shoes all in one size, to use a simplified example. Often, they could simply falsify bookkeeping records. They could then keep the money from the central government for themselves or distribute it among patrons and supporters.

But after many years of this kind of inefficiency and corruption, shortages of all types of goods began to appear. Housing shortages occurred because builders could not obtain lumber in sufficient quantities or nails of the correct size, for example. Clothing was in short supply because corrupt officials hoarded cotton to sell on the international market, even though it was a violation of Soviet law to sell anything for profit to outside markets. Food shortages were the most obvious problem. The Soviet Union accrued tremendous international debts to import grain and other essential food items.

Many turned to a black market system of barter to obtain necessary goods and services. A construction manager might promise to build a vacation home for another official in exchange for the lumber or nails to meet his established construction goals. But even this black market was inefficient, and it benefited only the corrupt Communist officials involved in directing the economy. Ordinary Soviet citizens and workers had to silently suffer the shortages of goods and food. As Mikhail Gorbachev would come to admit later, "The consumer found himself totally at the mercy of the producer and had to make due with what the latter chose to give him." Workers became lazy and discontented as their standard of living deteriorated and Party officials grew comparatively wealthy.

Afghanistan

Adding to the economic problems inside the country was the costly and unpopular war in Afghanistan, which borders the former Soviet republics of Turkmenistan, Uzbekistan, and Tajikistan. On December 26, 1979, Soviet troops were flown into Kabul, the capital of Afghanistan, at the "invitation" of the Communist government there. A Communist faction had taken over the Afghan government by coup in 1978. The Soviet invasion supported a second coup by a different faction of Communists. Though the Soviet army quickly established its presence throughout the country, control of the situation was difficult to maintain. In the mountainous regions of the south, small bands of determined Muslim fighters, called mujahedin, fought the occupying Soviet soldiers.

Beginning in 1981, the U.S. Central Intelligence Agency began to supply weapons to the mujahedin, including handheld surface-to-air missile launchers to shoot down Soviet planes and helicopters. Though the mujahedin were too few in number to engage the Soviets in a major battle, their campaign of harassment destroyed military supplies and inflicted heavy casualties. Over the ten-year occupation of Afghanistan, the Soviets lost tens of thousands of soldiers and millions of dollars of equipment. According to official Soviet figures, 13,310 Soviet soldiers were killed in the ten-year war, with more than 35,478 wounded and 311 listed as missing in action.

The war exacted many social costs from the Soviet Union, too. Soldiers returned from the war demoralized, bitter, and sometimes addicted to drugs. Drug abuse began to appear in Soviet cities and towns, and associated crimes, such as smuggling and stealing, also became a problem. As more and more soldiers were killed in Afghanistan, the war became increasingly unpopular at home. Young men began to avoid required military duty in order to avoid being sent to war. And soldiers started to desert the military as well.

But the most marked cost of the war in the early years was its drain on the Soviet economy. Whatever problems of corruption and stagnation existed in the production of consumer goods for the Soviet economy, the manufacture of military matériel had always been guaranteed. The cold war confrontation with the United States made it a necessity for the Soviets to maintain defense spending. It also obliged them to support the military expenses of a number of allied and proxy governments, particularly the countries of Eastern Europe. Since the end of World War II, the Soviet Union had kept the armies, governments, and economies of Poland, Hungary, East Germany, Czechoslovakia, Romania, and Bulgaria closely bound to its own through the Warsaw Pact. The division of Eastern from Western Europe, which the Soviet Union considered vital to its security interests, required expensive commitments to prop up the friendly Communist governments, socialist economies, and allied armies in those countries. The Eastern European countries' economies were in worse shape than the Soviet Union's. Having had socialism imposed on them in the wake of World War II, citizens of these countries were even more discontented than Soviet workers. Dissident movements were well established in many of these countries and were in contact with sympathizers in the West.

The Transition of Power

This was the situation inherited by Yuri Andropov when he succeeded Brezhnev as CPSU general secretary in November 1982. Andropov was a younger, more dynamic leader than Brezhnev. He was the former head of the KGB, the Soviet secret police, and he seemed to have firm control over the Party's system of *nomenklatura*. Also, he fully understood the need to revive the economy. He quickly implemented a campaign of worker discipline, severely punishing corruption, falsified bookkeeping, absences from work, and especially drunkenness on the job.

But his tenure as leader of the Soviet Union was brief. Andropov succumbed to heart disease in February 1984, only fifteen months after being named general secretary. His unexpected death sent a shock wave through the Soviet system. While Andropov had been a logical choice to succeed Brezhnev, he himself had no clear successor. After four days, the Party appointed Konstantin Chernenko to the office.

Chernenko had been second in command under Brezhnev, but he was also an elderly man in frail health. In public appearances, he often seemed infirm or confused, and more than once he fell asleep during official ceremonies. Chernenko's death on March 10, 1985, surprised no one. His selection as general secretary had been an interregnum to give the Party a chance to choose a real leader. The day following his death, Mikhail Gorbachev was named to replace him.

Gorbachev was the youngest man to become CPSU general secretary since Joseph Stalin. He had been a close associate and protégé of Andropov's, sometimes leading Politburo meetings during the elder man's illness. He was a dynamic and charismatic politician, and he vowed to continue the campaign to reform the Soviet economy. But he lacked the control over the Party's *nomenklatura* that Andropov had exercised. His first move, therefore, was to urge the retirements of a few of the most elderly Party leaders and to promote younger men to the Politburo. Among those he promoted were his close associates and friends Nikolai Ryzhkov, who also became chairman of the council of ministers, and Eduard Shevardnadze, who took the post of foreign affairs minister.

Gorbachev also signaled his intention to rejuvenate the leadership by beginning a personal public relations campaign. In a radical departure from the tradition of staid, secretive Soviet leaders, Gorbachev began to make appearances and deliver speeches in factories and public squares, talking candidly with workers and ordinary citizens about the problems and prospects of the Soviet economy and society. He introduced the policy of glasnost, openness, and called on citizens to publicly and earnestly voice their concerns about the economy, their criticisms of the leadership, and their suggestions for change.

The International Arena

Gorbachev's most far-reaching initiatives, though, came in relations with the United States. After forty years of cold war tension between the two superpowers, Gorbachev boldly made the first overture of change. He announced the unilateral suspension of a Soviet plan to deploy a new class of nuclear missiles in Eastern Europe. This gambit opened the way for Gorbachev and U.S. president Ronald Reagan to schedule a summit meeting in Geneva in November 1985. Then, as a prelude to the summit negotiations, Gorbachev offered a second overture, proposing that the Soviets and the Americans each cut their nuclear arsenals in half. Though the two sides eventually could agree only to hold more summit meetings in the future and to continue negotiations in Geneva, Gorbachev won international goodwill and praise for commencing this reduction in cold war hostility.

Gorbachev also sought to improve the Soviet Union's international standing in the area of human rights. Since the time of Stalin, the Soviet government had been criticized for its censorship of literature, its intolerance of religion, and its repression of political dissent. Gorbachev began to relax the government's stance toward dissent by first criticizing Stalin's rule and then reinstating or restoring the reputations of some of the victims of Stalin's cultural and political purges. Under the banner of glasnost, he also allowed the works of famous

Russian writers such as Boris Pasternak and Vladimir Nabokov to be published for the first time in the Soviet Union. He went further and began to allow Jews, a minority that had suffered a long history of Russian prejudice, to immigrate to Israel. Anatoli Scharansky, a famous Russian Jewish dissident, was among the first to be allowed to leave. Late in 1986, Gorbachev personally invited dissident Andrei Sakharov—the nuclear physicist who had developed the atomic bomb for the Soviet Union but later protested the government's stance on nuclear war—to return from exile. These highly publicized moves curried some consideration in the West for the Soviets. But Gorbachev's stated reason for initiating these changes was the need to focus on the lagging Soviet economy. He wanted to reduce international hostility and decrease Soviet defense spending in order to increase social spending.

Throughout 1985 and early 1986, Gorbachev focused on the need for radical reform of the Soviet economy. He continued the anticorruption and antialcohol campaigns started by his mentor, Andropov. But he went further and called for a restructuring, which he termed perestroika, of the centralized economic planning system. He wanted to grant more independence to factory managers and farm directors. But he also sought to promote economic discipline, enforce compliance with economic laws, and compel stricter adherence to central plans. His strategy seemed aimed at ending the system of *nomenklatura* and breaking the control of corrupt Communist officials. At the 27th Party Congress in February 1986, Gorbachev's cohort Boris Yeltsin gave a speech strongly denouncing Party members who used their positions to gain economic privileges and favors. The attack was unprecedented in the one-party system.

But the explosion of a nuclear reactor at Chernobyl interrupted Gorbachev's campaign for change. The worst nuclear accident in history, this incident clearly showed why mistrust and hostility remained between the Soviet Union and the West.

Chernobyl

The reactor explosion at the Chernobyl nuclear power facility near Kiev, Ukraine, occurred on April 26, 1986. The resulting fire raged out of control for days. A massive cloud of radioactive steam released during the explosion spread over the Ukrainian countryside and drifted northward over Belarus, the Baltics, and Finland. But high-ranking officials of the CPSU and the Soviet government said nothing about the event, and Soviet news agencies reported few details.

European countries quickly noticed the spike in radiation levels and tried to monitor the disaster with satellite surveillance. The Soviet government, however, initially resisted the West's demands for explanations and refused offers of assistance. The government also kept Soviet citizens in the dark about the accident. While the fire continued to burn and radioactive contamination spread, Party officials went on with scheduled commemorations of May Day, the international workers' holiday. The first day of May was traditionally the largest official celebration under the Communist system, marked each year with huge parades and massive displays of military weaponry.

Behind this wall of secrecy and official reticence, Soviet citizens mounted heroic efforts to cope with the accident. In the first days, only a few tens of thousands of people were evacuated from the immediate area. Eventually, though, more than 135,000 people from outlying areas had to be permanently resettled to other parts of Ukraine and surrounding republics. Soviet hospitals were swamped as thousands became sick from the contamination. At least 31 firefighters died in battling the blaze, most from radiation burns. After one week of the emergency, the Soviets were forced to accept help from the West. Teams of American and European doctors were allowed into the area to contribute their expertise. But the Soviet leadership still refused to offer official explanations or acknowledge the extent of the disaster. Despite international cooperation to face the medical emergency, the outcry over the incident from European governments continued.

Not until May 14, 1986, nearly three weeks after the start of the catastrophe, did Gorbachev (in an apparent contradiction to his commitment to glasnost) finally make a statement on Chernobyl. According to his official explanation, the accident was the result of an unauthorized experiment at the reactor. But many in the West as well as in the Soviet Union suspected that it was the result of dangerous flaws in the design of the facility. Many Soviet citizens were now forced to recognize the disastrous state of the Soviet economy reflected in the flaws in its nuclear technology. For his part, Gorbachev seemed galvanized by the incident to accelerate perestroika and consolidate his control of the system.

The Kremlin's handling of the Chernobyl affair resulted in a worsening in Soviet relations with the West, which was reflected in a series of international incidents during 1986. In July, the announcement of a withdrawal of Soviet troops from Afghanistan met with skepticism from Western governments. American analysts claimed that the Soviet army had beefed up its presence in Afghanistan only months before, so the withdrawal merely represented a return to the regular troop strength. In August, the Soviets accused an American reporter of being a spy, and the United States retaliated by expelling twenty-five Soviet representatives to the United Nations. In October, the second summit meeting between Gorbachev and Reagan, held at Reykjavik, Iceland, failed to make headway in arms reduction negotiations. But Gorbachev's greatest challenge came from within the CPSU and the Soviet government.

Conservative Communists

Gorbachev's endeavors to reform the economy and to consolidate his power were meeting stiff resistance from old-style, hard-line members of the Party. At a January 1987 meeting of a Central Committee plenum (quorum), Gorbachev introduced the first elements of his plan for political reform. He proposed holding free elections, with secret ballots and multicandidate races, to fill offices in city and republic governments and to nominate directors of economic enterprises. The plenum had been postponed many times due to resistance among the leadership over the pace of reform. Many conservative leaders, including Yegor Ligachev, the Politburo's chief of Marxist ideology, also objected to the growing attacks on Stalin's legacy and the criticisms of Brezhnev's leadership prompted by glasnost.

As 1987 progressed, infighting between reformist and conservative leaders became increasingly evident. In a May interview with an Italian newspaper, Gorbachev candidly confessed that there was resistance to perestroika among Communist leaders. Then in June, at another meeting of the Central Committee plenum, he took the unusual step of publicly reproaching two managers of the central economic planning commission, accusing them of incompetence and mismanagement. Nikolai Ryzhkov, Gorbachev's ally in reform, also openly criticized the system of central economic management. Gorbachev and other reform-minded Communist leaders then pushed hard to adopt and implement new laws granting independence to factories, farms, and stores.

At the next plenum in October conservatives reacted strongly to the continued criticism. Their response came when Boris Yeltsin berated Communist leaders (including Gorbachev and Ligachev) who he claimed were dragging their heels on reform in order to perpetuate the system of *nomenklatura* and privilege. The conservatives decried Yeltsin's remarks, and Gorbachev was forced to censure Yeltsin and remove him from the Politburo. The hard-liners then began to use the shield of glasnost to voice their opposition to Gorbachev's policies. Throughout the year, Ligachev made remarks condemning the contemptuous reappraisals of Stalin's and Brezhnev's reigns and openly contesting Gorbachev's leadership. And in March 1988, newspapers printed a letter ostensibly written by Nina Andreyeva, a schoolteacher, denouncing Gorbachev for his slander of Stalin's legacy. Conservatives who wished to oust him saw the letter as a veiled attack on Gorbachev's rule.

Stirrings of Discontent in the Republics

The central government and Party were not the only sources of resistance to Gorbachev's plans for reform and power consolidation. The first inkling of trouble came in December 1986 in the republic of Kazakhstan. Gorbachev moved to dismiss longtime Kazakh Communist Party leader Dinmukhamed Kunaev from the Politburo. Through his many years in the post of republic first secretary, Kunaev had garnered extraordinary power in the system of *nomenklatura* and had engaged in some of the most outrageous acts of corruption, including the sale of state-owned Soviet assets in foreign markets. But he had also gained a great deal of popularity among his fellow Kazakhs. Street demonstrations prompted by the announcement of his removal from power developed into outright rioting in the Kazakh capital of Alma Ata.

October 1987 brought more portents of unrest in the republics, this time in Yerevan, the capital of Armenia. Marches were held there protesting Azerbaijan's political control over the enclave of Nagorno-Karabakh, a region within the borders of Azerbaijan that held a sizable population of Armenians. Over the ensuing months, the demonstrations in Armenia grew and the agitation spread to Stepanakert, the capital of the Nagorno-Karabakh region. By late March 1988, widespread strikes and general disorder were reported in both Armenia and Nagorno-Karabakh, as well as incidents of ethnic violence. Azeris in turn began to dispute the Armenians' claims to disputed territory. In Sumgait, a port town on Azerbaijan's Black Sea coast, rioting led to the deaths of thirty-one local Armenians. But a decree precluding a transfer of authority in the region issued by the USSR Supreme Soviet, the highest lawmaking body in the country, failed to put the issue to rest.

In June the Armenian government formally declared its intention to annex Nagorno-Karabakh, a move that was quickly condemned by Azerbaijan's government. The Politburo's attempt to quash the issue by categorically ruling out Armenia's annexation of the enclave predictably failed to quiet the continuing demonstrations and violence on both sides. The volatile situation festered over the ensuing months.

Successes in International Relations

While he faced troubles at home, Gorbachev's initiatives in international affairs were beginning to bear fruit. The publication in late 1987 of the book *Perestroika: New Thinking for Our Country and the World*, which was aimed primarily at Western readers, demonstrated that the West was warming to Gorbachev's calls for an end to the cold war. In the book,

Gorbachev frankly detailed the economic problems that the Soviet Union faced, which he blamed on the economic and political system established by Stalin. He also proposed specific plans for reducing the tension and conflict between the West and the Soviet Union.

In December 1987, Gorbachev carried through on the arms control initiatives put forward over the previous two years. He traveled to Washington, D.C., for the third summit meeting with Reagan. There the two signed a ban on intermediate-range nuclear forces that had resulted from the Geneva negotiations begun in November 1985. While in Washington, Gorbachev won over American audiences. He met with and spoke to Americans—at one point stopping his motorcade to mingle with pedestrians—in an apparent attempt to advance his initiatives for peace. In May 1988, Reagan would pay a return visit to Moscow for the fourth and final summit between the two leaders.

Meanwhile, Gorbachev took a further step to promote peace. In February 1988 he proposed to withdraw all Soviet troops from Afghanistan. By mid-April 1988, this offer had been made concrete, and the United States and Soviet Union were signing an agreement to stop using Afghanistan as a stage for their cold war confrontation. On May 15, as agreed, Soviet troops began to retreat from the country. By February the following year, a month ahead of schedule, the last Soviet troops had left. This and other actions garnered Gorbachev a great deal of international respect and goodwill. In 1990, he would win the Nobel Peace Prize for his efforts to end the cold war.

Gorbachev's Maneuvering

Gorbachev's popularity and successes in the international arena were not matched at home, however. His antialcohol campaign resulted in a loss of tax revenue from alcohol sales, further sinking the Soviet government in international debt. Meanwhile, the sale of bootleg liquor increased, but the supply of food and consumer goods did not. The Soviet Union faced a budget deficit of 36 billion rubles (approximately $36 billion at the then-official exchange rate) by the end of 1989.

To pay the debt, the central government began printing more money, which reduced the value of the Soviet currency. With more money in circulation but few goods to spend it on, ordinary citizens began accumulating large piles of increasingly worthless paper. Without economic improvement, Gorbachev found little support within Soviet society for his program of perestroika.

With little popular support and strong opposition from conservatives in the Party, Gorbachev began campaigning for changes to the structure of political power in the Soviet Union. In May 1988 he implemented popular balloting to select delegates to the upcoming 19th Party Conference. By manipulating the procedure, however, conservative Communists managed to manufacture a majority among the conference attendees. Gorbachev had planned to break the Party's control of appointments to government offices by introducing elections to fill these slots—though not multiparty elections, of course.

Once at the conference, though, Gorbachev announced a more sweeping proposal than anyone expected. He called for the creation of a freely elected Congress of People's Deputies that would supplant the old Supreme Soviet as the most powerful legislative body. The twenty-five-hundred deputies were to be chosen from a broad range of associations within Soviet society, from factories to Communist Party organizations. The new congress would also provide balanced representation for the constituent republics. Gorbachev further called for this congress to choose a president who would become the highest executive authority within the Soviet Union. He announced that the representatives to the congress would be elected in March 1989 and that they would convene in May 1989 to select the president. It was clear that he expected to be the first such lawfully appointed president. In October, he adopted the post of chairman of the presidium, taking over one more position of traditional power within the old system even as he tried to create a new system.

Gorbachev used his new power to strike against his conservative opponents, demoting Ligachev and others from the leadership. But the conservatives struck back. They demonstrated their strength when the Party's Central Committee convened in January 1989 to select representatives to the new Congress of People's Deputies. A number of Central Committee members voted against Gorbachev's candidacy to the congress, endangering his bid to become president. Gorbachev eventually was elected president at the congress, but reformers within the Party had apparently lost faith in him. Beginning in 1989, reform-minded Communists began resigning from the Party to pursue change in the republics.

Rebellion in the Republics

The general elections to the Congress of People's Deputies proved a surprise to Communist Party leaders. Although conservative Communists successfully manipulated balloting for the preceding Party conference, they became the victims of free and fair elections to the congress. Despite balloting set up to guarantee a majority for the Communist Party, many individual Communist candidates lost their races. Some lost to independent candidates; others failed to obtain a sufficient percentage of the total votes cast, even when they ran unopposed, because voters crossed their names off the ballots. A great many Communist Party members in the republics lost to candidates from emerging nationalist parties.

The republics, particularly the Baltics—Latvia, Lithuania, and Estonia—had become hotbeds of nationalist political activity and had begun to press for independence from the Soviet system. In August 1988, under the policy of glasnost, the secret protocols of the 1939 Molotov-Ribbentrop non-aggression pact were made public for the first time. Negotiated between the Soviet Union and Nazi Germany at the start of World War II, the pact was an agreement between Hitler and Stalin to keep their armies at bay while Hitler attacked western Europe. The protocols outlined the Soviets' and Nazis' secret agreement to divide Poland between them and subject the Baltics to Soviet rule. Nationalist parties within the Baltics used the publication of these documents to claim that the Soviet Union had illegally annexed their countries.

In November 1988, Estonia's Supreme Soviet declared sovereignty, attempting to co-opt popular sentiment favoring independence from the Soviet Union. The declaration asserted Estonia's right to veto laws and decrees passed by the central Soviet government. Then early in 1989, Estonia's highest lawmaking body took another step toward sovereignty, adopting a measure that required citizens of the republic to learn the Estonian language. The law was designed to exclude Estonia's Russian minority, which made up one-third of the population, from citizenship. Within a week, Lithuania's Supreme Soviet passed a similar measure, and by the end of October 1989, six of the other republics had followed suit.

The March elections for the congress were the clearest demonstration of the strength of the independence movements in the Baltics. Estonia's Popular Front Party, which advocated rapid independence from the Soviet Union, won fifteen of the republic's allotted twenty-one seats. Lithuania's proindependence party, Sajudis, won thirty-one of the republic's forty-two seats. And Latvia's Popular Front Party won twenty-five of twenty-nine seats. The strength of the independence movements' showings prompted the governments of all three republics to take further moves toward sovereignty that summer as the congress met for its inaugural session. In turn, the congress's official recognition that the Baltics had been illegally annexed through the Molotov-Ribbentrop pact sparked mass protests on the fiftieth anniversary of the signing of the pact that August.

The other republics were also witnessing scenes of unrest. In April 1989 peaceful demonstrations in Tbilisi, the capital of Georgia, turned violent. Using clubs, shovels, and tear gas, Georgian police and Soviet army soldiers attacked a crowd of demonstrators, killing nineteen. In June ethnic violence between Uzbeks and Turks erupted in the republic of Uzbekistan. Thousands of Soviet troops were called in to quell the violence. And in July coal miners in Siberia and in Ukraine went on strike, asking for higher wages and better living conditions. In January 1990 the still-simmering conflict between Armenia and Azerbaijan again boiled over.

After days of rioting in Baku, Azerbaijan, that resulted in sixty deaths, Soviet military forces violently separated the two ethnic groups in the republic, causing sixty additional deaths.

The Fall of Eastern Europe

As alarming as the events in the republics were becoming for the Soviet leadership, events in Eastern Europe were perhaps even more shocking. The revolutions that overthrew the Communist governments of the Eastern bloc in 1989 were unexpected and swift. What was more surprising was Gorbachev's role in the matter.

The revolution in Poland was the most portentous for the future of the Soviet Union. It truly began in 1980 when worker strikes shut down the shipyards of Gdansk, on the Baltic Sea. From these strikes, the Solidarity union formed and Lech Walesa emerged as a leader of the anticommunist forces in the country. The situation then smoldered for years after the Communist government outlawed Solidarity and imposed martial law in 1981. Strikes and marches still went forward under the banner of Solidarity, while the Polish leaders used repressive police tactics suppress or stop them.

When Gorbachev came to power, he encouraged Poland's military government to follow his policy of perestroika. He urged them to negotiate with Solidarity, and in February 1989, the Communist leaders assented to talks with the union. These talks ended in an agreement to legalize Solidarity, to establish a new one-hundred-member Senate as the most powerful legislative body in the country, and to hold democratic elections for both the new Senate and the parliament (although the Communist Party would be guaranteed an uncontested majority of seats in the parliament). The June 1989 elections resulted in a thorough defeat of the Communist Party, and by August they were no longer able to lead the government. Gorbachev once again intervened to compel the Polish Communist leaders to accept a new government led by Solidarity. On August 24 the first noncommunist government was formed in an Eastern European country.

Poland set the stage for events in Hungary. Hungary had long been experimenting with free market economic reforms. In March 1989, one month after the start of the roundtable discussions in Poland, Soviet foreign minister Gennadi Gerasimov, an ally of Gorbachev's, proclaimed on Hungarian television that the futures of the Eastern European countries were in their own hands. The statement seemed to spark spontaneous demonstrations and marches in Budapest, Hungary's capital. The process of roundtable negotiations, the scheduling of elections, and the renunciation of the Communist Party's hold on power followed at a lightning pace. By October, the Communist Party of Hungary had disbanded.

Hungary's revolution had a domino effect on East Germany's Communist regime, and once more, Gorbachev played a part. In June 1989, as part of his campaign for peace with the West, Gorbachev proposed tearing down the Berlin Wall, long the symbol of the cold war division of Europe. But it was Hungary that took the first substantial move to end the division. In September, Hungary fully opened its border with Austria. This meant that for the first time since the end of World War II, Eastern Europeans could visit the West unfettered by restrictions imposed by the Communist regimes. Thousands of East Germans fled through Hungary to West Germany as refugees. Hundreds who stayed in East Germany began protest marches against the Communist rulers, despite harsh police crackdowns that resulted in the deaths of a number of demonstrators. In October, Gorbachev traveled to East Berlin to prod the Communist rulers of East Germany to accept the course of change. On November 9, 1989, the Berlin Wall was officially opened, and less than one month later, the Communist Party of East Germany abandoned its hold on power.

Czechoslovakia's revolution followed hard on the heels of the opening of the Berlin Wall. Czechoslovakia had a well-organized dissident movement that had been active since the 1970s. Peaceful rallies and demonstrations broke out in Prague, the capital of the Czech Republic, on November 19, 1989. Dissident groups immediately formed a united front, called the Civic Forum, to negotiate the end of Communist rule. With the demonstrations growing, the Czechoslovak Communist Party quickly capitulated to the demands of the Civic Forum. On December 10 the Communist leaders handed power over to a new noncommunist government. The transfer of power was so speedy and yet so peaceful that it was termed the Velvet Revolution.

Less peaceful and smooth, but just as swift, was the revolution in Romania. In mid-December, violent riots broke out in the town of Timosoara, in western Romania. The Hungarian minority in Timosoara, the principal town in the region of Transylvania, initiated the riots to protest domination by the Romanians. Security forces arrived quickly to quash the potential ethnic conflict before it could start, but the troops unexpectedly opened fire on the crowds and hundreds were killed. The demonstrations then spread to other Romanian towns and to the capital of Bucharest. Nicolae Ceausescu, Communist leader of Romania since 1965 and the most despotic ruler in Eastern Europe, immediately declared a state of emergency. But a faction of the Romanian Communist leadership, joined by the army, seized the opportunity to rebel against Ceausescu. On December 22 they overthrew the dictator and on December 25 executed him along with members of his family. Though they pretended to be inspired by the spirit of democracy sweeping Eastern Europe, it would take the new leadership two years to implement free democratic elections. In Bulgaria, the last of the Eastern bloc regimes, the Communist government quietly relinquished its hold on power in 1990.

The Union Drifts Apart

The breakup of the Soviet Union accelerated in the wake of the Eastern European revolutions. These revolutions seemed to inspire the independence-minded leaders in the republics; they stepped up their efforts to break away from the Soviet system. The primary issue in the emerging battle between the central government and the republics was the feeble state of the Soviet economy. For his part, Gorbachev, who had encouraged the Soviet satellites to find their own roads, acted desperately to rein in the republics and to tighten his grip over the fraying union.

Lithuania was the first Soviet republic to take up the example of the Eastern Europeans. With elections for local soviets and city councils scheduled throughout the Soviet Union for February and March, the Lithuanian government decided in January 1990 that all parties would be allowed to contest their local elections. The Lithuanian Communist Party felt certain it would lose the elections to Sajudis, the National Front, if it could not distance itself from the central Party. The Lithuanian Communists therefore unilaterally declared their independence from the CPSU. The affair was the most dramatic demonstration of the CPSU's continued decline in status and membership. But Sajudis won a resounding victory anyway. Lithuania then chose Sajudis leader Vytautas Landsbergis as president, the first noncommunist president of a Soviet republic.

On March 11 the newly elected Lithuanian legislature defiantly issued a declaration of independence from the Soviet Union. Gorbachev, in contrast to his image as a peaceful reformer, had to take openly repressive measures to counter the republic's secessionist drive. Soviet army troops moved into Vilnius, the capital of Lithuania, in tanks and armored personnel carriers and began to arrest young Lithuanians who had deserted the military or avoided the draft. Authorities from the central government also seized factories and Communist Party buildings. The central government then imposed an embargo on oil and gas shipments to the republic, threatening to ruin the small republic's economy. After two months of escalating confrontation, the Lithuanian government agreed to withdraw its declaration. Under intense pressure from the central government, the Lithuanian legislature in late June officially voted to suspend activities aimed at independence.

Gorbachev used the strong hand he gained in dealing with the Lithuanians to further maneuver to consolidate his hold on power. On March 13, 1990, at Gorbachev's insistence, the Congress of People's Deputies formally abolished the CPSU's constitutionally guaranteed hold on power and adopted a law expanding the power of the legally designated president. The congress also appointed Gorbachev to a full five-year term as president. Gorbachev had promised that he would use the expanded powers to institute sweeping economic reforms. But in late April, he suspended his plan to transform the ailing Soviet economy into a market system. The plan had been modeled on Poland's crash reform program, implemented in the wake of the October 1989 revolution. It would have quickly turned the Soviet economy into a fully free market system.

Despite Gorbachev's growing power, a new challenge emerged from the Russian republic. The Eastern European revolutions had inspired independence rallies and marches in Moscow beginning in early 1990. In the March local elections, Russian republic voters rejected conservative Communist Party members in favor of reform candidates, including Boris Yeltsin. On May 29, Yeltsin was elected chairman of the Russian Supreme Soviet, in effect making him president of the Russian republic. Yeltsin resigned from the CPSU and pushed the Russian legislature to adopt the same moves toward independence that the Baltic republics had earlier made. In July he went further and announced that Russia would adopt, independently of the rest of the union, the free market economic plan shelved by Gorbachev.

The Soviet Union's economy rapidly deteriorated as the republics began to go their own ways. Acute shortages of food and many other necessary goods began to appear in 1990. After Gorbachev set aside the radical program of reform, Nikolai Ryzhkov announced a program for gradual free market reform. The first phase of this new plan would allow many of the centrally established prices on consumer goods to fluctuate. This announcement sparked panic buying of food and other necessities throughout the union. Riots broke out in a few areas. To stem the disorder and to counter Yeltsin's economic maneuvers, Gorbachev was forced to negotiate an agreement on a unionwide plan for economic reform. Squeezed between the republics and the Party conservatives (who still dominated the central government and the congress), Gorbachev temporized for months about which plan he would follow—the radical plan adopted by Russia or the cautious plan put forward by Ryzhkov. Finally, in October 1990, he proposed a moderate plan that co-opted elements of both approaches. No one, however, found it acceptable.

The republics, with Russia now in the lead, increasingly went their own ways. All fifteen of the constituent Soviet republics had now declared their sovereignty over the policies and laws of the central union government. Attempting to stem the drift, Gorbachev further consolidated his authority. He pushed a proposal through the Supreme Soviet, the standing legislative assembly drawn from the ranks of the Congress of People's Deputies. The new law granted him the power to rule by decree during the transformation to a free market economy, in order to prevent further disorder and riots. Despite a flurry of presidential decrees ordering factories and farms throughout the various republics to deliver goods, though, he could not stave off the descending economic anarchy. Gorbachev's far-reaching accumulation of authority and power could do nothing in the face of the republic governments that supplanted him.

The New Union Treaty

By late 1990, signs of the union's disintegration were increasingly apparent. As the central government issued decrees to try to control the widening disorder, the republics continued to assert the supremacy of their laws over the union laws and to pursue their own economic agendas. In December, Kirghizia became the last of the fifteen Soviet republics to declare its sovereignty, and Latvia and Lithuania became the first republics to sincerely move toward secession. To try to preserve the vestiges of a unified system, Gorbachev drafted a new Union Treaty. The document was at first vague in the details of how power would be distributed between the central government and the republics. The draft of the treaty was used to gauge popular support for either abolishing or continuing the existence of the Soviet Union led by Gorbachev. The Congress of People's Deputies ordered a nationwide referendum, scheduled for

March 1991, to decide the fate of the new treaty. All Soviet Union citizens would be asked if they wanted to maintain the union structure.

Meanwhile, Gorbachev was coming under growing pressure from hard-line Communists to restore central control. Conservatives Boris Pugo, Gennadi Yanayev, and Valentin Pavlov joined Gorbachev's presidential cabinet over the objections of the few reformers who remained in the congress. While Gorbachev pleaded with the republics to maintain order and unity, the conservatives warned about the consequences of disintegration. The test of the resolve of both sides came in January 1991.

The Baltic republics had been the first to call for secession, and they now demanded independence from the Soviet Union. As negotiations between the Lithuanian government and the Soviet central government broke down, Soviet troops moved to reimpose central control over the breakaway republic. On January 2 the army shut down the main newspaper publishing plant in Riga, the capital of Latvia. Two weeks later military forces carried out an assault against the Latvian Interior Ministry. Four protesters were killed in the raid. In similar actions in Vilnius, Lithuania, during the second week of January, Soviet troops seized the Lithuanian television station and newspaper offices. Thirteen Lithuanians were killed in the attack as they tried to protest the military maneuvers. The crisis eased over the following weeks as the Soviet soldiers withdrew and the Baltic citizens toned down their demonstrations. Gorbachev denied ordering the actions, saying that the military had acted at the "invitation" of factions within the Baltic governments.

The March 1991 referendum on the new Union Treaty proved a boost to Gorbachev's efforts to prop up the disintegrating union structure. The results showed that an overwhelming majority of Soviet citizens throughout the union favored retaining a federation of the constituent republics. Gorbachev used those results to push forward his proposed union agreement. The finalized treaty called for maintaining and renewing the central government, with power vested in the Congress of People's Deputies. The union laws would once again outweigh those of the individual republics. But the republics would gain full control over the planning and running of their separate economies. Traditional trade ties and obligations among republics would again be revived. Gorbachev could convince only nine of the fifteen republics to join this arrangement. The Baltic republics of Latvia, Lithuania, and Estonia, and the Caucasus nations of Moldova, Armenia, and Azerbaijan refused. On April 23 in Novo-Ogarevo, the remaining republics signed a preliminary agreement to speed up implementation of the agreement. The final treaty was scheduled to be signed in August 1991.

The August Coup

In June the Russian republic held popular elections. Reformers were chosen to fill posts in major cities such as Moscow and Leningrad, and Yeltsin was elected to a full term as president. The election results gave Yeltsin a mandate to pursue radical economic reform and autonomy from the center. Though he participated in the negotiations of the Union Treaty, he pursued radical economic programs that circumvented the process.

In August conservatives attempted a last-ditch effort to preserve the central government's traditional power. Late in the evening of August 18, 1991, a group of hard-line Communists that included Pugo, Yanayev, and Pavlov arrested Gorbachev at his vacation home in the Crimea, on the Black Sea coast of Ukraine. The next morning, a group calling itself the State Committee for the State of Emergency declared that Gorbachev was ill, that Yanayev had taken his place, and that martial law would be imposed for six months. The committee ordered military forces into Moscow to surround the Russian parliament. Tanks took up positions throughout the city under instructions to keep protests and demonstrations from breaking out. But the Russian troops manning them refused to thwart the desires of their countrymen for freedom.

On the afternoon of August 19, Yeltsin broadcast a defiant message to Russian citizens asking them to resist the imposition of martial law. He called the actions of the emergency committee an unlawful coup d'état. He and other leaders of the Russian republic barricaded themselves inside the parliament building and issued a declaration of Russian independence. Yeltsin then began to issue presidential orders and decrees to the Russian people and soldiers, proclaiming his supremacy over the central government leaders. Twelve of the other republics followed Russia's lead, declaring their secession from the union. In the face of such resistance, the attempted coup collapsed, and the leaders were arrested.

The Collapse of the Soviet Union

Gorbachev returned from his brief captivity to find the Soviet Union in collapse. With his authority completely usurped by the republic governments, he attempted to distance himself from the traditional Soviet central government, which was still dominated by the Communist Party. On August 24, he resigned his position as general secretary of the CPSU and disbanded the Party's Central Committee. Two weeks later, the Congress of People's Deputies dissolved itself, leaving Gorbachev as the last stalwart of the central government. For his part, Yeltsin banned the Communist Party from the Russian republic.

Gorbachev attempted to resuscitate the Union Treaty as an economic confederation, with only a weakened central authority. But only eight of the republics were willing to consider the proposal. The three Baltic republics had gained international recognition as free and independent states. The Caucasus republics were in turmoil, and each pursued recognition as an independent nation. But it was the decision by Ukraine, the second-largest republic, to pursue independence that broke the back of the treaty negotiations. Following Ukraine's decision, Russia also withdrew from the treaty agreement. Together with Belarus, the republics declared the end of the Soviet Union on December 8, 1991. They invited the other former republics to form an alternative Commonwealth of Independent States that would preserve the union in name only. On December 25, 1991, Gorbachev resigned as president of the Soviet Union. The following day, the USSR formally ceased to exist.

The Aftermath

Russia, as the successor to the former Soviet Union, became the heir to many of its problems. Foremost among the problems was that Russia's economy was in shambles from the years of mismanagement by CPSU functionaries. The Russians were burdened with a large portion of the enormous international debts accrued by the former Soviet Union. They also inherited the former Soviet currency, the ruble, which had lost much of its value. Further, many of the goods produced in the outdated Soviet factories still operating in Russia could not be sold in foreign markets for hard currency. Russia attempted shock therapy to revive its economy from the doldrums, but a program of radical free market reform implemented in January 1992 did little to alleviate the situation.

Shortages of food and consumer items continued. Ordinary Soviet citizens could no longer rely on the guaranteed incomes provided under the Communist system, and they lost much of their savings as the currency continued to lose value. Many fell into poverty. But the free market reforms allowed some Russians to reap tremendous amounts of money. Those who could obtain foreign goods and sell them in Russia made fortunes, often, however, through smuggling and other illegal activities. Crime, particularly organized crime associated with smuggling enterprises, became an overwhelming problem in Russia.

Nationalism and ethnic conflict spilled over from the Caucasus republics to the southern regions of Russia. As the Soviet republics established their independence from the Soviet Union in the wake of the failed August coup, the region of Chechnya declared its independence from Russia. The small ethnic enclave, located on Russia's border with Georgia, had enjoyed semiautonomous status under the Soviet system. It now wanted to share the standing of the newly independent nations of the region. Barely noticed at first, the friction between the ethnic minority and the Russian government in Moscow would eventually erupt into a full-scale war. By 1994, the enclave's demands for independence were a challenge to Yeltsin's control over the Russian political system. Yeltsin sent Russian troops into the region and squashed the Chechen independence movement. By 1996 the Russian army had destroyed the Chechen capital, Grozny, and killed many members of the Chechen militia.

Russian society was also rife with nationalist parties that wished to restore the military and international prowess of the defunct Soviet Union. Many ordinary citizens were nostalgic for the orderliness and security of the authoritarian Communist system. But Russia and the other former Soviet republics continue to develop as democracies and as successful economies.

Chapter 1

Prelude to the Collapse

Turning|Points
IN WORLD HISTORY

The Death of the "Old Guard"

Seweryn Bialer

In the following article, published shortly after the official breakup of the Soviet Union, Seweryn Bialer maintains that economic stagnation and political corruption spread during Leonid Brezhnev's leadership (1964–1982), sowing the seeds of the Soviet Union's demise. Under Brezhnev's eighteen-year rule, he contends, bureaucratic elites, particularly those in the republics, became entrenched in positions of power and used their authority to pursue personal privilege and financial gain. Mikhail Gorbachev's attempt to reform the Soviet government and economy in 1995 was therefore necessary, in Bialer's opinion, but risky. By exposing the ineffectiveness and illegitimacy of the Soviet regime, he argues, Gorbachev's reforms deepened the existing crisis of leadership and accelerated the downfall of the Soviet government.

Seweryn Bialer is director of the Research Institute on International Change and a professor of political science at Columbia University. He is the author of *Politics, Society, and Nationality Inside Gorbachev's Russia* and *The USSR After Brezhnev*.

In the dark winter of 1990–91 many asked how the Soviet Union, trying to save itself, would end. With a bang or a whimper? King Solomon would have liked the answer that came after three historic days in August 1991: it ended with both. Those fateful days were obviously a potentially deadly putsch, but also a failure of such enormous proportions that

Reprinted from Seweryn Bialer, "The Death of Soviet Communism," *Foreign Affairs*, vol. 70, Winter 1991/1992 by permission of the author. Copyright 1991 Seweryn Bialer.

they cannot even be considered a full-fledged coup d'etat. While the putschists arrested Mikhail Gorbachev, their real targets escaped: Boris Yeltsin, Democratic Russia and the separatist republics. That failure has not only contributed to the myth surrounding the emergence of a new Russian state, but it also pushed the Soviet Union well beyond any parameters envisioned by the very process of reform the putschists were attempting to stem.

The Emergence of Gorbachev

Gorbachev emerged in March 1985 from the struggle among his Politburo colleagues to become general secretary of the Soviet Communist Party and the effective leader of the Soviet state. At that time the Soviet Union seemed a very weary yet immensely powerful country. It was decaying economically, but politically it still appeared to be stable. The crisis in the Soviet regime was over its domestic and international effectiveness; its survival was not in doubt. Even before they took power, however, Gorbachev and his closest associates realized their country was stagnating, but they termed it a "pre-crisis situation." So although they perceived some crisis of effectiveness in the regime, they did not yet comprehend its depth. They thought the regime only needed reform.

Six and a half years later the Soviet Union and Soviet communism were dead. What happened in those years that finally led to disintegration rather than salvation through grand reform? What happened to Mikhail Gorbachev? He once seemed an immensely energetic and attractive leader, speaking about national renewal by a new generation of leaders in words almost reminiscent of John F. Kennedy. Yet today one cannot forget the image of that worn man as he descended the ramp from the aircraft that brought him back to Moscow from his Crimean captivity.

To answer these questions one must first examine the various economic, social and political trends in place even before the Gorbachev leadership attempted its reforms. Only then can the response by Soviet leaders and institutions be assessed, and the summer's dramatic outcome be properly understood.

The Leadership Crisis

After Leonid Brezhnev's death in 1982, two extraordinary successions within a period of three years served to demonstrate the severity of the Soviet crisis that had been accelerating since the mid-1970s. Yuri Andropov, who immediately succeeded Brezhnev and who is considered Gorbachev's "founder," understood the need for change. During his short term he took both ideological and political steps to try to prepare the Soviet Union's ruling elites for a more efficient, disciplined and realistic communist regime. Under his tenure the brooding dissatisfaction of the regime's intelligentsia became more vocal and daring. This was the crucial gestation period for Gorbachev's views. Gorbachev's wife, Raisa, once pointed out to a visiting American first lady the picture of Andropov in her residence, saying, "This is the man to whom we owe everything." She was right.

But in some ways, and for very different reasons, the brief reign of Konstantin Chernenko provided the real catalyst for change. Chernenko's absolute grayness and incompetence engendered in the communist intelligentsia, parts of the elite and, of course, the Soviet people themselves a particular feeling of not only hopelessness but also deep embarrassment and shame. Hopes for a dynamic new leader who would make some change were completely buried.

The Soviet economic crisis was clearly visible in declining growth rates, increasing scarcity of exploitable resources and, most important, the worsening imbalance between military production and that for the general economy, especially consumer goods. The Soviet economy and society seemed mobilized for war, much more than even Nazi Germany at the height of World War II. In the consumer sector a very large portion of the capital stock was not only underproductive but was also simply at the limit of its physical capacity. Yet it was not being replenished. In the 10 years before perestroika began, according to Russian Prime Minister Ivan Silayev, only 15 percent of investment in the Russian republic went to consumer industries. Military industries, on the other hand, were continuously supplied with new technologies. Certain farsighted generals, especially those in technical services, tried to break the hold of traditional strategy that emphasized numerical superiority, only to be thwarted by high command.

The Bureaucratic System

The enormous Soviet bureaucracies, including the party apparatus, shifted from the limited autonomy of the Stalinist era toward a more corporatist system. They increasingly neglected their goal of service to the state and society in favor of self-aggrandizement. Political and economic corruption, which has existed throughout Soviet history—tempered somewhat by fear—increased systematically in the years before Gorbachev came to power. The size of the "second" or illegal "shadow" economy eventually accounted for 25 to 30 percent of the market and became essential to the functioning of the economy as a whole. Moreover corruption was less and less camouflaged, and by the end of the Brezhnev era many in the bureaucracy were almost openly accepting sizable bribes. It is likely that the party apparatus had previously been less involved in illegal enrichment than the administrative bureaucracy. But it, too, was becoming as bad as other bureaucracies, especially at its lower levels. In the mid-1980s a private Soviet "businessman" even commented, "You know, I would have never thought that there would come a time when I would walk into a Raikom [a regional Communist Party Committee] and talk serious business."

The corruption of the bureaucracies only separated them further from the people they were supposedly in place to serve. The actual depoliticization of the people themselves, in the world's most ceremonially political regime, went so far that cynicism, hopelessness and passivity developed as a shield against the authorities. It thus became increasingly difficult to mobilize the population in almost any sphere of life.

The quality of the Soviet leadership was deteriorating as well, especially at the top, but also in the middle. This was true not only in terms of intelligence and organizational talent, let alone commitment, but also in a physical sense. Members of the Politburo and Central Committee of the

Communist Party were aged, dogmatic and lacked spark. The respect and fear they once generated were rapidly declining in an increasingly young and educated country. Yet the party elites loved Brezhnev. Nikita Khrushchev may have given them security from threats to their lives, but Brezhnev gave them security in office, the good life, the blessing of domestic tranquility and tolerance—unless, of course, they crossed him personally. There were nevertheless many younger provincial party secretaries as well as officials of the central apparatus who were growing impatient waiting for promotion.

The weakness of political dissent within the Soviet Union was also important to the crisis. Under Khrushchev and in the early Brezhnev years political dissent grew rapidly and had great importance beyond its actual influence inside the Soviet Union. It planted seeds of antitotalitarianism and anticommunism in the native soil, especially among the young intelligentsia, and showed the West that the spirit of freedom was not dead in Russia. But by the late 1970s and early 1980s the most important dissenters were either silenced or abroad. Sympathy for their ideas was growing, but the political potential for active dissent inside the Soviet Union seemed to have sunk to a low. Dissent could have become immensely important to a process of renewal, if only internal conditions for its development would have changed.

The Nationalities Question

Finally the nationalities question in the Soviet Union—relations between non-Russian nations and ethnic groups and the Russian center—was also important. It was potentially the most lethal yet insoluble crisis in the system, because both modernization and backwardness worked against Moscow. To the extent that non-Russian ethnic regions maintained underdeveloped, peasant cultures, the depth of their attachment to traditional national culture and its religious context remained extraordinarily strong. These regions therefore were able to resist with surprising force subordination to Russian culture or submersion in the supranational conception of the Soviet state. Alternately, to the extent that non-Russian regions were swept up by the tide of modernization, they developed an intensely urban-centered orientation. The newly educated classes and the creative and managerial intelligentsia became the main carriers of this new kind of ethnic identity. Thus lack of development led to cultivation of old ethnic identities, while the process of modernization only created new strains.

Even by the time perestroika began, communism had not been able to create a Soviet "nation." Soviet federalism contained a potentially dangerous dualism. It denied all but the slimmest margin of autonomy to federated nationalities. At the same time, its symbolic institutions and administrative framework provided the base from which the struggle for national autonomy could be waged. There were communist elites and part of the intelligentsia who had diverse ethnic origins. But even here tension between Russian and non-Russian segments was quite pronounced. An overwhelming majority of non-Russian communist elites worked exclusively in their own native republics. Their careers stopped at their republics' borders, and their promotion to the center in Moscow was very limited. With their vertical mobility thus constrained, they pressed hard to extend control within their own republics, at the cost of the center.

Centrifugal Tendencies

During the late Brezhnev period a process described as "feudalization" became highly pronounced in the non-Russian republics, particularly in Central Asia and Transcaucasia. These republics became truly the fiefdoms of long-entrenched native communist leaderships and elites. These elites paid lip service to Moscow and enormous bribes to central inspectors; they amassed fortunes and engaged in an intricate network of private "business" contacts. (My favorite example is from Uzbekistan, where a harvest of one million tons of cotton was hidden from Moscow and sold for private profit.) These centrifugal tendencies of the native communist elites, combined with growing nationalism among the intelligentsia and broader population alike, became a major worry for the Russian center.

Even though the Soviet Union had lost its internal vitality, the powers of the regime were still immense. Decay was probably unavoidable, but disintegration did not at all seem to be an immediate prospect. Yet the crisis of effectiveness—absent major countervailing actions—did have the potential for becoming a crisis of survival. The irony is that the countervailing actions themselves—the deep changes initiated by perestroika—almost certainly accelerated the demise of communism and the disintegration of the empire. It was as Alexis de Tocqueville had warned: "The most perilous moment for a bad government is when it seeks to mend its ways."

Confrontation with the West

Richard V. Allen

At the start of the cold war, U.S. foreign policy was based on the strategy of containment. While avoiding direct conflict with the Soviet Union, the United States worked to prevent the spread of Soviet influence and military power in other parts of the world. During the 1950s and 1960s, the United States pursued containment backed up with aggressive production of nuclear weapons to match Soviet stockpiles. In the 1970s, the era of détente, the two superpowers negotiated a balance of conventional and nuclear forces.

Elected U.S. president in 1980, Ronald Reagan adopted a confrontational posture toward the Soviet Union as a deliberate, well-thought-out—and ultimately successful—move to win the cold war, argues Richard V. Allen in the following selection, excerpted from a speech originally presented in late 1995. According to Allen, Reagan calculated that the Soviet Union's economy was not strong enough to compete in a renewed arms race with the United States. To make certain that this was the case, Reagan set out to undermine the Soviet economy, he maintains.

Richard V. Allen, chairman of the Asian Studies Center at the Heritage Foundation, served as chief foreign policy adviser to President Ronald Reagan.

I am going to talk about how Ronald Reagan and his team—a team widely characterized at the time, both here and abroad, as a group of inexperienced and impractical right-wing ideologues and fanatics—prevailed in the Cold War. In

Reprinted from Richard V. Allen, "The Man Who Changed the Game Plan," *The National Interest*, no. 44, Summer 1996, with permission of *The National Interest*, Washington, D.C. Copyright © The National Interest.

doing so, I shall not be so foolish as to claim for them all the credit for victory. Clearly, much belongs to earlier American statesmen, from Harry Truman on; and one cannot deny a little to Mikhail Gorbachev, however unintended the consequences of his actions. But I shall offer what I believe is a reasoned defense of the proposition that the Reagan presidency can properly claim the lion's share of the credit—and, even more shocking for some, that the key factor in the winning side's team was the president himself.

Some of Reagan's critics still cannot understand how America and the world survived the eight years of his two administrations. After all, how could an aging actor, so untutored in the finer ways of thinking, so divisive and so rightwing in outlook, so unfamiliar with life inside the Beltway, [i.e., not a Washington political insider] be expected to tiptoe through (and a preference for tiptoeing was the very mark of sophistication for such critics) the nuanced strategic and diplomatic world of the 1980s? How could he run the world with his absurd 4x6 cue cards and a TelePrompTer?

Confrontation with the Soviet Union

Now it is true, President Reagan did initially take us into a confrontation with the Soviet Union. But he did so intentionally, deliberately, and in slow motion. Moving to confront the adversary in this way, Reagan followed a plan that he had thought through over many years. There were, of course, major glitches, detours, and reversals, but he never changed his basic outlook . . . and he did understand the importance of keeping it simple.

The fact that Reagan was prepared to use confrontation in this way is what has given credence to the view that, far from ending the Cold War, he actually prolonged and deepened it. There is a considerable body of revisionist history on this subject, including the work of our present deputy secretary of state, Mr. Strobe Talbott, the architect of the present administration's policy toward Russia and its former empire. One cannot help feeling that had Mr. Talbott been around in 1946, when Winston Churchill delivered his famous "Iron Curtain" speech at Fulton, he would have enthusiastically joined the many who accused Churchill of being a "warmonger."

When Churchill made that speech, we were busily demobilizing and withdrawing from Europe while Stalin stayed there, which meant that the United States was put in the position of reacting to Soviet advances in the postwar period, rather than seizing the initiative. It was only slowly and after much provocation—when, one after another, the Eastern European countries were taken over by a combination of highly effective internal subversion and external Soviet military pressure, and the Red Army did not budge from the eastern part of Germany—that the United States decided to react in earnest. When it did so, a long-term strategic plan began to take shape. . . .

Remember that [Paul Nitze] was the principal drafter of the 1950 document known as NSC-68. Signed by President Truman forty-five years ago, this landmark paper originated the policy of containment of the USSR. *How* we moved to contain the Soviet Union in various ways was a matter for successive presidents to decide, but this doctrine of containment remained essentially in place for the next forty or so years under both Republican and Democratic administrations.

In my view, however, the stage had been set for a deviation from containment and an eventual showdown with the Soviets—the showdown that was to come with Reagan in the 1980s—as long ago as the Cuban Missile Crisis of October 1962. While we breathed a collective sigh of relief in the wake of that crisis, two trends of great importance were set in motion by it. The first was the clear realization on the part of Nikita Khrushchev that, in October 1962, the Soviet Union was decidedly inferior to the United States in terms of military power. He vowed that it would not remain so, and embarked on the largest military buildup in history. We underestimated and misread this trend—badly.

The second trend was that the Chinese moved into an open and bitter dispute with the Soviets. I believe we badly misread the implications of this trend as well, for we concluded that the so-called responsible and sober Soviets were to be contrasted with the reckless and revolutionary Chinese, who were busy promoting "wars of national liberation" in the Third World and generally undermining U.S. interests. Of course, in reality it was the Soviets who were reckless, embarking upon a huge military buildup and themselves fomenting revolutionary strife in the less-developed world; while the Chinese talked a good game of revolution, but were in reality sober and careful not to extend themselves beyond their borders.

The Era of Détente

What was to occur later in the Nixon-Ford years is surely the subject of another discussion. Let me simply note that when détente became a policy, rather than merely a descriptive statement and a generalized hope, it amounted to little more—or less—than a reaffirmation of containment. Leading practitioners of détente (and especially Henry Kissinger) seemed to believe that the United States could never entertain a notion of "winning" the Cold War, and should instead seek the best arrangement possible under less than ideal circumstances. In fact, some believed that the Soviets were actually winning and that this necessitated a deal.

In 1976, you will recall, Ronald Reagan's primary campaign caught fire when he unleashed a powerful assault on the policy of détente, and the battle became so intense that Gerald Ford nearly lost the nomination at the Kansas City convention. So heated did things become that Henry Kissinger almost did not go to the convention, and when he did, it was to be booed by many of the delegates and to be met by a Republican platform that contained a repudiation of "détente" as the centerpiece of U.S. policy toward the USSR. (That platform document never saw the light of day; it was quietly deep-sixed by the Ford administration in its losing re-election campaign.)

Even in 1976, and for as long as I knew him, Ronald Reagan rejected the doctrine of "containment." This is not to say that he repudiated or demeaned its achievements, but that he believed deeply in its inadequacy if we were ever to be secure in the modern world. He believed in developing momentum through strength, and applying that momentum to the Cold

War equation. He knew that it would entail risk, but in his view a worthwhile and manageable risk, one that stopped short of outright provocation or war in order to achieve victory. He believed that a quantum change in East-West relations was necessary: no more passivity, no more reacting to Soviet initiatives, as we were clearly doing in the Carter years in Central America, Angola, and Afghanistan. He believed, simply, that democracy and freedom, resolutely asserted and eloquently articulated, could ultimately prevail.

Attempting to Gain the Upper Hand

Thus Reagan entered office in early 1981 with a clear strategy in mind. And that strategy, developed over the several years preceding his election, was, if we may use classic Soviet terminology, to change "the correlation of forces" in the world.

Reagan's program for dealing realistically with the Soviet Union was essentially a matter of getting the U.S. economy in shape, forging ahead with a comprehensive domestic program, strengthening America's defense capabilities through a sustained program of re-armament using modern and advanced technologies, and changing dramatically the way in which the country's foreign policy was conducted. There were those who said that Reagan "didn't have a clue" about how to conduct a coherent foreign policy. But he actually had more than a clue; he had a plan, and the resolution to put it into effect.

The major shift in U.S. policy was made formal in late 1982 and early 1983, through the adoption of NSDD-75, still today a secret document. The United States would no longer be content merely to shape and influence Soviet behavior, but would set out to change the Soviet system itself, and literally "roll back" Soviet advances and conquests outside its borders. The objective was to find weak points in the Soviet structure, to aggravate the weaknesses, and to undermine the system. This represented a sea change in U.S. policy.

A defense buildup would take a long time, Reagan knew, and it would be necessary to mobilize broad support for one. This he achieved by mid-year 1981, making choices for weapons and defensive systems and upgrades that sent a strong, unmistakable signal to adversaries and allies alike. Europe, with the clear exception of Mrs. Thatcher, did not much like what it was hearing; the United States was "rocking the boat", taking needlessly risky—even reckless—positions. It was "destabilizing" and "confrontational", "threatening" and "provocative." Establishment Washington agreed, and when Reagan said that communists would "lie, cheat, and steal" to get what they wanted, it went into a spasm of fright. Even some leading members of his own administration were said to be appalled at this bluntness. For their part, the Soviets sat up and took notice, and began to worry.

The Arms Race and Disarmament

There is a widespread but inaccurate view that President Reagan was transfixed by weapons, that he sought a military buildup in the belief that these weapons would be deployed and used. That is not so. He was, in fact, fundamentally a disarmer, so much so that by the time he got to the Reykjavik meeting with Gorbachev in the fall of 1986, some thought he nearly went overboard in that direction. He fervently believed that the doctrine of Mutual Assured Destruction, with its acronym "MAD", for so long the core of our declared nuclear doctrine, was fundamentally flawed and morally bankrupt because it offered the American people as hostages in a constant upward-spiraling arms race.

He believed the proper strategy to be one of clearly gaining the upper hand, and there negotiating from a position of strength—and the last part of that strategy, negotiation, was as important as the first. That the idea of seeking military superiority reduced the arms control community to a state of funk was of little concern to him; he aimed to build up this country's strength by relying on its economic and technological advantages, and translating those elements into measurable national power—all in order to convince the other side that it was hopelessly expensive, even impossible, to keep abreast. Only when the other side was so convinced, he reckoned, would it agree to come to the table. In other words, he believed that to disarm safely we first had to arm ourselves, deliberately and persuasively: the same sermon, not so incidentally, that Churchill had preached at Fulton.

Accordingly, by mid-1981, the president decided to move ahead with the deployment of a dazzling array of weapons systems: the B-1 bomber, Stealth technology in several forms, the goal of a 600-ship Navy, dramatic new cruise and intermediate-range missiles, the M-X missile, new Trident submarines, heavy R&D [research and development] funding, and more. In the first six years of this program, the U.S. procured 3,000 combat aircraft, 3,700 strategic missiles, and 10,000 tanks. In his 1991 book, *The Turn*, Don Oberdorfer quotes Rodomir Boigdanov of Moscow's Institute for the Study of the USA & Canada as saying, "You Americans are trying to destroy our economy, to interfere with our trade, to overwhelm and make us inferior in the strategic field." He was a perceptive man.

Reagan approached the Soviets on a dual track when it came time to decide whether to deploy intermediate range and cruise missiles in Europe in mid-1981. After several long, complex, and even heated discussions in the National Security Council (NSC), in which he met with resistance from surprising quarters inside his own administration, the president simply signed off on the option he wanted from the beginning, clearly signaling with hints and body language that he wanted a consensus position: The United States would deploy and at the same time negotiate intensely to make that deployment unnecessary.

As he was recuperating from the bullet that nearly took his life on March 30, 1981, President Reagan reached for pen and paper to hand-write a private letter to Leonid Brezhnev. In that and subsequent letters, as well as by his actions, Reagan tried to convey to Brezhnev both his belief that continuing an arms race would be counterproductive, and, that if there had to be one, the United States intended to win it. Brezhnev never understood the level at which Reagan made his appeal, and the responses always came back as Soviet boilerplate and bluster. By then the Soviets were clearly both baffled and alarmed at what they were seeing.

The Arms Race and the Soviet Economy

Reagan knew that he would have to squeeze the Soviets slowly and gently, but so they could feel it, as the U.S. programs to re-arm and modernize the military sector gained momentum. He never believed, as did many Western observers—including alleged experts—that the Soviet economy had the capacity to extract from its citizens limitless sacrifice for the sake of maintaining invincible military power. He knew instinctively that a healthy, growing, and productive American economy, with its scientific and technological excellence, would easily outpace the bankrupt "scientific socialist" system of the Soviet Union.

One of his key concerns was to deny the Soviet Union access to advanced technology. The objective would be to shut down, to the extent possible, the flow of scientific and technological data that migrated, legally and illegally, to the Soviet side. Some of it was simply stolen by a massive Soviet effort, and that would be difficult to stem. But much of it was sold openly, and Reagan was determined to put a stop to this, and to persuade the allies to follow suit. Accordingly, Bill Casey, the director of central intelligence, and others engaged in a major effort to close the doors from the United States and to persuade or, if necessary, cajole and pressure, our friends and allies in Europe and Japan to follow suit. It wasn't well received in Europe, as governments there really wanted to continue business as usual with the East, and resented U.S. interference. It wasn't always successful either, but the efforts during the Reagan years were persistent, even dogged, and people like Fred Iklé and Richard Perle at DOD, and Roger Robinson at NSC, worked hard with Casey to impede the eastward flow.

The weakness and inflexibility of the Soviet command economy were key factors in the Reagan strategy. To the extent that U.S. initiatives would place strains on that cumbersome machine, the Reagan administration sought to increase the pressures substantially. So, the screws were tightened, one turn at a time. At the outset of the Reagan administration, the Soviets were enjoying a bonanza through oil and gas sales to the West—for hard currency. During the 1970s, high oil prices had increased Soviet energy revenues more than tenfold. Western energy dollars were an important consideration in the ability of the Soviets to stay in the race, and so major efforts were undertaken, again principally by Bill Casey, to bring about a significant increase in global oil production in order to drive prices down. The benefit to the United States would be twofold: reducing the cost of energy to itself, while simultaneously undercutting the Soviet revenue stream. Every one-dollar drop in the price of oil meant a hard currency loss of between $500 million and $1 billion for the Soviets.

Led by Casey, this effort paid off handsomely as the Saudi government cooperated by increasing oil production from two million barrels to nine million. In short order the price of a barrel of oil fell from thirty to twelve dollars, inflicting a ten billion dollar annual "hit" on the Soviet Union. The machine tools, industrial robots, electronics, and computers that the Soviets needed to fulfill their ambitious Eleventh Five-Year Plan fell well beyond reach, and eventually put pressure on Moscow to plead for a "time out" in the arms race. They simply could not sustain a defense against the genuine and effective economic warfare being waged from Washington. A rapid succession of Soviet leaders—Brezhnev to Andropov to Chernenko to Gorbachev in relatively short order—did not make it easier for the Soviet side to respond effectively. Reagan used to say that he was trying to have a summit meeting with Soviet leaders, but it was hard to do because, as he put it, "they keep dying on me."

The Strategic Defense Initiative

The squeeze also included a new emphasis on strategic defense. Consistent with his basic views that defense is inherently superior in moral terms to offense and his abhorrence of "MAD", Reagan had long believed that the United States should not remain defenseless against a missile attack. Accordingly, a preliminary and informal study of the prospects for missile defense was begun in the first year of the administration. By 1983, an embryonic plan was ready and in late March of that year the Strategic Defense Initiative was announced. It soon became known by the pejorative term "Star Wars" and was roundly ridiculed and denounced both at home and abroad, especially by the Soviets.

Actually, it scared the hell out of the Russians. They were not sure whether they should believe it or whether it was a massive hoax. They rolled out all their propaganda tools to counter it, they blustered and threatened, but to little avail. After having worked for years since the Cuban Missile Crisis to find a breakthrough like this themselves, the Soviets had been outmaneuvered by the Grade B movie actor from California. Their antiquated command economy and pitifully weak technological base, at least fifteen years behind in computer technology, could not hope to sustain an effort against a determined and wealthy Western adversary. The necessary billions of rubles were just not there.

Afghanistan

But that was not all. The "squeeze" was also extended to other crucial fronts. The Soviets had an enormous presence and stake in Afghanistan, and the Reagan administration made the decision to engage by providing a reliable supply of money and arms to the Afghan *mujaheddin*. From late 1981 onward, the administration increased its efforts to open the flow of weapons, principally through Pakistan, and to get the Saudis and other friendly Arab states to finance that flow. Training, communications gear, intelligence from overhead satellite reconnaissance, rifles, mines, mortars, and eventually Stinger missiles for use against Soviet HIND helicopters—all of this converted the *mujaheddin* from a ragtag guerrilla outfit to a formidable military force. Heavy casualties—as many as twenty thousand by the spring of 1983—were inflicted on Soviet and Afghan regime troops, and the venture was turned into a Vietnam-like quagmire for the Soviets. The goals of U.S. policy were to inflict maximum casualties, to raise the price of the war—and to demoralize the Soviet high command. Remarkably, the war was also carried directly into Soviet Central Asia, and *mujaheddin*-supported strikes there became a veritable nightmare for Moscow. Late in 1986, after sustaining huge casualties and the loss of support from the Soviet people, Moscow retreated in defeat. . . .

So, it came to pass that the old fellow from California eventually prepared to leave Washington, his term expired.

He had come to town with a game plan, simple but under-standable. To be sure, it became a complex plan as elements were added to it and improvisations were made. Implement-ing the plan required a lot of money and a lot of courage, and in some respects it failed—as in the "loony tunes" of the Iran-Contra scandal, a tawdry sideshow to the main attrac-tion of the struggle with the Soviets. But in the end the United States called the Soviet hand, and the Soviets and their satraps folded.

Economic Stagnation

Leonard Silk

In the early 1980s, the Soviet economy was wracked by chronic shortages of food and consumer items. A few Soviet economists were calling for reform of the centralized economy.

In the following selection, Leonard Silk describes the economic situation within the Soviet Union and the plans for reform put forward in the early eighties. The problem with the economy, he claims, is the outdated system of central planning, which is producing malaise among Soviet workers and low productivity in Soviet factories. Economists, he says, are planning to introduce elements of a free market. But without political liberty, he argues, it is questionable whether such reform will work.

Leonard Silk, longtime economics columnist for the *New York Times*, died in 1995.

The whole hectic scene, with its long queues, surly saleswomen and shoddy goods, was as familiar as a recurrent dream. But it's one thing to read about the jumble of the Soviet economy; it's another to see it for yourself.

Here I was, in a general store in a small town in northeastern Siberia, and what I saw struck me as the heart of the mystery that had brought me to the Soviet Union for the first time in my life. Brassieres next to children's toys, fabrics next to souvenirs, fountain pens next to shirts and pants, pots and pans next to shoes and socks. Sofas and chairs that belonged in a thrift shop. Small refrigerators that could have come out of a 1924 Sears catalogue. And everybody—men

Reprinted from Leonard Silk, "Andropov's Economic Dilemma," *The New York Times Magazine*, October 9, 1983, by permission. Copyright © 1983 by The New York Times Company.

and women jamming the place after their normal working day—buying like crazy, as though the ruble were about to collapse.

The town was Neryungri (pop. 45,000), but the scene could have been duplicated all over the Soviet Union. Was this hidden inflation—too many rubles chasing too few goods, with the Government setting ridiculously low prices for its sparse consumer supplies and thus debauching the currency? Was it prosperity Soviet-style—the lusty consumer demand that kept the rickety supply side from breaking down? Was there some deeper riddle?

Shortages of Economic Goods

Yuri V. Andropov, the new Soviet leader, was proposing basic economic reforms. High officials in the Reagan Administration were contending that the Soviet economy was a basket case, or could be made into one if the United States stepped up the arms race and placed the Soviet civilian sector under increasing strain; this, they argued, could force the Russians to trim their military programs and adopt a less aggressive foreign policy. I decided that, given my background as both economist and journalist, it might be useful for me to take a look at the Soviet economy from closer up. With appointments arranged by the Soviet Embassy in Washington, I spent last May traveling across the Soviet Union, being received at some of the country's leading economic research centers, hearing much franker talk than I had expected to hear—and reaching certain conclusions!

The picture that hit me so hard at the store in the Siberian boondocks was complemented in the major cities. In Moscow, my wife and I were taken by our Soviet guide and interpreter to the capital's biggest bookstore to buy a Russian-English dictionary. There were no Russian-English dictionaries. We tried another bookstore; no luck. We tried in Leningrad, Novosibirsk, Yakutsk; none there, either. Where were the Russian-English dictionaries? Had they all been classified by the K.G.B.?

At a so-called free market in Moscow, where the collective farmers sell the produce of their tiny private plots at higher prices than those at the state stores, we found roses going at the equivalent of $5 per flower. Fruit and vegetables in stringently short supply at the official retail level sold for similarly exorbitant sums; I was told of a vegetable-craving wife of a foreign correspondent who paid $31 for a cauliflower.

Off Gorky Street, we saw a line for oranges, cucumbers and cabbages form before a stall and grow quickly halfway down the block. Illegal private enterprise? No, Government-controlled produce sold by a woman on outpost duty from a nearby shop. At GUM, the department store in the shadow of the Kremlin, more mobs, more lines. And the same everywhere we went in the Soviet Union—congestion, shortages, and queues, queues, queues.

Why, in the world's second-largest economy, is consumer-goods production so inadequate, so disorganized, so poor? Are the Russians simply lazy workers, as some Western observers say? That seems an unsatisfactory explanation, in view of the economic feats recorded during the country's industrialization. Yet it is widely agreed, even among Soviet experts, that the Soviet worker is no model of the work ethic today. In fact, slothfulness, absenteeism, drunkenness and other harmful attitudes were the object of Andropov's initial corrective action soon after taking power a year ago—his drive for greater work discipline. Yet, as an economist at the Institute of Economics in Moscow said to me, "discipline is only one of the ways of intensification."

"In the past," he went on, "discipline meant treating people harshly, putting them in jail. That won't work anymore. We cannot go back to the Stalin era. Now we have to find ways of giving greater incentives for work."

There, it seemed to me, lay one of the keys to economic betterment—motivating the Soviet worker to greater effort. But how?

"We've tried everything," confessed another Soviet economist, almost in despair. "This incentive, that incentive. Raises and bonuses if they will overfulfill the norms. Threats if they won't. We put out 'punishment books' if customers are dissatisfied with services. But nothing works."

Why?

Soviet Economic Experts

The city of Novosibirsk, in western Siberia, belies the image its location may have for most Americans. It is the site of an important branch of the Soviet Academy of Sciences, a research center where some of the country's most advanced economic studies take place. Shortly before my visit to the city, a group of economists there prepared a confidential report, later leaked to Western correspondents, which must be one of the most revealing Soviet economic statements of the post-Stalin era.

The economists argued that while the Soviet economic malaise was being attributed by different Soviet scholars to different factors—such as lagging investment, flagging work discipline, harder mining conditions and unusually frequent dry years in agriculture—there was a common underlying cause. That cause, they wrote, "lies in the outdated nature of the system of industrial organization and economic management, or simply in the inability of the system to insure complete and efficient utilization of the workers and of the intellectual potential of the society."

What a confession! But even a quick rundown of the system's workings is enough to give the indictment ample support. For ideological reasons, prices on goods in everyday demand are generally set below the level at which supply would equal demand; hence the hordes of people buying everything in sight. Excess demand makes it possible for Soviet industrial enterprises to be sunk in inertia and fouled up in red tape, and still survive. A Soviet business firm does not have to keep costs below selling prices and make a profit. What it does have to do is acquire the labor, materials and transportation to fulfill the production quota it receives from above. To prevent it from going broke in the process, it can be bailed out in a variety of ways. The managers' success commonly depends not on how well they manage but on whom they know out there, and up there.

In these conditions, the Soviet enterprise develops an insatiable appetite for resources. Each enterprise seeks to solve its problems by taking labor, materials, equipment and capital away from other businesses and industrial sectors. To do this, it uses *tolkachi*—pushers, what we used to call dogrobbers in the United States Army. Since all businesses do it to each other, they collectively intensify the shortages, bottlenecks, waste and low productivity of the entire system.

The Promise of Full Employment

And that is not all. These economic ills are worsened by a doctrinaire commitment to two goals reiterated as late as last August by the chairman of the State Planning Committee, Nikolai K. Baibakov. Moscow, he said, will continue to support money-losing plants rather than close them, because the Communist approach is to turn such plants into profit makers and save jobs; and the Government will not tolerate unemployment, even temporarily, since Soviet law requires that any worker who is dismissed be found another job.

Full employment is obviously a worthy goal. Unemployment and underutilization of industrial capacity are the abiding problems of capitalism, and they have led in recent years to sluggish growth and the wastage of human resources in the West. But the wastage of labor in the Soviet Union seems even greater and more demoralizing. I am thinking of those women sitting around the lobbies of hotels, watching and waiting; of the vast numbers of secret agents bugging and spying and informing on people for a living; of the oversupply of policemen stopping cars, watching the streets and guarding the compounds reserved for foreign diplomats, businessmen and correspondents; of all the supernumeraries in factories, offices and farms who, even if pushed out of a job here and there, have to be put into some other job elsewhere.

The system produces a sour, semicorrupt national mood—the grumpiness and indolence of those in undesired and undesirable jobs; the coats over the backs of chairs in offices signifying that their owners are nominally at work, though actually somewhere else, the incredible waiting times in restaurants, and the surliness of the waiters and waitresses. My favorite line, spoken by a waitress in response to a plea for an omelette at the National Hotel in Moscow: "*Omlyet—nyet!*"

I came to recognize some of the subtler side effects of the combination of no competition and jobs for all: the inescapability of earsplitting live music in restaurants from Leningrad to Yakutsk (full employment for musicians); the climate of laziness (the gardener sprinkling flowers while sitting in a truck, holding the hose in one hand, a book in the other); the filthy condition of public toilets (who wants to work in a toilet when you are sure of getting a job elsewhere?); the endless waits at airports, as Aeroflot, in its almighty and unfathomable ways, decides when to fly or whether to fly and whether to change you from one flight to another; the widespread drunkenness, on and off the job; the impossibility of getting anything done on time.

"We understand these problems," the economist Yuri I. Bobrakov, of the Institute for the Study of the United States and Canada in Moscow, told me. "They are the failures of success."

The accomplishments of the past six decades are undeniable—rapid industrialization, elimination of extreme poverty, slowly rising living standards—and, of course, full employment. But where has success gone?

The Decline of the Soviet Economy

Depletion of natural resources in the European part of the Soviet Union, the aging of the capital stock in industry and transportation and a manpower shortage traceable to World War II casualties have helped slow economic growth. From a peak of 5.2 percent during 1966–70, the period of the eighth five-year plan, average annual growth fell to around 2 percent during 1981–82, according to Daniel L. Bond and Herbert S. Levine of Wharton Econometric Forecasting Associates. (The Soviet calculations given me were not much different.) Soviet living standards are still only about one-third of ours, and the gap may be widening.

Soviet economists admit that the methods of the past, when the country lacked virtually everything and could be run on a forced-draft basis from Moscow, have lost their effectiveness and are breeding stagnation and decay. The economists I met told me the Soviet Union must now enter a new stage of development.

But can it? Some of the economists conceded that it won't be easy. As Georgi Skorov, a deputy director of the Institute for the Study of the United States and Canada put it, "There are some traditions it is difficult to overcome." Or, as another economist said, almost wistfully, "You Western economists are lucky. You can count on the discipline of the market. Managers know their businesses will fail if they don't manage better, make better products. Workers know they will lose their jobs if they don't produce or if their employers fail."

It would be difficult indeed for the Soviet planners to go in that direction. Once they started moving away from their taut economy, under which full employment and a tight balance between supply and demand are maintained by artificial means, they would be faced with some vexing new problems.

To start with, there would likely be an increase in the production of goods—both consumer products and capital goods, such as machinery—of better quality. But goods of the old shoddy variety would still be coming out of the spigot. Soviet consumers, offered an ampler variety, would be less ready to buy up the flow of junky goods, and massive gluts would develop. The producers of these unsaleable stocks would be forced into laying off their workers.

To cope with gluts and mass unemployment, the Government would be faced with a choice of unpalatable options. It could flood the economy with additional money for consumers to spend and for employers to pay out in wages. This would restore the original mess, a mixture of hidden inflation—hidden by price controls and subsidies but expressing itself in queues, shortages and black-market prices—and inefficient allocation of resources. Alternatively, the Government could establish a welfare system on Western capitalist lines to deal with waves of unemployment. But this would be admitting that—contrary to Soviet doctrine—the Soviet economy, like the capitalist one, is vulnerable to recessions. In a sense, the Soviet economy needs its inefficiencies to remain Soviet.

The Plan for Reform

The only way to minimize these problems would be to permit individual Soviet enterprises to make their own adjustments: improve the quality of their goods, change the product mix to meet current demands, set their own prices, cut labor and other costs, and fire incompetent managers no matter what their party status or who their friends at the top. This would require a drastic reduction in the power of the central planners. Is that what is meant by Andropov's economic directive of July 26, when it speaks of broadening "the rights of enterprises in planning and economic activity"?

Not from what I heard in the Soviet Union. The economists I talked to told me the essence of the planned experiments is greater autonomy for plant managers—and, at the same time, even greater control at the top. The shift of power to the factory level will not, they explained, be away from the central planners but from the middle-level bureaucracy.

This, in their view, will correct an unhealthy trend of recent years. According to the April memorandum of the Novosibirsk group, there has actually been a weakening of the powers of the State Planning Committee, at the economic apex, as well as of the industrial corporations and other economic enterprises at the bottom of the pyramid. "In stark contrast," the paper said, "the powers of the functionaries of the intermediate levels of management, the ministries and agencies, have grown out of proportion, giving rise to departmentalism, to disproportions in the economy, to a growth of economic activity outside the formal economic structure." The last phrase apparently refers to that peculiar semiofficial underground economy in which bureaucrats foraging for scarce resources behave like bandits. The basic idea is that both control at the top and initiative at the production level would be strengthened if the swollen powers of the bureaucrats in between were drastically reduced.

In short, the Soviet leaders appear to be searching for their own version of a mixed economy. The economists who advise them no longer see Western capitalism as the atomistic model of Adam Smith but as an effective mixture of business and government. Many of them seem ready to adapt the best Western models to their own use. Yet how can you give the plant manager more freedom of action at the same time that you augment Moscow's controls over what he does? It reminds one of the nursery rhyme in which the daughter asks if she may go out to swim and the mother replies, "Yes, my darling daughter. Hang your clothes on a hickory limb but don't go near the water." Are the proposed reforms basic enough?

The Soviet Leadership

We were driving through the suburbs of Moscow, past the heavily policed estates of the country's highest officials, when, suddenly, all traffic was brought to a stop and we were waved to the side of the road. Big black limousines with no license plates came roaring through at 100 miles an hour. The members of the Politburo were on their way home from work. We couldn't see them behind their curtained windows. When the limos and the guard cars had passed, the police waved us on.

On our last afternoon in Moscow, we were standing on the balcony of our suite at the National Hotel, my wife and I, watching the troops lining up before the Kremlin's south wall. They were rehearsing the funeral of Arvid Pelshe, the Politburo member and veteran of the 1917 Revolution who had just died at the age of 84. We thought we'd take some pictures of the historic scene. Instantly, a voice ordering us to put away our cameras came blaring over a loudspeaker from across the square.

The hierarchical, military style of the Soviet leadership reaches down through the system. It is hard to tell whether the cause is power hunger, officiousness or fear. It is just as hard to believe that such a society is headed for a democratic diffusion of economic power.

I seriously doubt that such a political structure is compatible with effective economic reform. The missing element is freedom. One does not have to look farther than the memorandum of the Novosibirsk economists for an indictment of what the Soviet industrial system does to human beings.

"The type of worker that such a system cultivates," the paper says, "not only falls short of the needs of developed socialism but fails to match the requirements of modern production. His common traits are low labor and productive discipline, an indifferent attitude toward work, a shoddy quality of work, social inactivity, a well-pronounced consumer mentality and a low code of ethics." What the economy needs, the paper said, are people who are more cultivated, who possess social and spiritual values, and who want—and should be granted—"greater leeway."

But the problem goes beyond stifling the worker's—or manager's—initiative; it involves the economic costs of the political repression that characterizes the whole society. What is the cost of inhibiting the imagination and daring of creative people by spying on them, cutting their communications with colleagues at home and abroad and letting them know that their colleagues have been punished for raising the issue of human rights?

In one of the Soviet institutes, at a seminar with a dozen economists, I was asked what I thought was the best and worst I had seen in the Soviet Union. I said the best were the Kirov Ballet in Leningrad, the Moscow Circus and some of the people I had met, and the worst things were the spying, the treatment of Soviet dissidents and of Jews who wished to emigrate, my inability to get the reading material I wanted and needed—in short, the lack of freedom.

The man who had asked the question looked at me solemnly and said, *"Khorosho"*—"Good." Neither he nor anyone else in the seminar tried to refute me. On the contrary, I have never felt such strong rapport with a group. They were silent and sorrowful. Later, they asked me to stay longer and join their institute for a year—"You would fit in."

Opposition to Reform

But my interview with the head of the Siberian division of the Academy of Sciences, Valentin A. Koptyug, made me wonder about that. While in Moscow, I had seen police guards before the entrance to the building where Andrei Sakharov lived before being exiled to Gorky in 1980, and where his wife still stays on her visits to the capital. I asked Koptyug why the police were necessary. "Did it ever occur to you that they were guarding her from the anger of the people?" he replied.

When I asked what the Nobel Prize–winning physicist and dissident had done to warrant such anger, he grew red in the face and said that Sakharov, for all his past contributions to physics, had lost the respect of his countrymen because of his "unprofessional" political activities. He claimed Sakharov was free to leave the Soviet Union whenever he wished, and offered to give me proof of that before I left Novosibirsk. The proof never came.

The outlook implicit in his remarks seems representative of the view at the economic pinnacle. The Andropov experiments, due to start next Jan. 1 in two machine and electrical equipment ministries and in selected industries in Byelorussia, Lithuania and the Ukraine, are an attempt to solve the economy's problems by purely technical means. In addition to greater local autonomy, they offer material incentives to producers to become more efficient. The hope is that this will gradually reduce the tautness of the economy, the source of low productivity, shortages, hidden inflation, low morale, corruption and the rest. To stimulate scientific and technological innovations, a critically weak area, the Government will set up a special fund and offer extra financial incentives for risk taking. But the experiments seem timid; they fall well short of radical reform. Andropov and his top aides hope to solve their economic problems without changing the political system.

I don't think it can be done. It does not seem to me that the Soviet Union's deep-seated economic troubles can be cured by material rewards alone. Either the Soviet leaders will be forced to permit a much wider degree of political and personal freedom than they are contemplating or their efforts at economic reform will fail.

The Chernobyl Disaster

Sergei Roy

On April 26, 1986, a reactor at the Chernobyl nuclear power plant near Kiev, Ukraine, exploded, releasing radioactive material into the atmosphere. At least thirty-one people died in the explosion and fire, and hundreds of thousands were evacuated from the immediate vicinity. Radioactive contamination spread over much of Europe, especially those countries north of Ukraine, prompting an international outcry.

Writing ten years after the accident, Sergei Roy argues in the following viewpoint that the Chernobyl disaster discredited Mikhail Gorbachev and the Communist government in the eyes of the Soviet people. Until then, according to Roy, Soviet cynicism toward the government was mixed with fear. News of the bungled response to and attempted coverup of the Chernobyl accident prompted citizens' fearless protest, he contends, which, along with the staggering costs of the disaster, led to the eventual overthrow of the Soviet regime.

Sergei Roy is an editor of *Moscow News*.

The reactor of the fourth unit of the Chernobyl ("Wormwood") nuclear power plant blew up on April 26, 1986. The time was 1:23:40 P.M. For the first time in the history of man, the mushroom cloud of a nuclear explosion sprouted over the earth's surface as a result of human error. The immediate cause was later officially stated to be an "unauthorized experiment"—which was a damn lie, for it lay in certain fatal defects of the reactor's design. If it hadn't happened at Chernobyl, it would have happened somewhere else, where the same RBMK (fast breeder) reactors were installed. I later learned that most plant managers walked in constant and very tangible fear of disaster, and on hearing that a nuclear explosion had occurred at some power plant, most of them automatically assumed that it had been at theirs.

All this came out much, much later, though. At the time, the first I heard of it all was through the BBC World Service, but the figures as to loss of life quoted there—hundreds and even thousands dead—amid the dead calm in the Soviet media left one guessing helplessly. What one felt most acutely was fury at an obvious attempt at a cover-up, the full scope of which only came out years later.

The Attempted Cover-Up

I read afterwards that the cover-up started from the very first telephone call from the Ukraine to Moscow: even the government was not told that the reactor had been destroyed—"to avoid long questioning by telephone," as the official who made the call later put it. This continued all along the chain of command: Shcherbina, chairman of the government emergency commission, did not report fully to Moscow, and the Politburo imposed an almost total information blackout, except for bland and palpably untrue TASS [news agency] statements, the first of which came out on April 28, two days after the explosion.

It was later rumored that the man primarily responsible for the clampdown on information about Chernobyl was Ligachev, and it looks like the truth, but the Politburo acted on the so-called "collective leadership" principle, at least in theory, so they are all collectively responsible for the untold misery of millions of people and the deaths of quite a few.

In real terms, Gorbachev could have put his foot down and put the facts that he himself knew before the nation and the world. Instead, he gave in to the Pavlovian dog's Soviet reflex of keeping all disasters under wraps until they are more or less dealt with. He thought of saving his political skin first, second and last, like perhaps every other politician in the world; unlike them, though, he thought that he could get away with any

sort of lie—and apparently still thinks so: on the tenth anniversary of the Chernobyl disaster he brazenly insisted that
there had been no cover-up at the time!

The international outcry, especially in countries that were
registering considerable radiation levels, like Sweden, and
the media hysteria about corpses lying about in the streets of
Kiev eventually put a stop to the attempted cover-up, and
Gorbachev spoke to the nation on TV—more than two
weeks later, on May 14, looking the picture of dismay. By
that time, though, a great deal of harm had been done: the
population hadn't been warned in time to take measures
against radiation in the first days after the disaster, when the
fallout was heaviest. Evacuation of the population from the
contaminated area was inexcusably delayed. Inadequate
measures were taken for the safety of the personnel sent to
fight the consequences of the disaster. And so on.

The Reaction of the Soviet People

The people reacted with fury to the facts that gradually came
out, passed on by word of mouth, inevitably garbled, and
gradually even penetrating the press. The Ukrainian Party
bosses, having packed off their own offspring to safety,
calmly allowed the May Day celebrations to proceed, smil-
ing benignly on thousands of children marching past on a
sunny spring day, amid flowers, music and flags, through
heavily contaminated streets. From then on, hatred for the
ruling nomenklatura among the masses soared. It was probably in those days that the jingle, so often chanted at later
mass rallies, was made up:

> *Pust zhivyot KPSS*
> *Na Chernobylskoy AES!*
> *(Long live the Communist Party*
> *At Chernobyl Power Plant!)*

Like all things in Russia, the issue became highly personal-
ized, and Gorbachev's credibility, what there was of it, was
wrecked by the whole episode—another fact about Gorbachev that the folks in the West, whose relatives never suffered from the rabid self-interest displayed by that individual,

do not seem to appreciate, as they accuse the ex-Soviet people of ingratitude toward the great man. Even at that time, though, his duplicity must have struck some Westerners who heard Gorbachev's call, in his May 14 address to the nation, for measures for swift notification of nuclear accidents—a feat of impudence that brought me to the point of apoplexy: the guy was "notifying" his own people about the disaster a solid three weeks after the event—and urging others to be "swift"!

A couple of years later, all sorts of damning facts about the antecedents of the disaster surfaced in the press. Some of the plant's construction defects were apparently due to the universal practice of doing things in a hurry in order to report to the Party superiors completion of construction by some celebration date.

But even releasing these facts to the press was yet another move in the cover-up campaign to conceal the defectiveness of all nuclear reactors of the Chernobyl type, not just the one in Chernobyl. A prominent nuclear physicist named Valery Legasov committed suicide after numerous unsuccessful attempts to convince the top leadership of the threat they posed, insisting that unless certain measures to change the design were swiftly taken, the world could expect two or three Chernobyls in the near future.

I learned of this from Ales Adamovich, the writer from Belorussia, the republic which, along with the Ukraine, was worst affected by the catastrophe, with hundreds of thousands, if not millions, suffering now from disaster-related diseases. Adamovich and Stanley Kramer wanted to make a film about Chernobyl and, as I translated Adamovich's script into English, we had some of those endless political arguments, but mostly I pumped the writer for facts that had not at the time been made public. Adamovich was then pursuing a career as a major anti-nuke campaigner in the Soviet Union, he had been Belorussia's representative at the United Nations, he was Director of the Institute of Cinematography in Moscow and knew quite a few people close to the top, so he was quite useful as a source of information in a country that still made do with the twin tools of rumor and bland, bare-faced official statements for hard news.

The Costs of the Disaster

The facts of the disaster and the handing of it are all fairly well known by now, so I need mention only the most salient points. The first people that went in to deal with the catastrophe were ordinary firemen who fought the fire at the nuclear plant after the explosion as just another fire, without a thought for radiation. Naturally, most of them died soon after. Then the soldiers went in, about 340,000 of them, to deal with the aftermath of the disaster, gathering and burying radioactive debris with spades and sometimes bare hands. I wonder if there is a single one among these people, called "liquidators," who have not suffered the consequences, sometimes fatal, of those days of heroism, incompetence and sometimes plain stupidity. Other major events there were the building of an outer shell, called the "sarcophagus," over the destroyed reactor and the (belated) evacuation of first 130,000 and then a further 100,000 people from the contaminated areas.

According to expert estimates, the Chernobyl disaster cost the country, in all the years since it happened, some $200 billion. No economy, least of all the Soviet one, could stand the strain—and it didn't. No political system that first made the disaster possible and then bungled the rescue effort, with reckless disregard for the expectations, feelings and very lives of millions, could stand the debacle, either—and the Soviet system didn't. It was plain doomed.

Closed Society Exploded

The Chernobyl disaster brought such irrefutable proof of actual, physical harm done to the nation by the Soviet spy mania and general paranoia that glasnost made enormous strides that year, changing the whole climate in the country. The catastrophe showed that all-pervading secrecy, suspicion and other unsavory aspects of a closed society were not just a nuisance for the populace, besides being the Party's tool for keeping that same populace in blinkered, totalitarian unanimity, but also a menace to the nation's economic well-being and national security itself.

Before Chernobyl, only the more educated public, mostly in the capital cities, suffered from the strictures of a hermetically sealed society. Trips abroad were, like nearly free housing or subsidized holidays, an instrument of encouraging loyalty to the-Party-and-the-government. The few lucky ones only went to foreign lands in groups, each of them routinely chaperoned by the KGB. Contacts with foreigners were not just discouraged or frowned upon but rather pounced upon by the same three-letter organization. Letters and parcels from abroad were routinely intercepted, opened, inspected and confiscated. Bibles were supremely suspect and seized as fiercely as Henry Miller.

The majority of the population, who had never heard of Henry Miller and had no hopes of or much desire for going outside, into the wide but reportedly hostile world, did not much suffer from claustrophobia, having never lived in any but a closed society. They might be breathing nothing but the fumes of a chemical plant nearby, but it never entered their heads to link up this fact with their right to know why it had been built there in the first place. That was just the way things were. Sure, an amorous couple from the sticks would be extremely annoyed at being kicked off a Crimean beach at night by the ever watchful frontier guards: it was forbidden to spend a night anywhere within 500 meters of the edge of the beach which marked the state frontier. These were but minor inconveniences, though, and in this, as in many other areas, the same rule applied as was formulated by Alexander Herzen early in the 19th century: the severity of Russian laws is mitigated by a general sloppiness in their application.

The End of Paranoia

The Chernobyl disaster showed, however, that the blight of secrecy was not always a joking matter, and that its consequences could be apocalyptic. Rudely awakened, Soviet society sat up and took notice, measuring itself not against the days of Stalinist horror but against the more civilized standards of open societies. The spectacle that presented itself to the eye was abominable. Paranoia started right at the core of the whole social structure—in the Party (and we must bear in mind that it was about 19 million strong): the whole oceanic flow of paper from local Party cells upwards and from the Politburo and Central Committee downwards was secret, top secret or plain old confidential, even if some little slip of paper contained nothing more than instructions on how the Party dues were to be paid. Come to think of it, it wasn't all paranoia, a throwback to the times when the Party was a bunch of conspirators or a tiny minority in power confronting a hostile population: the shroud of secrecy was also a useful tool of psychological domination. Ancient geographers had an apt saying: Where you know nothing, place terrors. So for decades the people saw the Party as a terrifying force—and when the fear evaporated in the rays of glasnost, the colossus came tumbling down like the statue of Dzerzhinsky in Lubyanka in August 1991.

The same hermetic situation prevailed in all the other state and social structures. No ray of glasnost ever penetrated into the inner workings of the armed forces, the Interior Ministry, or, *horribile dictu*, the KGB. The military-industrial complex was also impervious to view, and if you consider that that complex comprised about 60 percent of the nation's industry, if not more, that meant pretty much the whole country. These bureaucratic-industrial monsters made up their own laws called instructions, *instruktsii*, defying all rights—human, animal and vegetable—and lived by those rules. If any individuals got hurt by those monsters, so much the worse for the individuals: the monsters could always cite their own "instructions" which invariably proved them right—if they ever bothered to explain anything to anyone. In 1957, long before Chernobyl, there was a nuclear explosion in Chelyabinsk in the Urals, and no one was the wiser— I only learned about it when I went to the Urals in about 1971. The population of a huge area suffered—is still suffering—from the consequences of that much less publicized disaster, and their deaths were never diagnosed as anything remotely connected with radiation sickness. There were also rumors about a passenger ship on the Volga crashing into a bridge, with a loss of hundreds of lives, but there was never a murmur about it in the press.

The press, and anything ever printed in the country, was subject to the harshest censorship—which went to simply idiotic lengths. I remember being obliged to have my dissertation okayed by Glavlit, the state censorship agency, although it was on an abstruse subject in semiotics, light-years away from practical life, let alone any state secrets.

Glasnost and Chernobyl

I sometimes think that all this might have gone on for years, if it hadn't been for Chernobyl. Everybody would have been paying lip service to glasnost, because it was fashionable and the General Secretary told them to, and everybody who had the power to do so would be holding on to their precious "secrets" or rather the practice of never letting any outsiders know of what went on inside. Chernobyl put an end to that. On May 6, *Pravda* published an article on the disaster which broke with the cover-up tradition and was a real eye-opener to vast numbers of people. It became known much later that the man who insisted on its publication was Alexander Yakovlev, once exiled as an ambassador to Canada for being too much of a liberal (by Soviet Marxist standards), brought back by Gorbachev in 1983 and elevated to the Central Committee secretariat in February 1986. He became the motive force behind practically all moves that signaled the advance of glasnost and the crumbling of the hitherto relentlessly closed society.

Chapter 2

Attempts at Reforming the Government

Turning Points

IN WORLD HISTORY

Unmet Economic Expectations Under Gorbachev

S. Frederick Starr

Mikhail Gorbachev assumed the leadership of the Soviet Union as general secretary of the Communist Party in March 1985. In 1987 he embarked on a program of reform, under the rubrics *glasnost* and *perestroika*, intended to restructure the ailing centrally planned Soviet economy and revive the stagnant society.

In the following viewpoint, written in 1988 prior to the collapse of the Soviet Union, S. Frederick Starr argues that Soviet civil society had not succumbed to bureaucratic "petrification" or the stagnation of the official economy under Gorbachev's predecessors. The demands of the wealthier, more educated populace for consumer goods and services, he asserts, spurred the growth of an underground economy that outpaced the official economy and prompted increased criticism of the regime. Starr concludes that Gorbachev's perestroika is less a plan to initiate political reform than an attempt to harness these societal forces and modernize the Soviet economy.

S. Frederick Starr is President of Oberlin College and founding secretary of the Kennan Institute for Advanced Russian Studies at the Woodrow Wilson International Center for Scholars. He is the author of *The Legacy of History in Russia and the New States of Eurasia.*

What better way is there to initiate a program of reforms than to persuade the public that life stagnated under a predecessor's

Reprinted, with permission, from S. Frederick Starr, "Soviet Union: A Civil Society," *Foreign Policy,* vol. 70, Spring 1988. Copyright 1988 by the Carnegie Endowment for International Peace.

policies? There is no better evidence of Soviet leader Mikhail Gorbachev's political prowess than the thoroughness with which he has accomplished this discrediting. In his view, the vitality of the post-Stalin thaw gave way to a period of turgid bureaucratism during which not only the Soviet government and economy but also the society at large succumbed to a profound malaise.

Successful political slogans must contain at least a grain of truth, and the notion of general stagnation under the late Soviet leader Leonid Brezhnev meets this test. Long before the economy went flat about 1978, the regime had become petrified and oligarchic, thereby repressing the very forces that might have stimulated economic renewal. Where Gorbachev is seriously wrong—and where many Americans err in accepting his view— is in his claim that the manifest stagnation in the Communist party and bureaucracy pervaded Soviet society as well.

Social Ferment vs. Political Stagnation

Much of what happened in Soviet society under Brezhnev was bound to strike a provincial bureaucrat like the young Gorbachev as decadent, but this says as much about the mentality of officialdom as about the social dynamic itself. For while the official economy lagged, an entrepreneurial "second economy" burgeoned. In unprecedented numbers young Soviets became contributing participants in the global youth culture, forcing the government to accept what it could not alter. Individual citizens in countless fields plunged into innovative work, blithely ignoring official taboos and following wherever their interests led them. Torpor may have reigned in the official world, but Soviet society in Brezhnev's time experienced great ferment. To be sure, corruption abounded. But the rise of corruption must be laid directly to the regime's failure to open legitimate channels for the new energies rather than to some cancerous venality that had entered the body politic. Indeed, the social energies that were marginalized or suppressed under Brezhnev provide much of the impetus to today's economic and political reforms.

Gorbachev may be excused for playing down the dynamic element in Soviet society. To accept it he would be acknowledging that much of the initiative for change has shifted from the Communist party to society. Gorbachev then would appear not as the revolutionary leader calling a somnolent nation to action but as a conservative reformer trying to save a system facing pressures beyond his control.

Western analysts cannot so easily be excused for their narrow concern with Kremlin politics to the neglect of the social realities underlying them. To their credit, American researchers first identified the impact of alcoholism on the life expectancy of Russian men, as well as the demographic trends creating a labor shortage in European Russia and a baby boom in Soviet central Asia. But most have dismissed the broader changes occurring in Soviet society as not germane to explaining Moscow's actions to U.S. television viewers and members of Congress.

Gorbachev's June 1986 statement to Moscow writers that "Soviet society is ripe for change" exemplifies his sleight of hand and reveals the source of westerners' analytic errors. For Soviet society was already in the process of change; what is "ripe for change," but until recently unaffected by it, is the governmental apparatus. Economic stagnation, like its kin, corruption, occurred because the system failed to adjust to the emerging values of the populace, especially its best educated and technically most competent elements. Today Gorbachev is not creating change so much as uncorking it. The measure of his reform program is whether it adapts the party and government to the dynamic elements in Soviet society.

Causes of the Soviet Social Transformation: Urbanization

Fundamental shifts in Soviet society are going forward, and these increasingly define the national agenda. Since most recent analyses minimize this factor, a fuller review of the causes and character of the social transformations is in order.

Among the causes, none is more fundamental than the rapid urbanization of the past 30 years. A rural society at Joseph Stalin's death in 1953, the Soviet Union today is only about 10 per cent less urban than the United States and about as urban as Italy. This change occurred in spite of official policy rather than because of it. Boldly defying severe residency laws and internal passport controls, peasants flooded into the cities.

This great migration marked the waning of peasant Russia and the passing of a controversial national archetype. Long-suffering Russian peasants are a fixture of both Russian and Western writing. For centuries they seemed to epitomize all that made their country different and distinctive—they bowed to authority, engaged in elemental and anarchistic rebellion, were natural communists in their village communes, and strove desperately to escape the extended family's despotic might. In the eyes of Slavophiles they were noble savages, and to westerners, a barrier to Russia's integration into the community of modern countries. Today, fewer than one in four Soviets is a peasant, and the number continues to plummet.

City air may not have made all rural migrants free, but it has emancipated their offspring. Sons and daughters of Russia's collectivized peasantry have plunged into urban life with a vengeance, pulling strings to get their children into the right schools, hustling for better apartments, and cutting deals for everything from seaside vacations to birth-control pills. In the process, the new urbanites have grown more independent than their forebears. Those who have gained access to the best goods and services can give credit as much to their own initiative as to the largess of the system. As their expectations rose they grew more critical. Dissatisfaction is more common in the city than in the poorer countryside and is greater in large and more affluent metropolises than in smaller centers, where the peasant mentality still holds sway. Responding to their new environment, Soviet urbanites assert their individual rights in the face of what officialdom sees as their collective duties. As this happens they cross, albeit unconsciously, the ideological fault line running in Western political theory between the writings of Thomas Hobbes, who stressed the individual's need for security, and those of John Locke, who stressed the right to liberty.

Professionalization and Economic Growth

Rapid economic development spurred this shift in outlook. Notwithstanding its recent stagnation, the Soviet economy remains the world's second largest and has grown faster than the U.S. economy through the postwar years. Millions of new jobs have been created, many requiring great expertise and sophistication. Important responsibilities have been entrusted to tens of thousands of people far outside the narrow circles of party, bureaucracy, and military that controlled national life in the Stalin era. No longer does the Communist party enjoy the relative monopoly on skills it had when the economy was smaller and simpler. Today's professional elite is for the most part staunchly loyal but far less beholden to the party, and state bureaucracy than was its Stalinist predecessor. Brezhnev, by withholding from technocrats and intellectuals the rewards he extended to labor, hastened the growing autonomy of these elements.

The Soviet Union still lags behind the United States on many key educational indicators, but progress in this area, too, has been significant. Advances in education have fostered the individuation and sense of autonomy unleashed by urbanization and economic growth. In 1987, 245 million people, or 89 per cent of the Soviet population, had at least a 10th-grade education. The comparable figure in 1939 was 10 per cent; in 1959 it was 32 per cent. As the number of those able to read has expanded, so has the number of those capable of reading between the lines. Millions are now acquiring and assessing critically information that their grandparents would have found utterly inaccessible, the object of fear or awe. Not surprisingly, the rising levels of education have been accompanied by a proportionate erosion of faith in the state's ability to organize and micromanage such diverse functions as medicine, specialized manufacturing, and the provision of services.

Paradoxically, the recent economic slump has fostered the sense of individual autonomy that prosperity generated. As the sociologist Vladimir Shlapentokh showed in a 1986 study, applicants to Soviet universities now have less than one-half as good a chance of gaining admission as they did 20 years ago, and graduates have access to fewer positions in the ranks of bosses and managers. As the escalator of social mobility has slowed, especially at the upper floors, the young, educated, and ambitious increasingly have been thrown on their own resources.

The Rise of Individualism

The exercise of personal choice was once a privilege offered by urban life. Today it is a necessity. The State Planning Agency (Gosplan) may still bear formal responsibility for formulating comprehensive plans embracing all of the country's material and human resources, but in today's organizationally more complex environment it has lost the ability to carry out this task effectively. As a result, life decisions formerly made by the state—such as the selection of a career, employer, and place of residence—are either subject to personal influence or left fully to individual choice. The Soviet system of planning remains distinguished for its coerciveness and paternalism when compared with even the most socialized advanced industrial countries elsewhere. Compared with its own past, however, the Soviet system today devolves far more decisions to individual initiative.

All inhabitants of the peasant village knew where their neighbors were and what they were doing. But in the modern metropolis millions of urbanites rush about like unplottable electrons in an atom. Such circumstances have lowered the level of regimentation and surveillance the regime can expect to maintain. True, the Soviet Union remains a police state. Most of the laws and institutions created under Stalin are still in place. Now, however, the KGB has no choice but to focus its surveillance on a few individuals and groups. Many recent articles on criminality prove that police tactics often fail. That draft dodging could reach unprecedented proportions during the war in Afghanistan attests to the difficulty of operating a police state when the inhabitants are determined and resourceful in pursuing their own interests. The decline of fear as an instrument of control is both a cause and an effect of this situation.

Some future revisionist historian will remind the world how much Brezhnev and former Prime Minister Aleksei Kosygin did to reward the laboring men and women of the USSR. Whether from a sense of social justice or from concern that Soviet workers might follow the example of their Polish counterparts, they increased salaries steadily throughout their term in office. However, they failed to bring about commensurate growth in the supply of consumer goods, with the result that individual Soviet citizens had no choice but to salt away billions in savings accounts. Although total savings in 1960 equaled only 50 rubles for each Soviet citizen, by the 1980s this figure had risen to more than 600 rubles, equal to nearly three-fourths of the country's entire annual outlay for salaries.

The Second Economy

This development, too, has advanced the process of individuation. For half a century Soviet workers were encouraged to identify with the progress of a command economy in which the state was the sole producer. Now workers with bank accounts of unspendable rubles have a personal stake in prodding the economy toward responding to their own demands as consumers. Of course, the government would be foolish to alienate the owners of so significant a source of investment capital.

When the regime has failed to produce desired goods and services, citizens have not hesitated to create them. Thus enters the twilight second economy, which is estimated to account for one-seventh of the USSR's nonagricultural output. Whether semilegal or fully underground, this privatized economy has come of age. Pioneered by young people 30 years ago, it now touches every segment of the population. Hence when Gorbachev talks of expanding the small private sector he really means extending legal legitimacy—and taxability—to areas of the gray or black markets. After all, as a former general administrator, he scarcely can be ignorant of the fact that industrial firms and communes throughout the Soviet provinces rely on the services of semilegal *sabashniki*, free-lance teams of builders and laborers who outperform their official counterparts in spite of bureaucratic harassment.

During the Brezhnev regime Soviet society moved steadily in the direction of individuation, decentralization of initiative, and privatization. A virtual revolution in personal communications in that supposedly stagnant era dramatically strengthened these processes of change. Lenin and Stalin both labored to establish "top-down" vertical systems of communication. They nationalized and imposed strict political controls over such technologies as radio, film, sound recording, and modern postal services. More important, they limited or suppressed such horizontal technologies as the private telephone and the intercity telegraph. Their successors did the same with xerographic machines and desk-top computers. In the 1970s the USSR was the only country moving toward advanced industrialization that successfully braked the spread of private automobiles. All forms of international communication—radio, travel, mail, and telephone—were restricted or muzzled. As a result, society was left unable to communicate with itself. It was atomized and, in theory at least, rendered passive.

Extensive controls on the dissemination of information remain in effect today, yet millions of Soviet citizens routinely evade them. Over many years they have been astonishingly resourceful in their efforts to gain access to whatever information they desire. In the process they have taken advantage of such officially sanctioned major technologies as intercity telephones, whose number has increased rapidly but which are still in short supply. Equally important, they have skillfully exploited such seemingly innocuous "small technologies" as the cassette-tape recorder, the personal camera, the videocassette recorder (VCR), and the ham radio. In each case the state tried to suppress or strictly curb access to the new information technology. Outwitted by the public, it then sought a face-saving avenue of retreat. In the 1960s it had to reckon with a wave of illegally imported cassette-tape recorders that transformed their owners into publishers. The state then fell back on producing and selling its own. In the 1980s the process was repeated with imported VCRs. Eventually the Soviet government began producing its own VCRs in the hope that it at least could influence the use of a technology it no longer could prohibit.

Communications Technology and the Spread of Information

By such steps the Soviet state lost its monopoly on information. A privatized system embracing large segments of the population now exists alongside the controlled official system of communications. What one Soviet writer, Vladimir Simonov, called "technotronic *glasnost*" was a fact long before Gorbachev took up the latter word for his own purposes. Thanks to this *glasnost*, or "openness," instituted by the public itself, members of Soviet society have gained the ability to communicate with one another and, increasingly, with the outside world. With or without official *glasnost*, few events in the USSR or abroad long escape notice. Even the darkest corners of Soviet history eventually will be illuminated by the more resourceful members of society, whatever the party and state may desire.

Improved communications have made possible a degree of "networking" among Soviet citizens that would have been inconceivable a generation ago. Controls over the freedom of assembly are still in place and enforced sometimes with extreme severity. Yet persons with common interests throughout the Soviet Union can readily locate one another and enter into communication by means of the legal and semilegal technologies available to them. Whether model-airplane enthusiasts, rock music fans, Hare Krishnas, Afghanistan war veterans, or ecologists, interest groups of like-minded people form with relative ease and establish regular channels of communication among their devotees.

What began in the 1950s with networks of underground jazz fans spread in the 1970s to the sphere of public affairs. The Communist party newspaper *Pravda* acknowledges the existence of more than 30,000 *neformaly*, grass-roots voluntary associations dedicated to various types of civic improvement. What Western political scientists call "interest group articulation" reached a record high in August 1987, when a conference of some 600 politically oriented clubs and associations—in this case, all nominally socialist in their program—convened in Moscow under the aegis of the city's party boss at the time, Boris Yeltsin. . . .

Becoming a "Civil Society"

These, then, are some of the fundamental changes that took place during the otherwise stagnant Brezhnev era. Together they constitute part of the social reality that the Gorbachev administration will ignore only at its peril.

Clearly the new tendencies in Soviet life will soften many features of the social system forged by Lenin and Stalin. The old society's tendency was for everything outside the party and state apparatus to be turned into an amorphous mass, the whole country becoming "as if déclassé," in the words of the historian Moshe Lewin. The emerging society, by contrast, includes large numbers of autonomous and assertive personalities among both the rulers and the ruled. The sense of duty that the late anthropologist Margaret Mead found so characteristic of the Soviet public under Stalin is being balanced by millions of individuals actively trying to affirm their rights under law. People who formerly viewed themselves as subjects are taking on the mentality of citizens.

Gorbachev has declared his goal to be the democratization of society. But Soviet society already has moved far in this direction thanks to developments fostered or tolerated by his predecessors. The key question is whether the party and state will follow suit. To the extent they do, the Soviet Union will move toward becoming a radically different type of society than it has been for 70 years—namely, a "civil society.". . .

Can Gorbachev Reform Soviet Society?

Yet the suspicion remains that Gorbachev's démarche toward the new social realities is merely a tactic. What will happen when *glasnost* is directed not against the Brezhnev legacy but against Gorbachev's own record? How quickly will his administration pull back when the extension of openness to non-Russian peoples in the Soviet Union unleashes centrifugal forces incompatible with Great Russian pretensions? And how sharply will Gorbachev shift directions when the cycle of reform is played out, as must inevitably happen?

Such questions are intriguing but premature. Most of the announced reforms, particularly in the crucial area of law, are still being prepared. Until the first drafts emerge it will be impossible to determine how much substantive wheat is mixed with the rhetorical chaff. But there are serious grounds for doubting that legislation embodying principles

of a civil society will get very far. First, Gorbachev has declared his commitment to maintaining all the inherited prerogatives of the Communist party. Second, he fully shares
the traditional Marxist opposition to private property. Indeed, his limited acceptance of a private sector seems designed more to co-opt the unruly second economy than to
affirm the right to property that Locke posited as the basis
of citizenship in a civil society.

Third, and most important, Gorbachev's highest priority
is not to introduce liberal reforms but to revive the bedrag-
gled Soviet economy. That administrative decentralization
and sharp staff cutbacks in planning organs spell disaster for
thousands of bureaucrats is well known. Less often noted is
the way the economic reforms might hurt the interests of
labor. To put it bluntly, Gorbachev's economic program contains many facets that, if crudely imposed on the Soviet public, would sour the atmosphere for reform in other areas.
How, after all, is a Soviet worker to view proposals calling
for deregulation, the suspension of wage and price controls,
the expansion of the powers of local managers, compulsory
job reassignments for millions of blue-collar laborers, and
the stretching out of salary scales for the purpose of reward-
ing diligence and punishing sloth? The economy may desperately need such measures, but to the Soviet worker they
can only appear as a speedup.

Any other reforms put forward when such controversial
measures are being implemented will be tarred with an anti-
labor brush. If the economy fails to respond to Gorbachev's
stimuli—and 1987's results give little reason for optimism—
then many common Russians will pine for the good old days
when labor was not punished for the country's economic
malaise. That serious problems with poverty and unemployment in the USSR are only waiting to be discovered by the
public simply adds to the risks. It will be all too easy to draw
the conclusion that the inevitable price of political freedom
and civil rights is an unacceptable level of economic in-
equality. If embittered bureaucrats forge ties with alienated
labor, the reform program will face formidable opposition
that will test Gorbachev's powers as a political broker.

The Rise of Gorbachev: Perestroika and Glasnost

Richard Pipes

The economic and political policies of the Soviet Union were tightly controlled by the central government in Moscow, as were many other aspects of society and culture. The Soviet system was therefore considered by many political scientists to be totalitarian. Mikhail Gorbachev's initiatives perestroika (restructuring) and glasnost (openness) were intended to introduce limited economic and societal reforms to this system.

Writing in early 1990, five years after Gorbachev assumed office, Richard Pipes pronounces perestroika and glasnost failures; perestroika, because confidence in the economy could not be restored, and glasnost, because it permitted not only criticism of Gorbachev and the government but also the formation of opposition political parties. Pipes predicts that the Soviet Union will break down if Gorbachev does not move to restore totalitarian control.

Richard Pipes is Baird Professor of History at Harvard University. He is the author of *The Russian Revolution, Russia Under the Bolshevik Regime*, and *Communism, the Vanished Specter.*

On assuming office in the spring of 1985, Gorbachev and his associates expected to have a relatively easy time reviving the economy and reinvigorating society. In Gorbachev's own words: "We had initially assumed that basically the task was only to correct certain deformations of the social organism,

From Richard Pipes, "Gorbachev's Russia: Breakdown or Crackdown?" Reprinted from *Commentary*, March 1990, by permission; all rights reserved.

to perfect the entire system set in place during the preceding decades." The premise turned out to be wrong: before long, Gorbachev now concedes, it proved "necessary radically to alter our entire social edifice, from its economic foundations to the superstructure."

Once they realized the immensity of their problem, the reformers dropped the original slogan "acceleration" (*uskorenie*) in favor of "restructuring" (*perestroika*). The latter entailed reducing the grip of the bureaucracy on the country and concurrently stimulating private initiative in all spheres of national life. Essentially, it meant bringing society into a limited partnership with the ruling elite, making it an active participant in the life of the country without, however, abandoning the command method of political and economic management: a *perestroika* or "restructuring" rather than *stroitel'stvo* or construction.

From Totalitarianism to Authoritarianism?

In sum, the Soviet reformers undertook to transform the Soviet Union from a totalitarian into an authoritarian regime. They seem to have believed that the nation had stored in it a great deal of latent energy that would be released as soon as the shackles restraining and silencing society had been loosened. This belief accounts for the rather reckless manner in which they proceeded to dismantle many of the institutions of the Leninist-Stalinist regime before they were able to replace them.

To the historian of Russia this effort at limited reform is not unfamiliar. On two occasions when czarism faced similar problems (economic backwardness, social apathy, decline in international standing) it attempted to bring society into partnership without surrendering its autocratic prerogatives. This occurred in the 1860s and again in 1904. These attempts were, on the whole, unsuccessful because they failed to accompany the liberalization of the economy and of censorship with commensurate political concessions. They awakened expectations which the proposed reforms could not satisfy: in one case they ended in reaction, in the other in revolution.

Gorbachev's Task

There are indications that the Soviet Union is currently hovering between the same alternatives. Even as he is solidifying his personal power, Gorbachev is less and less able to govern effectively. The impression gains ground—it is prevalent in the Soviet Union—that while *perestroika* has done nothing to remedy the country's economic difficulties, it has created an added problem in the shape of a political crisis. Gorbachev himself now speaks of the "sword of Damocles" hanging over the Soviet Union, and accuses those who criticize his reforms for being too slow or too timid of "lighting matches while the Soviet Union is standing in a pool of gasoline." Such alarmist language, of course, serves the purpose of silencing the opposition. But even so, the Soviet Union is indeed in an exceedingly precarious situation. It is evident now that Gorbachev and his associates had vastly underestimated the task facing them: the structure which they had judged essentially sound and in need merely of an overhaul turned out to be rotten from top to bottom. First "acceleration" proved inadequate and had to give way to "restructuring"; now there is doubt as to whether anything solid enough remains of the old edifice to rebuild. The absence of a coherent domestic policy is becoming daily more apparent.

Turning a totalitarian regime into an authoritarian one is proving a far harder thing to do than transforming an authoritarian dictatorship into a democracy. Under Franco, Spaniards had been shut out of politics but they owned the country's wealth and were free to form private associations. When Franco died it was a relatively simple matter for democratic institutions to replace the dictatorship. Similar transitions occurred in Salazar's Portugal and Marcos's Philippines. It is a likely prospect for Chile after Pinochet's anticipated retirement. Gorbachev, however, is discovering that, underneath the ponderous superstructure of the Communist bureaucracy which he is seeking to reduce both in numbers and authority, there looms a vast void. In the Soviet Union, with its 290 million inhabitants, a new society must be created from scratch, for of that which had existed before 1917 not a trace remains. The question whether a totalitarian regime is capable of evolution remains, therefore, still open: the Soviet Union has as yet failed to make such a transition. In the end it may turn out that its alternatives are either collapse or reversion to totalitarianism.

The Soviet leaders are reluctantly concluding that their basic difficulties stem from human attitudes which are far more difficult to alter than institutions. Communist regimes have succeeded brilliantly in repelling all actual and potential challenges to their authority, but they have done so at the price of killing everything that gives life to the political organism: personal initiative, public spirit, trust in the government. Now when the regime calls on the population at large to come to its help, it encounters either indifference or outright hostility. The morale of the Soviet citizenry has been systematically destroyed and help is unavailable to the authorities now that they have concluded they can no longer do everything by themselves.

Opposition from the Elite

Gorbachev's problem is of a dual nature: in addition to the indifference of the citizenry, he confronts the opposition of the ruling elite which stands the most to lose from his reforms. To break bureaucratic resistance, Gorbachev had resort to two devices: the traditional one of purges, and the innovative one of using the state apparatus as a counterweight to the party.

Over the past five years, he has methodically replaced both civilian and military personnel inherited from the previous administrations with his own, with people who may or may not share his outlook but who owe their careers to him. Nearly all the current members of the Politburo and secretaries of the Central Committee are his appointees. The purges reach deep down into the provincial branches of the party and state apparatus and form the basis of Gorbachev's personal power which shows no signs of weakening despite the failures of the reform program. Gorbachev has pledged to eliminate 40 percent of the country's bureaucracy by

1991; if implemented, such retirements will afford him ample opportunities to be rid of many more opponents.

His boldest stroke, however, was to bring into play the Communist state apparatus which since Lenin's days had been confined to carrying out the party's directives and bearing the blame for whatever went wrong. The creation of a new body, the Congress of People's Deputies, elected on a fairly democratic franchise (two-thirds of the seats chosen by secret ballot, the rest reserved for the party and its organs), and the introduction into the Supreme Soviet of genuine public representatives, had been originally intended as a limited operation. It was to give the population a sense of being involved in the political process, and, at the same time, serve as a lever against the hardliners in the *nomenklatura* [ruling elites]. The local Soviets, which Lenin had reduced to impotence within months of taking power in their name, are to be revived as well.

In this instance, too, the reformers underestimated the difficulties. After seventy years of dictatorship, the politically active minority of the population was not about to accept the role of consultant to the one-party regime. The leadership was clearly unprepared for the electoral defeats of its candidates which revealed in stark figures the regime's unpopularity: in many districts official nominees could not obtain the required votes even when they were running unopposed. The shattering of the carefully nurtured myth of popular support is something for which the Communist cadres are not likely to forgive Gorbachev.

Equally unexpected was the dispatch with which the reformed Supreme Soviet assumed legislative functions, once some of its deputies came to look on themselves as representatives of their constituencies. Through the system of guaranteed seats, Gorbachev controls enough votes to have his way whenever he considers the issue to be sufficiently important. But there is no assurance that the new parliamentary bodies will always be accommodating.

The Emergence of Political Parties

Indeed, although the Soviet Union still acknowledges only one lawful party, the caucuses which have emerged in the

Congress of People's Deputies in the guise of "groups" or "clubs" have for all practical purposes assumed party functions. The most influential of them is the Inter-Regional Group with some 400 deputies (out of a total of 2,250): it is committed to a democratic platform. The Group resembles the Progressive Bloc formed in 1915 in the Duma, which with its relentless criticism of czarism's conduct of World War I paved the way for the February Revolution. Like the Bloc, the Inter-Regional Group is divided into radical and moderate wings: a victory for the latter was the decision, taken hours before the death of Andrei Sakharov, its titular leader, to call off a general political strike. The hard-line deputies in the Congress have responded with *Rossiia*, a caucus of some 100 members.

Gorbachev has thus created a monster that step by step encroaches on the Communist political monopoly.

To some extent this also holds true of the diverse associations, some 60,000 in number, which had been authorized in yet another effort to infuse life into a moribund Soviet society. For the most part they are politically innocuous (a good many of them are youth organizations devoted to sports and rock music). But in some instances, especially in the non-Russian areas, such associations have become a distinct threat to the status quo. The Democratic Union, which advocates a multiparty system, free trade unions, and the right of the ethnic minorities to secession, is the most prominent example. Others are *Rukh* in the Ukraine, *Sajudis* in Lithuania, and the Pan-Turkic *Birlik*, each of them a nationalist party in all but name. Although frequently harassed and persecuted by the authorities, they manage to carry on and gain in local influence.

The political evolution of the Soviet Union since 1985 has been filled with contradictions which are difficult to unravel. Side by side with the incontrovertible measures of democratization is the concentration of power in the hands of one man. It is by no means clear whether Gorbachev involves the populace in the political process in order to share power with it or merely to use it against his personal rivals. He not only staffs the civil and military administration with followers, but gathers in his hands the reins of formal authority. In December 1988 he assumed the title of President of the Supreme Soviet, which gives him considerably greater prerogatives than were enjoyed by his predecessors, designated Chairmen of the Supreme Soviet Presidium. He is both General Secretary of the party and head of state, which endows him, at least nominally, with immense authority. Sakharov worried greatly that such accumulated power could be used for other than reformist purposes.

Economic Reform

The centerpiece of *perestroika*, economic reform, has failed and may be said, for all practical purposes, to have been abandoned. The bold plans to reinstate private property in the means of production were given up because they could not be reconciled with the maintenance of a planned economy and the one-party system. The reconstruction of the free market was indefinitely postponed because it required a fundamental pricing reform which was certain to cause inflation and result in social unrest. The Five-Year Plan for 1991–95, as recently announced, faithfully treads beaten paths. The central institution of the Leninist-Stalinist economy, the State Planning Commission or *Gosplan*, retains its grip on the nation's resources. Promises have been made of major shifts to consumer goods and cooperatives are to be encouraged, but the outlook for the next five years is more of the same.

The situation with consumer goods is becoming insufferable. Staple foods are in short supply, and even when available are shunned because of saturation with pesticides, nitrates, and other chemicals. The press reported not long ago that Soviet cats snubbed sausages produced for human consumption. The main victims are the Soviet poor, defined by the authorities as citizens earning less than 78 rubles a month ($5 at the current free-market rate). Government sources indicate they number 43 million. With such a low income, survival is possible only by shopping in state outlets where prices are kept artificially low by government subsidies. However, the burgeoning cooperative market which *perestroika* encourages siphons off these goods to the private sector, with the result that many Soviet citizens are now living in a condition of permanent undernourishment and not a few pensioners slowly die of malnutrition.

Economic Downturn

The population's lack of confidence in the national economy is reflected in the drastic fall of Soviet currency on the black market. As recently as the summer of 1988, the ruble, officially pegged at $1.61, sold for 20 U.S. cents. In the past year it suffered a further and precipitous decline. As the government in November 1989 adjusted the exchange rate for foreign tourists and businessmen to 16 cents per ruble, the free market once again overtook it: at present, the ruble fetches 7 cents, which represents a 300-percent devaluation.

Various factors account for the failure of the economic-reform plans. There is the inherent difficulty of grafting private initiative onto a centralized economy. Soviet citizens do not trust the government to honor promises to respect the rights and earnings of cooperative enterprises. But above all there are the vested interests of the party bureaucracy to whom state (i.e., bureaucratic) ownership of the national economy assures an easy and comfortable living; the bureaucracy fears the political consequences of the accumulation of wealth in private hands. The risks to which the Communist diehards expose the country with their sabotage of economic reform plans are incalculable: their triumph over liberal economists spells disaster. *Perestroika* aggravates social inequalities in a country where they are poorly tolerated. It also increases unemployment which is supposed not to exist under Communism. There are at present several million jobless in the Soviet Union and officials expect that by the year 2005 they will number between 15 and 16 million. Such inequalities and such unemployment, on top of generally declining living standards, create a situation laden with revolutionary potentialities.

The Soviet leadership seems to have no clear idea how to extricate itself from this predicament. It cannot, of course, openly commit itself to full-scale capitalism, which some of its economic advisers privately confess they would prefer. It speaks of adopting the Swedish Social-Democratic model, which the population at large would find most attractive, but it neither knows how to bring it about nor seems to realize that such a system requires centuries of cultural maturing.

Loosening of Censorship

Nothing has won Gorbachev greater admiration in the West than the policy of *glasnost*, the loosening of the absurd censorship designed to propagate images totally at variance with reality no less than with the private opinions of Soviet citizens. (Censorship has been loosened, not abolished, since its organ, *Glavlit*, continues to operate, although under more liberal guidelines.) This policy caught most experts by surprise, since many if not most of them (myself included) had regarded the imposition on the populace of what Alain Besançon has called "surreality" as essential to the survival of Communist regimes. In time *glasnost* may indeed turn out to have been a fatal mistake: for how can one permit open criticism of the government and yet make it illegal to work for a change in government? The czarist government learned this lesson every time it relaxed censorship.

Yet a certain degree of free speech was unavoidable. The Soviet regime had been assuring its citizens for decades that they lived in the most progressive and prosperous country in the world. If that was the case, why change? To justify perestroika it was necessary to tell the truth about the country's desperate condition. Apparently the Communist leaders, once again victimized by their own propaganda, believed that it would be enough to blame the country's ills on Stalin and Brezhnev. They exposed the regime to criticism in the expectation that it would be confined to the implementation of Communism but respect its principles. The criticism was to be constructive: destructive criticism was to be channeled back, into the past.

The leaders were quickly disabused of these expectations. Freedom of opinion, once unleashed, proved exceedingly difficult to keep within approved bounds; it acquired a life of its own and pushed outward, probing the limits of the permissible. Thus questioning of the past inevitably led to questioning of the present. Every exposure of a lie, every breaking of a taboo, opened a breach in the fortress of official mythology through which poured critics ready to assault the next bastion. The censors, confused by vague directives, lost their bearings.

The limits of free speech are continually being tested. On the whole Lenin is still beyond the pale of criticism, although on some occasions he has been assailed for instituting concentration camps and dissolving the popularly-elected Constituent Assembly. But the Nazi-Soviet pact, the Katyn massacre, the murder of the imperial family have all found their way into Soviet media. So has the true condition of Soviet society. Denigrating the current leadership, however, is not tolerated. Gorbachev lost his temper when *Argumenty i Fakty*, the most widely read journal in the Soviet Union, if not indeed the world, with a circulation of over 30 million, published the results of a readers' poll which indicated that not he but Andrei Sakharov was the country's most popular figure. Even so, Gorbachev failed in his attempt to dismiss the editor of the offending journal.

At the end of 1989 there were in the Soviet Union over 300 independent publications, the majority of them of a democratic and pro-Western orientation.

The coexistence of a relatively free press alongside a one-party regime is clearly anomalous. It contributes to the widespread feeling in the country that the present ambiguous situation is not likely to last and will end either in full freedom or no freedom. . . .

The Failure of Reform

Gorbachev, hailed abroad as a statesman who has dared to challenge the very fundamentals of the Leninist-Stalinist regime, a liberal and a man of peace, inside the Soviet Union is held in low regard as someone who has failed to make good on his promises and brought the country to the brink of anarchy.

It can hardly be disputed that the Soviet government is losing authority. Of this, there are many indications. Although strikes in the energy sector have been declared illegal, Moscow could do nothing but equivocate and negotiate with the miners of Vorkuta when they struck in October 1989 to protest its failure to honor promises to them. All around the country, demonstrations are taking place daily, many if not most of them unauthorized. On November 7, 1989, the anniversary of the Bolshevik coup, demonstrators carrying anti-Communist banners paraded in Moscow and other cities in front of stony-faced bureaucrats. In several republics, dissidents disrupted official celebrations on that occasion; in Georgia and Armenia they forced the authorities to cancel them. More ominously, the armed forces are encountering open defiance. In certain districts, 10 percent of those called for induction fail to show up. In the Baltic republics and Transcaucasia, draft centers have been blocked by protesters. The Chief of the General Staff has complained that men in uniform are frequently assaulted by hooligans: in 1989, 53 officers lost their lives as a result. The violence in Azerbaijan, in the course of which police stations were raided by fully armed men and local security forces were unable to restore order, has been widely reported in Western media. These are occurrences without precedent in the Soviet Union over the past half century. They are ominous developments for a system whose authority has always rested on force.

The Possibility of Crackdown

With each passing day, the Gorbachev regime resembles the ill-fated Provisional Government of 1917 more and more: long on words, short on deeds, uncertain what to do as the structure which it has undertaken to reform collapses all around it. And like Kerensky, Gorbachev enjoys greater popularity abroad than at home.

Gorbachev has taken a number of preventive measures which in the eyes of Russian reformers presage a crackdown. He has organized special Worker Detachments to Support the Police (ROSM). These units, linked to the Ministry of the Interior, are supposed to help fight crime, which is rising at an alarming rate. But fears have been voiced that their true function is to serve the same role as the notorious

ZOMO's in Poland in 1981 during the crackdown on Solidarity. Someone has also taken the trouble to establish a hard-line Communist trade union, the United Front of Workers of Russia, which opposes reforms and assails intellectuals as exploiters. The authorities have shown a leniency which occasionally resembles patronage toward the anti-Semitic *Pamiat*, whose more extreme followers spout Nazi slogans. The *Rossiia* faction in the Congress of People's Deputies, ROSM, the United Front of Workers of Russia, and *Pamiat* are instruments available to Gorbachev or his replacement should it be decided to stage a crackdown.

Prospects for Success

Whether the Soviet Union will make a transition to a modern civil society, collapse in revolution and civil war, or, like China, resort to repression cannot be foreseen at this time. The most desirable solution for everyone concerned would be for an orderly, institutionalized transfer of all the authority traditionally claimed by the Communist party to democratically elected institutions. This is what Gorbachev seems to have had in mind in his address to the Central Committee Plenum on February 5, 1990, in which he called for the abolition of the Communist party's monopoly on power, the creation of a presidency (presumably elective), and the introduction of a multiparty system. These revolutionary proposals, if implemented, would undo the political work of Lenin. Can this be accomplished? Gorbachev himself seems unchallengeable: he has accumulated more personal power than any Soviet leader since Stalin. But since he assumed office in 1985 the Communist party—his principal instrument—has lost a great deal of authority and prestige. For this reason, the process of transition may prove beyond his or anyone else's capacity to carry out. The masses support Gorbachev in his struggle against entrenched party interests, but their vision of a new Russia is not necessarily the same as his own. As power slips from the party's hands, politics may become polarized between the forces of reaction and those of anarchy and separatism.

Aware of the incompetence as well as the unpopularity of Communism, Gorbachev is seeking to jettison it in his own country as he has done in Eastern Europe. But it is by no means certain that the Russian empire with its multinational population has the cohesion necessary to make a peaceful transition from totalitarianism. Nor is it clear whether Gorbachev, for all his professions of democracy, would be willing to abide by the will of the nation once his reforms were in place. For it is one thing to invoke the *vox populi* against one's opponents and another to obey it when it goes its own unpredictable way.

Cooperation with the West

Stephen Sestanovich

During the détente of the 1970s, the United States and the Soviet Union sought to ease cold war tensions and began negotiating treaties on a wide range of issues. But following the Soviet invasion of Afghanistan in 1978, discord once again increased. Ronald Reagan, elected U.S. president in 1980, initiated a renewed arms race. When Mikhail Gorbachev came to power as leader of the Soviet Union in 1985, he immediately sought an end to this renewed conflict.

In the following selection, first published in 1993, Stephen Sestanovich acknowledges that the conditions for peace imposed on the Soviets by the United States and other Western governments brought about the demise of the Soviet regime. As proof of peaceful intentions and prerequisites for arms reductions, the West demanded that the Soviets introduce democratization and recognize human rights, such as allowing political dissent, Sestanovich notes. He contends that this pressure, promoted in an atmosphere of cooperation rather than cold war hostility, undermined the legitimacy of the Soviet regime and brought about its collapse.

Stephen Sestanovich is director of Russian and Eurasian Studies at the Center for Strategic and International Studies. He is the author of the book *Rethinking Russia's National Interests*.

On our crowded planet there are no longer any internal affairs. The Communists say, "Don't interfere in our internal affairs. Let us strangle our citizens in peace and quiet." But I tell you: Interfere more and more. Interfere as much as you can. We beg you to come and interfere.

—Alexander Solzhenitsyn, 1975

The Cold War, it was often said, was a struggle not merely between states but between incompatible social and political systems. There was as a result no issue of Western policy more important, more persistent or more controversial than whether external influences might alter the internal evolution of Soviet communism. In different ways and at different times, the problem preoccupied and divided realists and moralists, liberals and conservatives, militarists and appeasers, businessmen and legislators, Europeans and Americans, those who claimed to know what kind of pressure would work and those who said the effort was futile, even dangerous. Most recently, of course, with communism in ruins, the problem has also come to preoccupy those who want a share of the credit— or want to dispute someone else's.

Containment Strategy and the Cold War

In 1947, when George Kennan sketched out the strategy of containment in his legendary "X" article, he promised a gigantic payoff—a remade Soviet Union. Moreover, he suggested, the transformation of the system could be pursued indirectly. Western policy had only to be steady enough to check the Russians "at every point where they show signs of encroaching upon the interests of a peaceful and stable world." The resulting frustration of communist designs would "promote tendencies which must eventually find their outlet in either the breakup or the gradual mellowing of Soviet power."

Although it was the intellectual bedrock of containment, this theory of how communism would come to grief never enjoyed universal support. Over time, it had to contend with the growing suspicion that the Soviet system, far from being vulnerable, was just as powerful as it said it was. For some, a competing conception of Soviet change suggested itself, according to which it was international tension that kept the system intact. In this view (now supported by Kennan himself), communism coped fine with conflict, but could not endure normalcy; improved relations and increased contacts with the West would inevitably rob dictatorship of its rationale; "mellowing" would ensue.

Fully understanding the external sources of communism's demise, in other words, means weighing the impact of both conflict and conciliation. In particular, it means comparing the internal consequences for the Soviet system of the two most distinctive Western policies of the past twenty years: the would-have-been "era of negotiation" known as detente, and the military buildup and harsh anti-Soviet rhetoric of the Reagan administration.

At first glance, this comparison between the 1970s and the 1980s may not seem like much of a contest. Certainly if the question is whether the USSR was shaken more deeply by victories or by defeats, the answer has to be relatively obvious, and the 1980s, a truly miserable time for Soviet foreign policy, will be judged the easy winner. Nevertheless, two important qualifications—one for each decade—have to be added to this verdict. The acute international tensions for which the early 1980s are usually remembered tell only part of the decade's story. They were followed by a half decade of growing coziness between Soviet and American leaders, and this too contributed to the happy result. As for the detente of the 1970s, its claim to have begun digging totalitarianism's grave is weak. All the same, this was the moment when the Soviet Union agreed to treat human rights as a principle of East-West relations—an act of real importance for the disaster to come.

The oscillations and unpredictability of democratic decision-making are frequently said to produce poor performance in foreign policy, and to compare the 1970s and the 1980s is certainly to confirm the incoherence of Western attempts to influence the Soviet Union. Yet the story's successful denouement is a powerful reason to think again about the presumed costs of erratic policy. The infuriatingly inconsistent West turned out to be an opponent that Soviet communism simply could not understand, much less subdue. In the end, the democratic weakness that so many bemoaned may actually have helped to bring victory in reach.

The Hard Eighties

No one disagrees that Russian revolutions of the past were set off by international defeats—1917 by the First World War, 1905 by the loss to the Japanese; even the end of serfdom in 1861 is commonly traced to the Crimean War. "Explaining" a revolution in this way doesn't mean that defeat created social strains where none existed (abolitionist intellectuals, for example, had been promoting freedom for the serfs for decades), nor that in the war's aftermath events could only move in one direction (the Bolsheviks' victory was a matter of incredible luck). But any serious interpreter of the historical record begins by recognizing that in all three of these cases, war fundamentally altered the political balance of forces at home. If the causal links are so straightforward when we analyze the past, what (apart from churlish feelings toward Ronald Reagan) makes anyone dispute them in our own time?

Admittedly, the Soviet Union suffered no outright military defeat in the first half of the 1980s. Nevertheless, by the middle of the decade, the outlook on almost every front of Soviet foreign policy was poor and clearly deteriorating. The list of failures needs very little elaboration: INF [intermediate-range nuclear forces] deployments in Europe and successive large increases in the U.S. military budget; Afghanistan, Grenada, and the emergence of the "Reagan Doctrine," which put new pressure on Soviet clients in Africa, Asia, and Latin America; Moscow's exclusion from Middle East diplomacy, and the humiliation of Soviet-made weapons in the Lebanon war of 1982; the Solidarity challenge in Poland; robust Chinese economic growth against a background of continuing Sino-Soviet hostility. And all this bad news before even mentioning the Strategic Defense Initiative (SDI), which threatened a new round of military competition and highlighted Soviet technological inferiority. Eduard Shevardnadze summed up the situation as follows: Soviet foreign policy had been "out of touch with the fundamental vital interests of the country."

Merely to recite this list of Soviet setbacks is to underscore the West's role in discrediting the policy of Gorbachev's predecessors. Naturally, Georgi Arbatov, in his recent memoirs, describes as "absolute nonsense" the idea that Western toughness "helped alter Soviet policy and demonstrate the futility of its warlike course," but there is no need to take this view too seriously. After all, Soviet policy was not inherently "futile"; it was made so by the strong external opposition it produced. Had there been no such opposition, the warnings of experts like Arbatov, about how the United States would respond to this or that action, would have had no credibility. Similarly, had there been successes to balance the failures of Soviet policy—had, for example, the Afghan operation gone relatively smoothly, with the West quietly ceding Moscow a sphere of influence; or had NATO's INF policy unraveled in the face of mounting European street protests—it would have been harder for Gorbachev and his colleagues to make a comprehensive critique of past policy. Instead of proposing a completely new approach to dealing with the outside world—what they grandly called "new thinking"—they would have been much more likely to propose *ad hoc* adjustments of specific policies.

Soviet policy was particularly vulnerable because it had made a mess everywhere. This argument, if correct, implies that the unrelenting approach of the Reagan administration was probably more effective than a better balanced Western policy—beat up the Soviets here, conciliate them there—would have been. By "overdoing it," the United States gave extra credibility to individual policies that might have lacked real force on their own. This is particularly true of SDI, which raised the specter of vast increases in Soviet military spending. Although its partisans sometimes talk as though SDI brought down the Soviet regime all by itself, it was always a somewhat hypothetical threat, based on military systems that had been neither developed nor tested nor deployed. What made it impossible to laugh off SDI was the Reagan record as a whole.

Stability and Change in Soviet Policy

The Brezhnev regime had come into being in 1964 on a platform that elevated stability over Khrushchevian impulsiveness. By the early 1980s, however, this stability became outright petrification: policy was hard to change without the pressure of a crisis. Confrontational Western policies provided that pressure.

There was, of course, nothing automatic about the Soviet response to crisis, and a tightening-up of the system was at the very least conceivable. Hawks on both sides of the struggle, said some commentators, had to protect their common interest in keeping the conflict going. Arbatov has gone so far as to say that U.S. policy in the early 1980s created "further obstacles on the road to reform" and almost led to a "restoration of Stalinism."

There is no doubt that the Soviet propaganda apparatus answered the policies of the Reagan administration with some of the most blood-curdling invective of the Cold War, but Stalinist rhetoric can hardly be treated as proof of Stalinist politics. Arbatov himself observes that the military-industrial complex had "escaped control" a full decade earlier, thereby refuting his own claim that U.S. policy was responsible for the "Frankenstein monster" of Soviet militarism in the first half of the 1980s. On balance, the tensions of this period seem to have *weakened* those within the Soviet leadership who argued that the best response to crisis was more of the same. It should be remembered that the notorious Marshal Ogarkov, the loudest advocate within the military of running harder to keep up with the West, was ousted even before Gorbachev came to power.

The rigidity of the Soviet system made it more likely that pressure would lead to crisis. In recalling this period for the Hoover Oral History Project, two members of the Politburo (both of them Gorbachev allies) have described the internal debate about how to respond to SDI. The commitment of resources needed to run the arms race at all was already crushing, and in the first phase of Gorbachev's tenure—when he proposed to fix the economy through resource re-allocation rather than radical reform—the idea of shifting *more* resources to the military was simply not viable. Yet the high command refused to consider "quick-fix" responses to the SDI threat. Their determination to have a full-blown strategic defense of their own dramatized the internal price of the arms race and made clear the need to shake the system up.

Gorbachev, of course, presented his program somewhat differently. In December 1984, three full months before he took over as general secretary, he assured Party conservatives that his goal was to guarantee that the Soviet Union entered the twenty-first century "in a manner worthy of a great power." For many, this statement became a kind of proof that, from the very beginning, perestroika was meant to serve geopolitical aims. There is little reason to doubt that the general staff and captains of industry saw it this way, but the picture is far less clear when it comes to Gorbachev himself. He may have spoken the language of the military establishment so as to neutralize it politically. (He had the help of in-house propagandists: as late as 1990, when reforms were already taking a severe toll on Soviet power, military billboards continued to proclaim: "The main goal of perestroika is to strengthen military readiness!") That Gorbachev could credibly claim to be serving military goals testifies again to the impact of a hostile international environment. By showing that past policies had led nowhere, Western toughness altered the internal power balance of Soviet politics in favor of fundamental change.

The Soft Eighties

Although he was the beneficiary of international tensions, Gorbachev had to show that he could do better than his predecessors, lest the power balance turn against him again. As he put the point to *Time*'s interviewers shortly after he took power, he needed a calm international environment to put his reformist plans into practice. This remark was scorned by many as a clever appeal for a time-out in the East-West competition, but it accurately described the logic of Gorbachev's position. He got convincing support, moreover, from no less than Andrei Sakharov, who—though he had publicly supported U.S. deployment of the MX while Yuri Andropov was in power—argued that the United States needed a very different approach for dealing with Gorbachev. In the early Reagan years, Sakharov had stunned Western arms controllers by making the heretical suggestion that an arms race (by which he meant a U.S. buildup) could help prevent nuclear war. Now he worried that, if the race continued, "the process of democratization and liberalization will stop."

In the first half of the 1980s, then, Western contentiousness provided the right backdrop for Soviet re-thinking. By contrast, the congeniality of the second half of the decade created a setting in which reforms steadily expanded and eventually became uncontrollable. The impact of this detente, it should be added, did not derive from its concrete achievements, which were rather meager. Soviet-American relations had never been so warm, but in contrast to the detente of the early 1970s few agreements were reached, there was no mutual acceptance of the status quo, and the idea of resolving disputes by splitting differences never took hold. In fact, Western demands tended, if anything, to escalate, and the criteria for believing perestroika to be "serious" grew stricter. In June 1987 Reagan, never having talked much about the Berlin wall, suddenly called on Gorbachev to tear it down. The West Germans, who had long since learned to live with East Germany, began to question the division of Europe. And in 1989, acceptance of East European revolution became the test Gorbachev had to pass to preserve good relations with the West.

These adverse developments had little impact on Gorbachev's internal position and policies, for with every passing year the course of reform became steadily less dependent on external conditions—and certainly less dependent on individual Western actions. It makes little sense, for example, to argue that perestroika might have been aborted by the conclusion of a strategic arms reduction treaty in 1987. The same is true of the idea that there was a causal link between the failure to sign an arms treaty at the Moscow summit in June 1988 and Gorbachev's turn to radical political reform (that is, elections) in July. Such notions confuse Gorbachev's very strong general interest in lower international tensions with his much weaker specific interest in this or that agreement. He turned to elections in the summer of 1988 because he didn't have a solid majority in the Central Committee of the party. No START treaty, no matter how skewed in his favor, would have given him such a majority.

Gorbachev's International Prestige

The detente of the late 1980s—marked by more or less annual declarations that the Cold War was now really, finally, conclusively, irreversibly over (such announcements have continued into the 1990s)—had highly uneven effects in East and West. Although Soviet spokesmen announced with malicious glee that the West was being robbed of the "enemy image" on which its anti-Soviet policies had allegedly been based, Soviet decision-making itself was far more thoroughly transformed. Struggle against the Western world, now off its head with admiration for Gorbachev, simply could no longer be an organizing principle of society. Similarly, Gorbachev's popularity in the West may have had less impact on Western policy than on his own vanity. Did "Gorbomania" encourage him to ignore the doubts of fellow Politburo members, taking risks with the stability of the Soviet system that a less flamboyant leader, his head not turned by global celebrity, would have instantly recognized as imprudent?

The hard international environment of the early 1980s obliged the Soviet leadership to consider change, but tough Western policies alone could not finish the job. Reagan, Thatcher, Bush, and the other Western leaders who dealt with Gorbachev had only limited leverage over him. What they did, in effect, was hand him a gun and suggest that he do the honorable thing. As is often true of such situations, the victim-to-be is more likely to accept the advice if it is offered in the gentlest possible way and if he concludes that his friends, family, and colleagues will in the end think better of him for going through with it. For Soviet communism, the international environment of the late 1980s was a relaxed setting in which, after much anguished reflection, to turn the gun on itself.

Cultural Ferment

Geoffrey Hosking

Although the Soviet regime went to great lengths to censor and control political dissidence, it could not thoroughly stamp it out. A few dissidents, such as Andrei Sakharov, made their views widely known both within the Soviet Union and in the West. When Gorbachev introduced the policies of glasnost and perestroika in 1987, these dissidents quickly became the nuclei of budding reform movements.

In the following article, first published shortly after the disintegration of the Soviet Union in December 1991, Geoffrey Hosking describes the transformation of these dissident movements into the formal political opposition that eventually contrived the defeat of the Communist government and the downfall of the Soviet Union. Informal groups originally formed around environmental and historical issues, Hosking notes, but nationalist movements also quickly emerged. As perestroika progressed, these movements organized to field and elect candidates to a new Russian parliament, the Congress of People's Deputies and to the governing bodies of the constituent republics: Leading dissident figures then used the congress and the republican governments as platforms to propose political alternatives to the Soviet Communist regime.

Geoffrey Hosking is the author of many books, including *The First Socialist Society: A History of the Soviet Union from Within*, *The Awakening of the Soviet Union*, and *Empire and Nation in Russian History*.

Reprinted from Geoffrey Hosking, "The Roots of Dissolution," *The New York Review of Books*, January 16, 1992, by permission of David Higham Associates, London, as agents for the author.

The first people to challenge the Party's political monopoly were a few long-haired youths with guitars, rather contemptuously known as "informals" (*neformaly*), a label they accepted with cheerful defiance. When they appeared in the mid-1980s, they seemed to have not the slightest hope of bringing about serious change; indeed, that was not their aim, initially at least. They took up causes like the defense of a seventeenth-century merchant's house in Moscow (one of very few to have survived the great fire of 1812, and in 1986 threatened by urban redevelopment), or the Hotel Angleterre in Leningrad, where the much-loved peasant poet Sergei Esenin committed suicide. They organized picket lines, collected signatures for protests, paraded with placards, and once or twice appeared on glasnost-conscious television. Some were longstanding hippies or pacifists, some were members of barely tolerated rock groups, others were students attracted by the freer atmosphere of the new era.

The Birth of Informal Politics

A bit later the *neformaly*, joined by more students, moved on to ecological concerns, protesting about the noxious fumes of a factory here, the construction of a nuclear power station there, the damming of a river for a hydroelectric project somewhere else. The Chernobyl explosion of 1986 gave powerful impetus to their efforts. Gradually they began to attract impressive crowds of people who were becoming aware of the carelessness with which bureaucrats had adulterated their food, poisoned their air, and contaminated their drinking water. The authorities were acutely embarrassed by these protests. In the age of glasnost, they could not simply suppress them. It was difficult to deny the facts of ecological degradation, and environmental health is like motherhood: you can't be opposed to it.

The next stage of informal politics came when members of academic institutes began to get involved in these campaigns. To understand what this means, one must realize that scholars enjoyed much higher prestige in the Soviet Union than they do in Britain or the US. The rulers need pure scientists and technologists to foster economic growth, while scholars in the humanities and social sciences used to help them produce the ideological pap they fed the people. That need, even under Brezhnev, gave scholars a certain independence, which some could use to shut themselves away in small groups, or even alone in their offices, and investigate subjects which had nothing to do with Marxism-Leninism but a great deal to do with the market economy, constitutional politics, religion and theology, folklore and ethnography. They could not publish their results at the time—or only in muffled and distorted fashion—but the results of their work are evident in the rich and varied intellectual life which suddenly blossomed, as if from nowhere, when censorship was lifted. The academic institutes in the republics also harbored future leaders who have since come to power: the musicologist Landsbergis in Lithuania, the orientalist Ter-Petrosian in Armenia, and the literary scholar Gamsakhurdia in Georgia.

Academics and Dissent

By and large, it was younger scholars, rather than their prestigious seniors, who first went into informal politics. For example, in the early months of 1987 the so-called Klub Perestroika emerged from an ongoing seminar at the Institute of Mathematical Economics in Moscow. It brought together economists, jurists, sociologists, political scientists, and others, mostly research assistants and junior scientific workers in their twenties and thirties, to discuss the drafting of a new law on economic enterprise. The discussions were expert and wide-ranging, and soon outgrew the original theme, throwing light on the failure of the whole Soviet economy. Discussion of this stimulated in many participants the desire to move beyond academic debate and do something practical. They organized specialist task forces to give shape to these aspirations. A group concerned with "social self-administration" was set up to advise workers on how to make use of their rights under the new enterprise law; a "civic dignity" group undertook to advise citizens whose civil rights were threatened; another called *Memorial* solicited public support for the idea of a memorial center dedicated to

Stalin's victims. Analogous initiatives were undertaken in a number of cities, but Klub Perestroika was especially important. It is remarkable how many of Yeltsin's closest advisers today—and also some of his leading opponents in the democratic camp—began their political careers there.

Informal Politics Becomes Nationalist

The next important stage took place in the Baltic republics, where the first popular fronts were organized in the late 1980s. Their appearance marked the moment when members of the Party-state apparatus began to transfer their allegiance to the "informals." It was characteristic that this development took place not in Russia but among peoples who had long felt they were being oppressed by Russia. In circumstances of national oppression, any grievance, whether it had to do with the environment, education, the economy, the mass media, or whatever it might be, could be presented as an ethnic issue. Some Ukrainians, for example, were beginning to think of the Chernobyl explosion, not inherently an ethnic matter at all, as the product of a Russian policy of genocide directed against the Ukrainian people—a continuation, in fact, of Stalin's elimination of the kulaks and his purges of the Communist Party.

So devastating had been the effects of Communist misrule that a great variety of issues were accumulating to be taken up by political movements that could construe them as challenges to Soviet Communist rule over the republics. In those circumstances, the proconsuls of the empire—the leading Party-state apparatchiks in the non-Russian republics—had to reassess the sources of their power. Hitherto they had mediated between Moscow and their home populations, but always on the assumption that real power derived from Moscow, and that serious disputes would ultimately be settled there. That assumption now had to be called into question. Increasing democratic participation gave them a stronger position in relation to Moscow, but also made it more difficult for them to deal with inflamed public opinion in their own republics.

After considering the new situation, some apparatchiks in

the republics decided to throw in their lot with those whom they had hitherto considered "nonconformist" or even "dissident" intellectuals in their own homeland. The first to do so was Edgar Savisaar, a senior planning official in Estonia. Indignant at the undemocratic way in which delegates were being "elected" (in fact appointed), for the 19th Party Conference, he appeared on Estonian television on the evening of April 13, 1988, calling for the formation of a mass movement to press from below for the genuine democratization which Gorbachev was promising from above. He immediately received thousands of letters of support, and formed a new organization called the Popular Front in Support of Perestroika.

The idea was soon taken up in other republics, swiftly in the more urbanized ones where national feeling was strong and united, such as Latvia, Lithuania, Georgia, Armenia, Azerbaijan, and Moldavia, more slowly where national feeling was weaker or more divided, as in Byelorussia and the Ukraine, or where there were fewer urban centers, as in Central Asia. During 1988 and 1989, with different emphases in different republics, these movements presented demands for their economies to become self-governing, their languages to have official status, their environment to be protected, their histories and cultures to be properly taught in schools, their victims under Stalin to be commemorated. In some republics, notably the Baltic nations, Moldavia, and Western Ukraine, the Popular Fronts received many votes in the elections of 1989 and 1990 and moved into positions of local power during 1990.

Full Independence Movements

Before the beginning of 1991 nearly all of them were demanding "sovereignty." This was a capaciously ambiguous concept—it might mean anything from full independence to the right to run your own refuse collection: but it had the advantage of providing an issue on which intellectuals and the local apparatchiks could cooperate. For the former, the word stood for their dreams of national self-determination and democracy; for the latter, it meant they would at last have real power—including the power to repel unwelcome measures of perestroika emanating from Moscow.

An excellent example of such an alliance of convenience was Ukraine's virtually unanimous declaration of sovereignty in July 1990. This was in many respects surprisingly radical in tone, including demands for human rights, full-scale multiparty democracy, and a separate national army. But many Ukrainians remained distrustful, suspecting that the apparatchiks still in a majority in the Ukrainian Parliament had no intention of turning the words into reality. So a few months later students went on a hunger strike in the main square of Kiev to try to compel the Ukrainian government to do what it had already declared was its policy. The struggle to turn a theoretically sovereign Ukraine into an independent state has finally been won with the referendum of December 1. The struggle to transform the newly independent ex-apparatchiks into democrats, however, is likely to go on much longer. . . .

Russia's Informal Movements

In Russia things have been more complicated. There was no nationwide Popular Front, for there was no obvious ethnic target to protest against, and no unified feeling that a national liberation movement should be directed against the empire. Indeed, most Russians over the centuries have automatically identified Russia with its huge multinational territories to the extent of confusing nation and empire. It followed that not all Russian national movements were democratic in aspiration either: *Pamyat*, the first one to be widely publicized back in 1987, was decidedly authoritarian, and anti-Semitic as well. And even those that *were* democratic have been deeply divided over whether to try to keep the Union together in some form, or to allow the non-Russians to go their own way into full independence, if they wanted.

The Russian movement that most nearly took on the characteristics of a Popular Front was *Memorial*. Its founders, like the historian Ury Afanasyev, believe that troubling questions about nation and empire could be put aside in the face of the overwhelming need to investigate the truth about Stalin's repressions, and to make that truth known in order to commemorate the victims and ensure that nothing comparable could ever happen again.

Memorial had a very powerful emotional impact. In November 1988 it sponsored a "week of conscience" in many towns. In Moscow a "wall of memory" was erected, to which thousands of photographs of the victims were pinned. People came to see it to seek out relatives they had lost, and to leave forlorn notes asking, for instance, "Does anyone know my father?" In front of a huge map of the USSR marked with the islands of the Gulag Archipelago stood a convict's wheelbarrow in which visitors could place their donations toward a fitting memorial.

This project of a memorial, to be accompanied by a library, archive, and exhibition hall, led such prominent and established figures as the writer Anatoly Rybakov and the actor Mikhail Ulyanov to support ideas that until very recently had been outlawed. *Memorial* held impromptu polls in the streets, to find out who the public thought should lead the project. It was a kind of unofficial popularity test for public figures. Significantly, nearly all those who received large numbers of votes were writers or scientists. The lone politician to be thus honored was Boris Yeltsin, whose outspoken attacks on privilege and corruption, followed by his expulsion from the Party Central Committee in 1987, had given him enormous appeal to ordinary people.

Some of the leaders of *Memorial* began the process of rescuing Yeltsin from the political wilderness into which he had been cast when he was purged in 1987. Together with other "informals" that had emerged from the Klub Perestroika, they organized political meetings for him before the elections of March 1989. Among those involved were some of the leading figures of post-Communist Russia: Alexander Muzykantsky, later chairman of the Moscow Association of Voters and now one of Yeltsin's "prefects"; Sergei Stankevich, now a Russian State Councilor; Lev Ponomaryov, of the Moscow Association of Voters and Democratic Russia; Pavel Kudyukin and Leonid Volkov, of the Social Democratic Party; Igor Chubais, of the Democratic Platform and the Republican Party. At the climax of their campaign, on the eve of the poll, they are reckoned to have gathered some 20,000 people in the Luzhniki Stadium.

Support for Boris Yeltsin

In his autobiography, Yeltsin gives a brief picture of his "informal" helpers and supporters, and acknowledges his debt to them:

> I shall always be grateful to them for their selfless support, their sincerity, devotion and loyalty. Many people asserted that I was making a terrible mistake by choosing as my campaign aides people who were not professionals—not politicians, not experts, but plain, intelligent, decent human beings. I knew none of them before the election campaign started; they either rang up or came to see me, saying that they wanted to be my campaign assistants. I was grateful for this, but warned them that it would be extremely tough going. They knew this, of course, and many were dedicated enough to have taken unpaid leave to help in my campaign. And they worked, without exaggeration, literally night and day.

Not only did the "informals" work hard for him, they also began his political reeducation. During the 1989 campaign he had little more to offer than general democratic notions combined with denunciations of privilege, corruption, and incompetence. At the time that was sufficient, and he won by a vote of nearly 90 percent. But once he was in the Congress of People's Deputies, where he was recognized as a kind of unofficial leader of the opposition, he had to offer some coherent alternative to Gorbachev's policies on a wide variety of issues.

This was where Yeltsin first met some of the country's leading intellectuals, elected, like himself, through the campaigning efforts of the "informals." Their relationship was not easy at first. There were many reasons why a former apparatchik should distrust university professors, and vice versa. But together they formed the Interregional Group of Deputies to coordinate an opposition strategy; and they began to tolerate and even respect each other. As one of his associates later commented: "What Yeltsin knew much better than the others was the inner-Party kitchen and what they were cooking up. I think he added some intellectual qualities to his natural wolflike intuition, and became the fully formed personality he is today."

Important though it was, the Interregional Group suffered from the way ethnic claims became imposed on virtually all political issues during 1988 and 1989. Although the alliance in principle united deputies from different nations and republics, it was torn apart by stormy interethnic rivalries. Besides, the Interregional Group made up only a small minority of a legislature still dominated by what Yuri Afanasyev called the "aggressively obedient majority" of deputies nominated by the Party-state apparatus.

Yeltsin Comes to Power

So the Interregional Group was an unsatisfactory power base for Yeltsin, and early in 1990 he decided to shift his position and take advantage of the upcoming republican and local elections. With his sure instinct for power, he had seen that "sovereignty," troublesome enough for Gorbachev when claimed in Estonia or Moldavia, would revolutionize Soviet politics generally if it were declared in Russia. The Russian Supreme Soviet, hitherto a pale legislative shadow, could become a new strategic vantage point from which to challenge both the Communist Party and the Soviet president.

There was no Russian Popular Front to organize his campaign, and *Memorial* was withdrawing from politics to concentrate on its cultural and historical mission. But a substitute for both appeared when the various "informal" groups, though riven with disputes about nation and empire and about what kind of democracy was appropriate, managed to create an electoral bloc called "Democratic Russia," with branches in all the major Russian towns. Its program invoked the memory of Andrei Sakharov, and commended his proposals for a new Soviet constitution. In line with Yeltsin's new program, it proposed that "the Congress of People's Deputies of Russia should do what has not yet been achieved at the all-Union level and assume the full power of the state in Russia."

The upshot of Democratic Russia's campaign was a legislature much more evenly balanced than the all-Union parliament elected the previous year: the "aggressively obedient majority" was no longer a secure majority. Yeltsin was elected as the parliament's speaker by a narrow margin but, once he was installed in that post, he was able to use it to launch his bid to become, the following year, the popularly elected president of Russia. Thus he reached the position from which he was able to defy the coup.

What is also remarkable about the Russian Parliament is that many of its members who originally seemed to be faceless apparatchiks, have gradually been "infected" by the ideas of the democrats. As in the non-Russian republics, this infection has taken place through the notion of "sovereignty." During the prolonged sterile disputes over the numerous economic reform programs that were put forward but not carried out during 1990, many deputies came to feel that no single program would work for the whole of the Soviet Union (whether a Union Treaty were signed or not) but that it made sense to try to adapt reform programs to each republic individually.

When Yeltsin was under pressure in the spring of 1991 from the army and the Communist Party, a small but decisive number of Communist deputies in the Russian Parliament deserted their colleagues and supported him. Their caucus, the "Communists for Democracy," led by former Afghanistan hero Colonel Rutskoi, threw their weight behind the democrats and ensured that Yeltsin would not be removed from his position as speaker.

Both parliament and president of Russia, then, owe their current power and legitimacy to the process of political fermentation that started with the meetings and protests of long-haired "informals" back in 1987. Yeltsin was rescued from the political wilderness by the "informals" and the academic and other reformers who joined with them. They gave him a new kind of political program, and organized his campaigns. The Russian Parliament too owes many of its reformist ideas and much of its public support to them.

Chapter 3

Disintegration of Empire

Turning Points

IN WORLD HISTORY

Retreat from Afghanistan

Anthony Arnold

After the Soviet Union invaded neighboring Afghanistan in December 1979 to shore up that country's Communist regime, the U.S. Central Intelligence Agency began supplying arms to Afghan mujahedin (Islamic militants) who were fighting the Soviet invaders. Though the mujahedin won few battles, they inflicted severe casualties on Soviet forces. Nine years later the Soviets pulled out without resolving the situation. As of 1998, Afghanistan remains embroiled in a civil war, though a faction of the mujahedin has gained control over most of the country.

In the following selection, written in 1993, Anthony Arnold argues that the debacle in Afghanistan was a major factor in the downfall of the Soviet Union. The Soviet citizens became less willing to endure economic sacrifices for the aggressive foreign policy of a regime that was perceived to be decrepit and powerless.

Anthony Arnold is the author of several books on Afghanistan, including *Afghanistan: The Soviet Invasion in Perspective* and *The Fateful Pebble: Afghanistan's Role in the Fall of the Soviet Empire*, from which this viewpoint is excerpted.

> *A dead-tired man may stumble over a pebble and fall; but his weariness, rather than the pebble, is the cause.*
>
> —George Stewart, *Storm*

Stewart may have been right, but he fails to give the pebble its due. How much farther might that dead-tired man have staggered on before collapsing of his weariness alone? How much more serious might the consequences of his fall have been after his last reserves of strength had been exhausted, and he was unable to cushion his fall?

I submit that the Soviet Union, beset with a myriad of economic, social, and political problems in the waning years of Leonid Brezhnev's reign, was analogous to the weary traveler, and Afghanistan to the pebble that brought him down.

If it had not been for the Soviet setback in Afghanistan the next challenge to Moscow's hegemony almost surely would have been met with the same resort to arms. That challenge (from Poland, later in 1980) in fact very nearly did trigger an invasion, first in early 1981 and again in December that year; a Soviet general has stated that his troops were ready to occupy the entire country "within one day or at most two," and Polish Communist leaders have generally contended that only General Jaruzelski's imposition of martial law stayed the Soviet hand at the last moment. Surely, however, another major element in the Kremlin's decision not to intervene must have been the embarrassment they were suffering in Afghanistan.

What the international repercussions of a Soviet invasion of Poland might have been can only be conjectured. Even without that fateful step, however, it is arguable that a quick victory in Afghanistan might have meant that: the Communist party of the Soviet Union (CPSU) traditional apparat would still be in full command of the USSR; its general secretary would be someone a good bit more intransigent than Mikhail Gorbachev; the military budgets of both the United States and the USSR would be continuing their mad expansions of the 1970s and 1980s; active Soviet involvement in Africa, Asia, and Latin America would still be the order of the day; the reform movements that have exploded throughout the Marxist-Leninist world would be the stuff of dreams; and international tensions would be at an all-time, virtually unbearable high.

This suggested alternative to today's reality, although impossible to prove or disprove, is but a logical extension of old Soviet policies whose single virtue was—until Afghanistan—demonstrable success. Since World War II, at tremendous cost to the Soviet people, Moscow's export of Marxism-Leninism had been pushed relentlessly, if not always successfully, throughout the world and had sparked equally costly defensive moves from the West. Meanwhile, in areas already won to Moscow's side, opposition had been suppressed by ruthless police action or, when necessary, by force of Soviet arms (East Germany in 1953, Hungary in 1956, Czechoslovakia in 1968), thus increasing Western concerns still further.

Ultimately, the inherent weaknesses of the old Soviet system were bound to cause a major reform movement, but as long as the empire could be perceived as successfully expanding, the Kremlin leaders had few incentives for changing their policies. Despite a falling standard of living, even the common Soviet citizen would probably have been prepared to accept many more years of privation for the greater glory of the realm. There doubtless would have been some popular grumbling about conditions, but the three basic pillars of Soviet society—the party, the military, and the KGB—would have continued to suppress dissent and enforce discipline. It was only when the corrosive effects of the unwinnable war ate into each of those pillars that the empire they supported began to come apart.

Many books have been written about the fate of empires. Most fail to touch on one vital politico-psychological aspect:

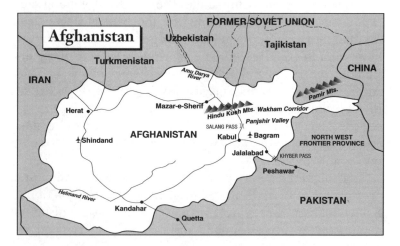

the perception of imperial failure, both within and without the empire. Regardless of how much economic progress is being sacrificed to military needs, the problem only becomes acute when it becomes self-evident. In this respect, the war in Afghanistan occurred concurrently with a world revolution in communications, a revolution wherein the old Soviet system of information control simply broke down. When Soviet dissidents could simply fax their works to the West by telephone, censorship became a largely outmoded tool.

A third factor that undermined the old Soviet system was the U.S. hard-line response to Soviet military muscle flexing and its willingness to go head-to-head with the USSR in an arms race. The critical element here was the fulfillment of a pledge in the late 1970s to deploy ground-launched cruise missiles (GLCMs) and Pershing II ballistic missiles in NATO countries if the Soviets proceeded with deployment of SS-20 missiles aimed at Western Europe. The Soviet response was to ignore the warning, proceed with deployment, and pull out all the stops in a massive overt and covert political action campaign to prevent the U.S. countermove. This campaign failed. The United State deployed its missiles in the early 1980s, and the USSR wound up in worse strategic shape than before.

Although this drama unfolded far away from Afghanistan, it is arguable that both the U.S. firmness and the failure of the Soviet campaign were results of the December 1979 invasion, which the West accepted as a more convincing demonstration of basically aggressive and expansionist Soviet intentions than any propaganda could negate.

Although all three factors were important in triggering the collapse of the Soviet empire, a key element was the erosion of public support for the Kremlin's aggressive policies. Popular perceptions are difficult to analyze in a society where until recently the legal media have been entirely government controlled, political nonconformity has been treated as a criminal offense, and the image of public support for Kremlin policies has been foisted on both domestic and foreign audiences.

Revolutions in Eastern Europe

Coit D. Blacker

In the aftermath of World War II, the Soviet Union created a "sphere of influence" for itself in the eastern half of Europe, which it had liberated from Nazi Germany's control and occupied in the immediate postwar period. The Soviet Union established military bases in Poland, Czechoslovakia, Hungary, Bulgaria, Romania, and East Germany and set up allied socialist regimes in these countries. When Mikhail Gorbachev came to power in 1985 and initiated his policies of perestroika and glasnost in the Soviet Union, he pressured the Eastern European governments to adopt similar courses of reform. In 1988, as part of negotiations with the West to reduce military forces in Europe, Gorbachev agreed to the withdrawal of Soviet troops from these countries. With the loss of Soviet military support, the unleashing of political dissent in 1989 toppled one Eastern European socialist regime after another, in rapid succession.

Writing in 1990, prior to the collapse of the Soviet Union, Coit D. Blacker argues in the following article that the downfall of the socialist governments in Eastern Europe came as an unpleasant surprise to Gorbachev and the Soviet leadership. The loss of control over these allied regimes drastically reduced the influence of the Soviets in international affairs, he contends. The demands of the new Eastern European governments for the withdrawal of Soviet troops obviated negotiations with the West on this issue, according to Blacker: Gorbachev's attempts to remake

Soviet foreign policy had resulted in a loss of international influence.

Coit D. Blacker is a professor of international relations at Stanford University. He is the author of *Hostage to Revolution: Gorbachev and Soviet Security Policy, 1985–1991.*

Soviet military power has been an enduring preoccupation of U.S. policymakers for better than forty years, its presumed menace one of the great constants of the age. Our understanding of that power and the perceived menace have changed dramatically, however, as a direct consequence of Mikhail Gorbachev's program of radical economic and political reform. Nowhere has the changing face of Soviet power been more apparent than in Europe. The presence of almost 600,000 Soviet troops in Europe symbolized and sustained for several decades the grim reality of the continent's postwar division. Today the partial withdrawal of these forces, coupled with the expectation of additional reductions, signals the start of a new era. With these redeployments begins a period of profound political change in Europe, the most significant, in fact, since the defeat of the Axis powers at the conclusion of World War II.

Collapse of the Postwar Division of Europe

If the rapid disintegration of the postwar order in Europe took Western leaders by surprise, it stunned, confused and demoralized their counterparts in Moscow. What began as a well-conceived strategy to recast the tone and substance of Soviet security policy in Europe all but dissolved in the face of an extraordinary political upheaval that the Soviet leadership appears not to have anticipated. As a result, Kremlin leaders now confront the virtual collapse of Soviet power on the continent. Moreover, this collapse comes without a corresponding erosion of authority and influence on the part of Moscow's erstwhile adversaries to the west.

Gorbachev and his colleagues did not labor to attain supreme power in the U.S.S.R. only to expedite their country's decline. They were seeking instead to ensure that the

Soviet Union would enter the 21st century, in Gorbachev's words, "in a manner befitting a great power." But upon assuming power, they discovered their nation's decline was already well advanced, largely as a consequence of a deeply troubled economy. Only through substantial reform, they thought, could this precipitous slide toward economic ruin be halted and then reversed. Exactly how far-reaching that reform had to be in order to accomplish economic renewal became apparent only in retrospect. By that time, however, the process threatened to consume not only the architects themselves, but the very system it was designed to save.

Key to Gorbachev's ambitious strategy was a period of peaceful, evolutionary political change. It was essential that Moscow's allies and adversaries, including the United States, recognize the processes underway in the Soviet Union, welcome and facilitate them, and adjust their own policies accordingly. Since the fall of 1989, however, events have overtaken Moscow's carefully constructed plan for Europe, resulting in a kind of policy "free-fall." Today, the Kremlin leadership has all it can do simply to respond to events as they occur.

Soviet Foreign Policy Goals

From the mid-1940s to the late 1980s two goals lay at the heart of Moscow's European policy: to safeguard the territorial and political gains attained at such enormous cost in the final phase of World War II; and to secure admission to, and influence in, the remainder of Europe. Confronted with a cohesive community of Western states able to arrest the advance of Soviet power beyond the line that came to demark the continent's division, the Soviets were forced to settle for their first objective—hegemony in the East—to the long-term detriment of their second—an institutionalized role in the West.

As Europe's de facto East-West split solidified, the Soviets invested significant resources to garrison a community of "socialist" states in Europe, remade in all important ways in the Soviet image. Thus by the mid-1950s, eastern Europe was securely linked to the U.S.S.R. through a complex series of reinforcing bilateral and multilateral ties that affected virtually every aspect of the region's political, military and economic life. Yet Moscow's larger vision of Europe never faded. The Soviet leadership repeatedly in the 1950s called for the convening of an all-European conference to overcome Europe's division, specifically by implementing a multilateral nonaggression pact and a series of bilateral security guarantees. The United States, as a non-European power, was to be excluded from these arrangements. Once in place, the new system would supplant NATO and the Warsaw Pact, and all foreign military forces, including those of the United States, would be withdrawn from the continent. The Soviet Union, then, would be *primus inter pares* [first among equals] politically and militarily.

The resounding lack of support in the West for these initiatives did not deter the Kremlin from offering them, at irregular intervals. At a meeting of Warsaw Pact foreign ministers in Bucharest in 1966 the call went out once again— this time shorn of its blatantly anti-American tone— and the result was different. Much reduced in scope, and with the United States and Canada as central participants, the Conference on Security and Cooperation in Europe (CSCE) finally got under way in the fall of 1972 in Helsinki. That this conference failed, utterly, either to legitimize the Soviet position in eastern Europe or to enhance its influence in western Europe was not apparent to the Brezhnev leadership for a number of years. Soviet leaders at that time looked upon the CSCE as an ideal instrument for attaining a position in European affairs fully commensurate with what they termed the "worldwide shift in the correlation of forces" in favor of the allied socialist states.

What Soviet leaders failed to understand was that, in order for them to reap substantial rewards from détente, the West required a perceptible and sustained reduction in the Warsaw Pact's military threat. It also needed to see a measurable loosening of the Kremlin's political hold over eastern Europe. Absent these steps, Moscow's proclamations of pacific intentions toward the noncommunist states of Europe rang hollow. Moscow's attempts to overcome the continent's postwar schism under a Soviet aegis were thus rendered stillborn.

The Arms Race

Between the mid-1970s and early 1980s the Kremlin undertook a far-reaching and expensive effort to modernize its conventional and nuclear military capabilities in the European theater. This move provoked deep alarm in Western capitals. Among other consequences, the Soviet buildup resulted in NATO adopting the Long-term Defense Program in 1978 to enhance its ability to withstand a Warsaw Pact conventional military attack. The following year NATO also made its famous "dual track" decision, in which the Western allies agreed to field a new generation of nuclear-armed intermediate-range missiles in Europe if a negotiated solution to prevent their deployment could not be reached.

The Kremlin also continued to lend strong support to the repressive regimes of eastern Europe, most of which did their best to quash the kinds of dissenting political expression supposedly guaranteed by the 1975 Helsinki Final Act. Thus with the rise of the Solidarity trade union movement, the Polish government imposed martial law in 1981 with at least Moscow's blessing, if not at its instigation. By the time Soviet leader Yuri Andropov died in February 1984, the Kremlin's political fortunes in Europe were at their lowest ebb in several decades. The abbreviated tenure of Andropov's successor, Konstantin Chernenko, witnessed only a modest change for the better. The two superpowers announced in January 1985 that they would resume negotiations on intermediate-range nuclear forces (INF) and the Strategic Arms Reduction Talks (START), which the Soviets had broken off 13 months earlier. It was in these far from auspicious circumstances that in March 1985 the Soviet Central Committee elected Mikhail Sergeyevich Gorbachev general secretary of the Communist Party. At 54 years old, Gorbachev was twenty years younger than the man he replaced.

Gorbachev's Shift in Foreign Policy Priorities

Within four years Gorbachev transformed Soviet foreign policy beyond recognition. In short order he abandoned many of the principles his predecessors had routinely invoked to justify their country's international conduct. He jettisoned as atavistic existing Soviet positions in several arms control settings, including the INF negotiations and START. He also displayed a willingness to entertain foreign-policy outcomes that previous leaders had consistently rejected as detrimental to Soviet interests.

Gorbachev moved with particular alacrity to overturn the Brezhnev legacy in Europe, where twenty years of rigid and shortsighted diplomacy had produced by the mid-1980s a policy conundrum. On one hand, to continue along the present path seemed certain to prolong the impasse in East-West relations. On the other, to change course by acceding to Western demands in INF negotiations, for example, was equally unpalatable: the Warsaw Pact's theater military posture, including its nuclear dimension, was central to Moscow's European policy.

To resolve this dilemma Gorbachev essentially reversed Soviet priorities in Europe. In other words, he placed the fostering of fully normalized relations with Western countries, long the second-order goal of Soviet policy, ahead of what had always been the Kremlin's primary objective on the continent, the maintenance of virtually absolute control over the east European glacis.

Gorbachev selected two vehicles to signal this sea-change in policy. The first was the decision to eliminate the Warsaw Pact's superiority in nuclear and conventional military capabilities through a combination of unilateral measures and negotiations with the West. With the successful conclusion in September 1986 of the Stockholm Conference on Confidence-and Security-Building Measures in Europe, the Soviets hinted broadly at their interest in restructuring the NATO–Warsaw Pact balance. They even harkened back to proposals made by the West 13 years earlier in the long-running, and ultimately fruitless, Mutual and Balanced Force Reductions negotiations. This nascent dialogue was furthered in 1987–89 during the so-called Mandate Talks, convened to prepare the way for a new set of negotiations on limiting conventional forces in Europe. At the Mandate Talks the Soviets communicated their readiness to accept military parity "from the Atlantic to the Urals," an offer that, if backed by action, would require them to make deep, asymmetrical reductions in areas of traditional advantage, such as deployed manpower, tanks, armored personnel carriers and artillery.

Reduction of Troops in Europe

The Soviets coupled these measures with a series of pronouncements on military doctrine underscoring the "defensive" character of the Eastern alliance. The Warsaw Pact's Political Consultative Committee, for example, declared in May 1987 that "the military doctrine of the Warsaw Treaty . . . is subjugated to the task of preventing war, both nuclear and conventional." The pact also emphasized support for reductions in forces and armaments "down to the level where neither side, in ensuring its defense, would have the means for a sudden attack against the other side, for starting offensive operations in general." Gorbachev then announced to the U.N. General Assembly in December 1988 plans to reduce unilaterally the size of Soviet armed forces by 500,000 troops within two years, including the withdrawal of 50,000 troops from eastern Europe. Thus by the time NATO and Warsaw Pact countries gathered in Vienna in March 1989 for the start of talks on Conventional Forces in Europe (CFE), the Soviets had indeed effected a dramatic volte-face in their European arms-control policy. Moscow had set the stage for what most observers felt confident would be the most productive series of exchanges on East-West military issues in postwar history.

The second signal of the sea-change in policy was the Soviet leadership's decision to encourage a process of indigenous political reform in eastern Europe. This initiative, however, precipitated revolutionary rather than evolutionary change and all but eviscerated the logic that inspired Moscow's initiatives on arms control and defense doctrine. It appears Gorbachev believed he could control and direct the forces of reform in order to produce a fundamentally new political order in Europe—one denoted by greater cooperation and mutual stability.

The Soviet Union's Warsaw Pact allies, however, declined

to play the part Moscow had scripted for them. The political disintegration of East Germany in late 1989, followed less than a year later by the unification of the two German states—and on terms set by the Federal Republic no less—was particularly traumatic for the Kremlin. These and other developments in the region constituted mortal blows to the Soviet position in eastern Europe.

The Helsinki Agreement on Human Rights

Given the enormous stakes for the Soviet position in Europe, what possible combination of factors could have impelled the leadership to undertake such a high-risk strategy? The first factor was the continuous decline in Soviet political fortunes in Europe between the late 1970s and the mid-1980s, colored by the gnawing sense that the European military balance was evolving in ways disadvantageous to the Warsaw Pact. The second was the precipitous decline of the Soviet economy.

The Kremlin's position in Europe never looked more secure than in 1975 at the conclusion of the CSCE. Moscow had attained formal Western acceptance of the political and territorial status quo in eastern Europe—or so it seemed—in the first several paragraphs of the Helsinki Final Act. The Brezhnev leadership doubtless also found to its liking the second part of the document, which encouraged the 35 signatories to develop more extensive economic and trade relations. Only the inclusion of the call for "the freer movement of peoples and ideas" and respect for fundamental human rights gave Moscow pause. The Soviet leadership appeared to believe that it could look to its stalwart allies in eastern Europe to contain the seemingly moderate pressures for political reform, and thereby extract from the CSCE process most of the benefits and few of the costs.

Ten years later, however, the bargain struck in Helsinki looked very different. While conservative regimes still held sway in eastern Europe, they did so through increasingly repressive measures that widened the gulf between the rulers and the ruled. In Poland that gulf became a yawning chasm, resulting in Solidarity's spectacular rise, and apparent fall, in

1980-81. Elsewhere, most notably in Czechoslovakia and Hungary, governments also found themselves under constant siege from reform elements that drew much of their legitimacy from the phrases embedded in the Helsinki Final Act. . . .

Soviet Defense Spending

The most salient and time-urgent factor promoting change in Moscow's European policy, however, was the steep decline of the Soviet economy. The cost of maintaining the largest military establishment in the world, including 31 combat-ready divisions in eastern Europe equipped with the most modern weapons the Soviet system was capable of producing, was an enormous drain on the country's industrial and technological resources. As Soviet economic growth slowed during the last decade, the share of the national income devoted to military requirements actually increased. This was true even though the rate of increase in military spending between the late 1970s and the early 1980s was cut in half, from 5 percent a year to roughly 2–3 percent. By the second half of the 1980s, even this modest increase in military expenditures could not be sustained.

Military spending imposed an obvious and onerous burden on the Soviet economy. It absorbed resources that, in the judgment of Soviet and Western economists alike, would have been better spent on the modernization of the country's aging and inefficient industrial, transport and agricultural sectors. To compound the problem, the economic reforms introduced between 1985 and 1989 were extraordinarily costly in material terms, demanding the identification and utilization of additional capital and human resources. For perestroika to succeed the government had to reorder radically the country's economic priorities. One key to that strategy was the reallocation of resources from defense to investment and consumption accounts.

To date the results of perestroika have been disappointing, to say the least. Eagerly anticipated increases in productivity have mostly failed to materialize. This has served in turn to increase the allure of the Soviet Union's own "peace dividend"—the capture for more productive purposes of some of the resources hitherto earmarked for the military. While reductions in defense expenditures of 25 to 50 percent for armed forces and military industries cannot be achieved without significant near-term strategic costs to the Soviet Union, the long-term benefits could be considerable. The current leadership understands this better than anyone. This fact partly explains its haste to shrink both the size and attendant costs of Soviet armed forces, particularly those in Europe and Asia. Hard economic necessity, as well as the desire to convince the West of the seriousness of Moscow's "new look," may thus have inspired Gorbachev's dramatic demobilization edict of December 1988 and his assent to the November 1990 CFE accord.

New Thinking and East European Revolutions

Since many of Moscow's troubles appeared to stem from the decision after World War II to seal off the "socialist community" from contamination by the West, Gorbachev may have considered greater openness to be a solution. Glasnost for the Gorbachev regime has had several distinct meanings. Among other things, it has meant a greater tolerance for diversity in political opinion, a less restrictive cultural milieu, and less secrecy in military and national security affairs. It also implied a new receptivity to social, political and economic forces long deemed subversive to the interests of Europe's communist states. Gorbachev began to speak and write of the importance of "universal human values" in defining Soviet interests and security. He also noted the sterility of such time-honored Marxist-Leninist concepts as "the international class struggle" and "proletarian internationalism." Soviet authorities and academics thus called for "new thinking" in the formulation of foreign policy, and challenged allies and adversaries alike to join in the search for novel answers to old problems.

The use by senior Soviet officials of a vocabulary that their predecessors would have found wholly unintelligible was designed to signal an important departure in policy. The theories and practices of Stalin, Khrushchev and Brezhnev had divided the world into two camps, with each side irreconcilably opposed to the values, purposes and goals of the other. Gorbachev, by contrast, described in February 1986 a world of converging interests, a world both "interdependent" and "integral." Such allusions to the notion of intersystemic integration—the gradual overcoming of the political and economic barriers separating East and West—were for seventy years a cardinal heresy among orthodox communists. That Gorbachev seemed eager to sanction a process of integration reflected his deepening conviction that the Soviet Union would fall still farther behind the rest of the world economically, socially and politically if it continued to remain in a self-imposed exile.

Diagnosis, however, is no cure. To end the Soviet Union's isolation Gorbachev needed to sanction the elimination of the twin pillars of Moscow's postwar security policy in Europe: its vise-like hold over eastern Europe and the offensive military posture of the Warsaw Pact. Gorbachev has already completed the first step, deciding not to intervene militarily within eastern Europe to arrest the process of revolutionary change. This decision could not have come easily. But the disastrous state of the Soviet economy, the growing political and social restiveness of its own population and the perceived need not to delay in opening a new and more cooperative East-West relationship all deprived the leadership of any real choice in the matter. The second step is now underway: the complete withdrawal of Soviet forces from Czechoslovakia and Hungary scheduled for mid-1991, and eventually from eastern Germany, as well as the signing of the CFE agreement.

Some Soviet leaders may regret the decisions to accept military parity with the West and to allow eastern Europe to chart its own political and economic destiny. But the process cannot be halted, let alone reversed, at this late date. The issue, then, for Gorbachev and his allies is not how to recover what has been lost, but how to take advantage of the opportunities that induced them to take such an extraordinary gamble in the first place.

Growing Autonomy for the Republics

Martha Brill Olcott

The Soviet Union, founded on the remnants of the czarist Russian empire, comprised fifteen national republics. Each republic (with the exception of Russia) maintained its own Communist Party and government structure, but leaders were chosen and policies were set by the central government in Moscow.

In the following article, written a few months after the unsuccessful 1991 coup against Gorbachev, shortly before the official breakup of the Soviet Union, Martha Brill Olcott argues that Gorbachev's plan to reform the economy and Communist government of the Soviet Union failed to take into account the problem of nationalism in the republics. In the wake of the attempted coup and the resulting power vacuum in Moscow, she argues, the republics seized the opportunity to declare independence.

Martha Brill Olcott is a professor of political science at Colgate University. She is the author of *The Kazakhs* and *Central Asia's New States: Independence, Foreign Policy, and Regional Security* and the editor of *Russia After Communism, The Soviet Multinational State*, and *Religion and Tradition in Islamic Central Asia*.

When Mikhail Gorbachev became Soviet Communist party general secretary in 1985, he seemed confident that he had the vision and the talent to imbue the Soviet political system with the legitimacy needed to goad the population into ac-

Reprinted, with permission, from Martha Brill Olcott, "The Slide into Disunion," *Current History*, October 1991; © 1991, Current History, Inc.

cepting possibly disruptive but nonetheless necessary economic reforms. His assessment was partly correct—the Soviet Union's political survival depended on the regime's ability to reform the economy. But the Soviet leader woefully underestimated the complexity of his task. Political and economic reform were not only intertwined with, but also complicated by, the Soviet Union's "nationality problem."

In his early calculations Gorbachev simply overlooked this problem. Even after he realized that nationalism was an important political force, he continued to underestimate its disruptive potential. Until the failed coup in August, Gorbachev believed that economic recovery—based on preserving the Soviet Union as an integrated economic unit—would cause the nationalist movements to lose their political legitimacy.

Thus the basic tension between economic and political reforms escaped Gorbachev's attention; his decision to open the political process brought to power nationalists who opposed a united country. Given this flaw in his thinking, Gorbachev consistently stumbled over nationality relations by offering the republics too little, too late.

The Eruption of the Nationality Issue

During his first years in office, Gorbachev was influenced by his late mentor, General Secretary Yuri Andropov. Like Andropov, Gorbachev believed that economic reform could not succeed without the removal of corrupt Communist party cadre who were preventing the Soviet economy's modernization. On coming to office in 1985, Gorbachev launched an anticorruption campaign against the powerful political bosses who ran the Soviet republics. One by one the longtime republic overlords were disgraced and forced to retire. Some were ousted with relative ease, but a few demonstrated their political skill by successfully parrying Moscow's best efforts to bring about their dismissals.

Dinmukhammad Kunayev, a member of the Politburo for 15 years and head of Kazakhstan's Communist party for more than 25 years, proved among the most tenacious republic leaders. However, on December 16,1986, at a session of Kazakhstan's Central Committee that had been convened at Moscow's order, Kunayev announced that he was retiring and that his replacement would be Gennadi Kolbin, a Russian from outside Kazakhstan. As news of Kunayev's retirement spread, protesters demanding an explanation for Moscow's actions began to fill the main square in the republic's capital of Alma-Ata.

The demonstrators stayed in the square overnight. The next day special troops, armed with attack dogs and sharpened spades, were sent to disperse the crowd. After two days of skirmishes, the protests came to an end. Gorbachev and Kazakhstan's prime minister Nursultan Nazarbayev, condemned the disturbances as "nationalist"-inspired violence. According to official reports, one demonstrator and one policeman died, but unofficial sources say these figures are far too low.

The Alma-Ata riots strikingly demonstrated the cost of ignoring the "national" factor. The Moscow-based Russian reformers regarded Kunayev as an aging despot who had benefited those in his immediate circle at the expense of the masses. However, as protests of his removal showed, he was a hero to many Kazakhs.

Criticism of Stalin and His Nationalities Policy

Gorbachev learned his lesson. In the aftermath of the Alma-Ata riots, republic party leaders won greater discretionary authority to control their territories. The long dead Joseph Stalin now became Moscow's principal target. Gorbachev planned to dismantle the Stalinist system, although no one knew quite what this meant. Glasnost, or openness, was encouraged. The people were told to speak their minds and even to join new, unofficial political groups to push for sweeping reforms.

Stalin's victims included millions of non-Russians, among them the Balts, the Crimean Tatars, and other north Caucasian peoples whose populations were forcibly deported during World War II. In spring and summer 1987, first the Crimean Tatars and then the Balts organized protests locally and in Moscow. The Crimean Tatars demanded the return

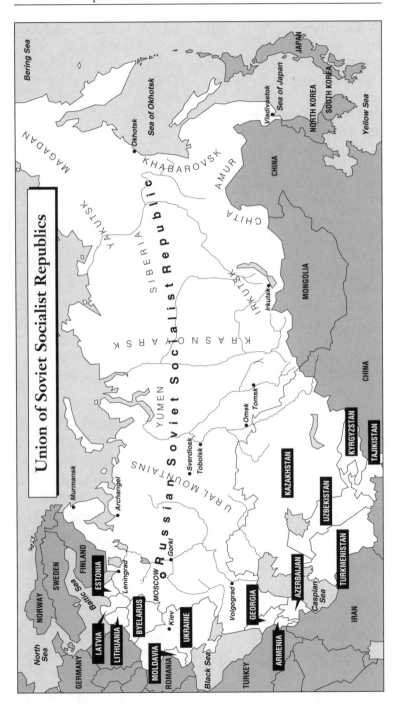

Union of Soviet Socialist Republics

of their homeland; the Balts, official recognition that their lands had been illegally annexed to the Soviet Union. Moscow's relatively benign treatment of the protesters led other nationalities to demand real rather than symbolic political reforms.

The situation became particularly serious in the Caucasus, where tensions between the Armenian and Azerbaijani populations spiraled out of control in early 1988. In February the Politburo voted to allow the republic of Azerbaijan to retain control of Nagorno-Karabakh Autonomous Oblast, an Armenian enclave within Azerbaijan. The Armenians believed they had been cheated by the Politburo decision, and more than 1 million Armenians in Yerevan protested Moscow's decision; a general strike was also organized in Nagorno-Karabakh. Tensions ran high, and in a town near the capital of the oblast, Stepanakert, two young Azerbaijanis were killed by local Armenians. In retaliation, more than 30 unarmed Armenians were killed during an Azerbaijani rampage in Sumgait, an industrial center near Baku. The central government sent troops to Nagorno-Karabakh in early 1988 to quell the disturbances. The situation has remained more or less out of control; the troops are still in the oblast, and armed Armenians and Azerbaijanis continue to fight.

The violence in the Caucasus helped bring home the message that further political reforms were necessary to transform the stagnating Soviet political system. Gorbachev still thought in terms of revitalizing old institutions. But his efforts to reinvigorate the Communist party—marked by the July 1988 nineteenth party conference, the first extraordinary session of the party since the 1930s—proved to be little more than sloganeering.

Popular Elections Become Nationalist Demonstrations

By this point Gorbachev had recognized that for perestroika to succeed, the rules of the political game had to change. He called for the popular election of a Congress of People's Deputies, which would convene in May 1989. The Communist party, however, organized the elections to predetermine the winners and losers.

The party's electoral plans backfired in the three Baltic republics, where party candidates won only a handful of seats, and these mostly in Russian enclaves. In dozens of other elections throughout the country, officially orchestrated campaigns went awry—including those in which Russian republic politician Boris Yeltsin and the dissident Andrei Sakharov competed. But less than 10 percent of the seats in the Congress were won by the regime's critics.

About the time of the elections, Moscow encountered unexpected problems in Georgia when a pro-independence movement staged demonstrations in the capital of Tbilisi. On April 9, 1989, Soviet special forces using sharpened spades and, allegedly, poisoned tear gas broke up a crowd of nationalist demonstrators, resulting in the death of 20 civilians.

The chain of command in the decision to deploy the troops has never been firmly established. Gumbar Pastiashvili, Georgia's Communist party leader, was found responsible but he claimed that he had acted with Moscow's approval. Evading responsibility for this and other attacks became a hallmark of the central government. Gorbachev was out of the country at the time, but Yegor Ligachev, the ranking Politburo member, later claimed that there was full Politburo approval for the decision.

The use of troops in Georgia was intended to warn nationalists throughout the Soviet Union that the Communist party would not tolerate actions that threatened its rule. For reformers nationwide, April 9 became a symbol of the repressive underside of glasnost and perestroika. For Georgians the events of that date became a catalyst for declaring independence two years later, on April 9, 1991.

One month after the breakup of the Georgian demonstrations, the newly elected Congress of People's Deputies held its first session. The new Congress and the Supreme Soviet did not provide miraculous solutions for the Soviet Union's economic problems or shore up Gorbachev's seriously eroding political power base. The Congress proved to be neither an effective legislative body nor a popularly elected rubber stamp for the Kremlin leadership.

Increasing Violence Between Nationalities

In June 1989, as the first Congress session drew to a close, fighting broke out between Uzbeks and Meskhetians in Uzbekistan's densely populated Fergana Valley. The fighting stemmed from rumors, which had begun to circulate in the spring, that the Meshketians, who had been deported to the area as a "suspect" people during World War II, would be awarded homesteads and sent back to the north Caucasus. These rumors infuriated local Uzbeks, many of whom were unemployed and living in overcrowded conditions.

Official accounts said the fighting broke out over the cost of a basket of strawberries. Whatever the cause, Uzbek youths turned on the Meshketians. Within days whole Meshketian settlements had been razed and nearly 100 people had been killed. Official reports maintained that local authorities who tried to suppress the rioters became the next target. Police stations and local party headquarters were severely damaged. Uzbekistan's party organization—already racked by the dismissals of officials implicated in a scandal involving the annual theft of much of the republic's cotton crop—was left to restore order in the republic.

The ugly side of political spontaneity manifested itself repeatedly during the summer of 1989. While cleanup operations were still proceeding in the Fergana Valley, fighting erupted between Kazakhs and migrant north Caucasian workers in the Kazakh republic town of Novy Uzen. Less than a month later there were riots in Sukhumi between Georgians and local Abkhazians who wanted to sever their ties with Georgia.

These outbursts helped strengthen the position of law-and-order proponents in the Communist party who claimed that they, not the new "democrats," could best protect the public. While party diehards tried to limit the influence of their critics, popular front groups formally opposed to Communist party rule began to attract large memberships.

In September 1989 the Communist party finally convened a long-awaited special meeting on nationality problems at which the party seemed united in its impotence. Gorbachev offered the increasingly rebellious republics only vague promises of an unspecified form of political sovereignty and warned that these new powers would have to be exercised to fully protect the rights of national minorities.

The Siege of Baku

Near the end of 1989, it was obvious that the political status quo could not survive much longer. Along with the nationalities problem and independence movements, Gorbachev now faced a nearly nationwide miners strike. To end the strike, Gorbachev promised that popular elections for local and republic legislatures would be held by the spring of 1990.

On January 19,1990, in the midst of the election campaign, Baku was placed under martial law. The decision followed several months of demonstrations after the Azerbaijani government had again received control of Nagorno-Karabakh from the Gorbachev-appointed "special commission" that had administered the region since early 1988.

When the transfer occurred, there were immediate protests by Armenians that grew in intensity. Encouraged by the Popular Front, Azerbaijanis countered with their own demonstrations, filling Baku's main square and demanding the resignation of the local party bureau and the appointment of a sovereign Azerbaijani regime. The party-led government of the republic, headed by an unpopular and ineffective political reformer, lacked public support; the Popular Front thus appeared likely to win control of parliament in upcoming republic elections.

However, in mid-January, alongside the peaceful demonstrations, Azerbaijanis in Baku began attacks on the city's by now small Armenian population. Determined to keep Soviet troops out of Baku, the Popular Front managed to restore an uneasy peace. The front maintains that the city was relatively tranquil when martial law was declared. But within hours of the declaration, tanks rolled into Baku to drive demonstrators from the city's main square. More than 90 civilians—most of them unarmed—were killed during the recapture of the city. Despite countless eyewitness reports to the contrary, official Soviet government statements have consistently justified the use of force as necessary to restore order and protect unarmed civilians.

During the first days of the Red Army occupation, chairman of the republic Council of Ministers Ayaz Mutalibov was appointed to replace disgraced first party secretary Abdul-Rahman Vezirov. In Azerbaijan, as in the other republics, the first secretary also became president. Mutalibov slowly acquired popular support, aided in part by the popularity of his own successor as chairman, Gasan Gasanov. Baku, however, remained under martial law until April 1991.

The Baltic Revolt

The siege of Baku greatly influenced Lithuanian president Vytautas Landsbergis, who saw the attack as a warning of what half-steps toward independence might produce in Lithuania. After the Lithuanian Communists voted to sever all ties with the central party in December 1989, a collision was bound to occur. Algirdas Brazauskas, who was now both party leader and chairman of the republic parliament (Sejm), saw the break with Moscow as necessary to preserve the credibility of the Communist party.

But Brazauskas failed to convince Gorbachev of this when the two men met in December and January. Gorbachev traveled to Lithuania, but returned undeterred in his commitment to preserve the nation's unity and the Communist party's primacy. Gorbachev recognized that the party had to carve out a new role for itself and expected that the popular elections he had promised for the spring of 1990 would rejuvenate the republic and central governments. But once again Gorbachev's plans went seriously awry.

Lithuania was one of the first republics to hold its parliamentary election. Candidates endorsed by Sajudis, a mass organization formed in 1988 that supported Lithuanian independence, easily won a two-thirds majority. Until the very last minute Gorbachev thought that the Lithuanians were bluffing about independence. On March 8, 1990, two days before the newly elected parliament met for the first time, Gorbachev offered Brazauskas one last concession: a promise of confederate status for Lithuania, a form of semi-independence that would be introduced at an unspecified future date.

Since Gorbachev had recently demanded that the Supreme Soviet create the office of president, which gave him sweeping new powers, and pass a harsh law on republic secession, Lithuania's new leaders believed they should quickly proceed with their plans. On March 11, 1990, Lithuania's Sejm voted to restore the republic's independent statehood.

Gorbachev countered by demanding that Lithuania obtain its independence through "lawful" means—by adhering to procedures enacted by the Supreme Soviet on April 25. Thus until Lithuania rescinded its March 11 declaration, Gorbachev said, there could be no negotiations between Moscow and Vilnius.

A campaign of intimidation was quickly organized. Soviet garrison commanders in the Baltics staged tank "drills" in Vilnius, and planes dropped pamphlets attacking the Landsbergis government and warning that Soviet law would be enforced. The Baltic military district quickly made good on this promise by entering a Vilnius hospital and beating up young Lithuanian nationals who were resisting induction into the Soviet army as a protest against Soviet rule.

Gorbachev soon grew impatient and began to threaten direct military action to crush the Lithuanian government. However, mindful of international public opinion, the Soviet president instead established an economic blockade of the republic, cutting off oil and gas supplies. But Gorbachev's actions backfired again. The Lithuanians rallied behind Landsbergis with the spirit of a war-besieged people, and new democrats throughout the Soviet Union accepted the plight of the Lithuanians as their own. The Latvians and Estonians, who had passed their own declarations of independence, joined the Lithuanians in an economic union. Georgians shipped medicines, the Moscow and Leningrad city councils promised to trade meat for Lithuanian manufactured goods, and Byelorussians and Ukrainians trucked in black market gasoline across the border.

The Russian Revolt

The center of political protest moved to the Russian republic. The Russians, who had seen other nationalities demonstrate for two years, were no longer fearful of asserting their own nationalism. The discontented increasingly began to identify with a single opposition leader, Boris Yeltsin. In May 1990 the country watched Yeltsin struggle and win control of Russia's new parliament over the combined opposition of Gorbachev, professional party functionaries, and the leadership of the new Communist party of Russia. Yeltsin promised that if he won, Russia would be freed from central government control. On June 12, 1990, the newly elected Russian Congress declared the republic's sovereignty.

Yeltsin's ascendancy posed a potential threat to the Communist leaders who led the other Soviet republics. Only Latvia, Lithuania, and Estonia were headed by non-Communists. The remaining republic leaders were Gorbachev loyalists. The Soviet president needed to find a way to help these men survive politically and retain their loyalty. Moreover, he needed to do so quickly, before the twenty-eighth party congress in July.

Gorbachev feared that what was initially planned as a victory celebration for reform-minded Communists would turn into an opportunity to repudiate his leadership or, worse yet, irrevocably splinter the party. So within days of Yeltsin's election, Gorbachev became a proponent of republic sovereignty. The leaders of the Ukraine, Byelorussia, Kazakhstan, and Uzbekistan all reversed their earlier positions and also became vigorous champions of republic autonomy.

The Soviet president called for a new union treaty, which would delineate the powers of the central government and the republics. Having helped insulate the republic party leaders from their outspoken nationalist opponents, he wanted to retain some power over how they would exercise their increased new authority.

Gorbachev maintained control of the party at the congress in July, but at a price. Yeltsin and several other prominent reformers quit the party, and the hard-line Communists in the party—men like Soyuz (Union) faction leader Colonel Viktor Alksnis—pressed Gorbachev to crack down on pro-secession nationalists. The Soviet leader's political problems intensified throughout the summer. Moscow and the Baltic republics were unable to start formal negotiations. Communists were roundly defeated in elections in Armenia and fought for their political survival in Georgia. Moldavia was on the verge of splitting into three parts: pro-independence Moldova, pro-union "Pri-Dnestra," and pro-autonomy (but within the union) Gagauzia. Even longtime allies like Kazakhstan's Nursultan Nazarbayev and the Ukraine's president, Leonid Kravchuk, called for real autonomy for their republics as they struggled to make the transition from Moscow-designated to popularly supported leaders.

Popular Elections for the Russian Parliament

Martin Malia

During 1990, many rank-and-file Communist Party members resigned their memberships, substantially reducing the size and influence of the party. As Gorbachev moved to relegitimize the CPSU, he allowed the republics to hold free elections for leadership posts. This forced remaining Communist officials to campaign against democratic reformers.

Writing in mid-1991, six months before the collapse of the Soviet Union, Martin Malia compares the July 1991 Russian republican elections to the 1989 elections that brought about the end of Communist rule in Poland and other Eastern European countries. Just as in the previous Eastern European elections, the Russian elections pitted Communists who supported Gorbachev's plans to reform Soviet rule against democrats who advocated the dismantling of the Communist government, according to Malia. The resounding victory of the democrats, he argues, signaled the beginning of the end of the Soviet regime.

Martin Malia is professor of Russian history at the University of California, Berkeley. He is the author of *The Soviet Tragedy: A History of Socialism in Russia, 1917–1991*.

In the six-year-long disintegration of communism euphemistically known as "restructuring" (the meaning, after all, of perestroika) the Russian elections of June 12 will surely count as a revolutionary turning point. In presidential and municipal balloting, the homeland of Leninism elected three anti-Leninist leaders—Boris Yeltsin, Gavriil Popov, and Anatoly Sobchack—by between 60 and 65 percent of the vote, against less than 25 percent for three Party presidential candidates combined. This occurred, moreover, in a contest that explicitly pitted "democrats" against "communists," and in which the declared goal of the democrats was to liquidate definitively the country's crumbling "totalitarian" structures in favor of the rule of law, private property, and the market. And the citizens of Leningrad voted by 55 percent to change their city's name back to St. Petersburg, thus symbolically repudiating the entire Soviet experience.

The Collapse of Communism

It would be idle to view this epoch-making turn of events as a matter of rivalry between Gorbachev and Yeltsin, real though that rivalry is. It would be equally superficial to continue to talk of Soviet events as a process of "reform" in which Yeltsin and Gorbachev must ultimately cooperate for a tidy "transition to democracy," as if this is what perestroika had been about all along. For we are not dealing here either with a personal feud or with mere reform, but with the collapse of a total system. Nor are we dealing with some bland transition, but with a revolution by implosion. In short, the process taking place is analogous to what happened in Eastern Europe in 1989.

The events of 1991 can be seen as the second, Soviet phase of the anticommunist revolution that swept through Eastern Europe in 1989, and the Russian elections of June 12 are the rough equivalent of the Polish elections of June 4, when Solidarity unexpectedly won a semi-rigged vote, thereby bringing to power Europe's first postcommunist government, a breakthrough that soon led to the fall of the Berlin Wall, the Czech Velvet Revolution, and the end of Ceausescu.

Thus beyond the particular events of the experiment with perestroika it is now possible to understand better the historical process of the end of communism, its structure and stages. Solidarity in Poland was the pioneer in setting the pattern during the 1980s. The Democratic Russia Movement headed by Yeltsin is now attempting, and quite consciously so, to follow the same route. But how did Russia pull abreast of Eastern Europe so quickly? And what are democratic Russia's chances of success?

Reform Communism

Nothing makes sense in this process unless it is first recognized that Gorbachev's perestroika was never anything more than reform communism. Following the precedents of Khrushchev, Dubček, Kadar, and Jaruzelski, Gorbachev undertook to revive a Stalinist system in dire crisis by what he hoped would be controlled liberalization. The model for such a program, for Gorbachev as for his predecessors, includes an expanded but still limited right to tell the truth about the past and to criticize the shortcomings of the present; a measure of participation in public affairs by groups outside the Party; and a modest degree of managerial and financial autonomy for state enterprises, together with the emergence of a small sector of semi-private businesses providing services. But reform communism never was intended to mean full cultural freedom, constitutional government, or a market economy with private property. And it never envisaged abandoning the hegemony of the Party, even though other political groups might be tolerated as part of a reform "popular front."

Such a program, obviously, is always ambiguous. On the one hand, the leadership naively thinks it can mobilize society to revive the system and yet not lose control. On the other hand, some temporary allies of reform—Andrei Sakharov is the most prominent example—are in fact working to liquidate the system. And between the two, matters always get out of hand, with the result that attempts are made to restore "real socialism" by force, with the result taking the form of Brezhnevite stagnation.

The most vulnerable and crisis-racked part of the system, moreover, has been Eastern Europe—the weakest link in the communist chain, to paraphrase Lenin—for the obvious reason that the system was forcibly imposed there as an alien order. And the most vulnerable part of Eastern Europe has been Poland, for cultural and historical reasons that have long been apparent. So, with Solidarity, there emerged the first movement that explicitly renounced reform communism as an illusion and sought instead to fashion what it called a "normal" post-totalitarian society.

The Polish Example of Communism's Defeat

Solidarity got its chance to do this in 1988 and 1989 with the failure of Jaruzelski's reform communism—which had been stimulated by Gorbachev's perestroika. Confronted with strikes and economic collapse, the Polish generals accepted Round Table negotiations with Solidarity for an "anti-crisis pact" involving limited power sharing, but a full sharing of responsibilities: that is, the pact provided that Solidarity members could take part in elections to the Sejm and the Senate that were partly rigged to yield a Communist majority (as were Gorbachev's concurrent elections to the first Soviet Congress of People's Deputies in March 1989). The Polish population, however, turned this occasion into a referendum on communism by denying to the Party's candidates, on the first round, most of their allotted seats. As the party and the regime began to unravel under this blow, the astonished leaders of Solidarity were obliged to form a new government on the principle of "your [Communist] president, our [Solidarity] prime minister." And Solidarity soon took over the whole government.

Elections, even partly controlled ones, have thus proved to be the Achilles' heel of reform communism. The formula of the Round Table was next taken up in Hungary, with similar effects leading to the liquidation of the Party. By the end of the year, the Round Table strategy had come to mean throughout the communist world the negotiated, phased transfer of power from the Party to the democratic opposition. As a tactic and a goal, therefore, it was taken up by the Russian opposition in early 1990, once the complete collapse of Eastern European communism made it clear that the days of the Party-controlled system were now numbered everywhere.

Gorbachev's Perestroika and Economic Problems

Gorbachev's version of reform communism, which dominated the Soviet scene and captured the world's attention between 1985 and 1989, was the most far-reaching ever in communist history, largely because the Soviet economic crisis was far deeper than any in earlier decades. Perestroika was strong on political change allowing the unprecedented cultural freedom of glasnost and semi-free elections to central and local soviets, or legislative councils. But perestroika was weak on economic change, permitting only "self-management" and "self-financing" for state enterprises, together with modest encouragement of cooperative enterprises. This was so in part because such measures were all that Gorbachev and his prime minister, Nikolai Ryzhkov, believed in, and in part because the Party apparat resisted any serious reforms since this would threaten the control of the nomenklatura. The failure to perceive the contradiction between the political and economic aspects of perestroika brought the entire program down in 1989. As the radical dissident Sergei Grigoriants commented at the start, "Gorbachev doesn't know what he's ruling over."

In the economic sphere, the limited autonomy of self-management and self-financing soon destroyed the vertical chain of command by which the state plan had always been carried out, without creating the arrangements for horizontal exchange among producers, distributors, and consumers which characterize a market system. The result, not only for farm and consumer products but for durable and capital goods as well, was that most economic activity became localized, and the country moved to an ad hoc barter system. Meanwhile the growing budget deficit was "covered" by printing more money and by accelerating inflation.

Glasnost and the Formation of a Democratic Opposition

On the other hand, glasnost and democratization made it possible for people to complain about this state of affairs, as well as about seventy years of their accumulated grievances of every kind. Glasnost was exploited by increasingly radical intellectuals to expose the crimes of the past and the evils of the present. This, together with growing awareness of the economic gap between Russia and the outside world, soon

destroyed what was left of the myth that socialism was leading to a "radiant future." Most of the people began to feel
swindled by "seventy years on the road to nowhere," as a
popular slogan had it. The system was desacralized and dele-
gitimized, and by 1990 only criticism of Lenin remained
taboo.

The democratic opening also permitted a nascent opposition not simply to express dissident views but to make a bid for
power. At first, in 1988 and 1989, Gorbachev organized par-
tially contested elections to the soviets because he wished to
create a power base for reform communism separate from the
recalcitrant main-line Party. But this maneuver backfired even
worse than glasnost. It is true that Gorbachev obtained the
support, as the historian Yuri Afanasyev said, of an "aggressively submissive majority," which dutifully elected him "president"—to give him an aura of democratic respectability
abroad and to make him seem the equal of George Bush at
home—and regularly voted him sweeping but ineffectual decree powers, as the country's general crisis worsened. But the
elections to the soviets also permitted the emergence in the
central Congress of People's Deputies of independent political blocs, such as the "Interregional Group" of Andrei
Sakharov, Gavriil Popov, and Anatoly Sobchak. And these
groups moved increasingly away from reform communism toward outright repudiation of the system.

This turn to open opposition began during the spectacular first session of the Congress in June 1989 (at the same
time as the Polish elections), which convinced the emerging
Russian democrats that Gorbachev did not contemplate
sharing power, and that he would therefore have to be
drawn, or forced, into a "left-center coalition" against the
conservatives of the apparat, and then by stages into a more
radical economic and political program. In consequence,
tension mounted between the government and the opposition movement—indeed between the government and "civil
society" generally—as the country moved toward the local
soviet elections set for the following spring. Although the
"radicals" did not publicize their intentions, it became increasingly clear, especially in private conversations, that

their goal was to wrest power from the Party and to move toward genuine constitutional government, a market system, and private property. By the end of 1989 this postcommunist program was basically ready, although not yet widely published or broadcast on television.

Then at the beginning of 1990, the Soviet situation was suddenly and sharply affected by the aftershock of the collapse of communism in Eastern Europe. For this event demonstrated that, contrary to Party dogma and the alleged logic of history, "the conquests of socialism" were in fact "reversible," that subjection to the system was therefore not inevitable, and that hope for true liberation, as opposed to mere reform, was at last possible.

This realization produced a great leftward surge across the country, which was expressed, first of all, in a series of "declarations of sovereignty," beginning with the Baltic states, among the fifteen constituent republics. This "parade of sovereignties," as the hard-line commentators called it, was accompanied by a "war of laws," in which the republics, municipalities, and even districts voted measures to take take economic and administrative power from the Party and the "center," as Gorbachev's government was now called. By the end of the summer of 1990, the Soviet Union had virtually collapsed as a cohesive structure, and Gorbachev's primary concern came to be working out a new union treaty to salvage state unity.

At the same time the demise of Eastern Europe's communist regimes produced the first concrete economic program for postcommunism. This was the "shock therapy" of Finance Minister Leszek Balcerowicz's "big bang" plan to install a market system and to privatize industry in Poland. Hitherto these subjects had been taboo in Soviet public discussion. Suddenly, in the spring of 1990, they were actively discussed within the government. Experts began drafting proposed laws, and momentum started building toward what would become by summer the 500-Day Plan of Stanislav Shatalin and Gregory Yavlinsky, Russia's first program of genuine economic transformation. . . .

Gorbachev's Turn Toward Authoritarianism

By the autumn of 1990 the rising strength of the opposition forces supporting sovereignty for the republics, the market, and Yeltsin himself produced, as was only to be expected, a reaction that led to a six-month attempt to roll back the gains that had been made. In October Gorbachev abandoned the 500-Day Plan. By November he was moving close to the army and the KGB. In December Eduard Shevardnadze's resignation sounded an alarm against possible "dictatorship." In January Prime Minister Ryzhkov gave way to the even more conservative Valentin Pavlov, an economist in the most primitive Soviet command tradition. During the same month the army and the police moved against Lithuania and Latvia, killing some twenty people, in what appeared to be a prelude to martial law. The central government also acted to bring Soviet television under direct control. By February it seemed that a planned crackdown was being carried out. By March it appeared as though Soviet reform communism would end, as all such previous efforts had, in repression, and that Gorbachev would turn out to be his own General Jaruzelski—in the style of 1981, not of 1989.

Although there is still much that is mysterious about this episode, it is at least clear that Gorbachev was leading as much as he was led. He is consistently on record as holding fast to the principle of "one and indivisible" union and as being opposed to private property. As he puts it, his principles are "the socialist choice made in 1917" and "the communist perspective."

In veering toward authoritarianism he was also, and quite understandably, anxious to stave off the seemingly imminent collapse of the economy. This concern could explain Pavlov's inept policy of confiscating rubles, imposing a new sales tax, and setting up a traditional Soviet-style "anti-crisis program." Such a combination of measures suggested to some Soviet commentators that Gorbachev was contemplating an authoritarian market economy, a policy known in Russia variously as the Pinochet scenario or the Chinese model. Whatever his real intentions, the new policy of the "iron fist" fizzled ignominiously in March and April, and the democrats came back in force.

The Democrats Press for a New Union Treaty

They did so because they mobilized actively against the creeping *coup d'etat*. Although some, including even Sobchak, wavered during the winter, declaring that authoritarian government might after all be necessary, most liberal intellectuals publicly abandoned Gorbachev for Yeltsin: most of the best political minds of Russia are now firmly in his camp and on his councils.

And Yeltsin provided superb leadership. On March 17 Gorbachev held a meaningless referendum on preserving the Union, and to it Yeltsin appended a proposition calling for direct election of the Russian president. When this passed easily, he took the matter to the Russian parliament for implementation. There the near majority of Communist members tried to impeach him, certainly with Gorbachev's support, since Yeltsin was calling for the Soviet president's resignation. Yeltsin beat back the impeachment attempt, split the Russian Communist party, and obtained a June date for elections. He won this victory in large part because on March 28 several hundred thousand Muscovites defied a ban on rallies issued by Gorbachev, and backed by fifty thousand troops, in order to demonstrate their support of his cause.

At the same time Yeltsin backed a two-month-long miners' strike in Siberia, which put forth not just economic but also political demands, including Gorbachev's resignation. When this strike movement spread in April to hitherto quiescent Byelorussia, the balance of power was tipped decisively in Yeltsin's favor. The result was the "9 plus 1" agreement, negotiated in secret on April 23 between Gorbachev and nine republic presidents led by Yeltsin.

Although formally a compromise, the April 23 accord gave far more to the nine than to the one. Two concessions were made to Gorbachev: a call for "work discipline" and a ban on strikes, and both of these angered some of Yeltsin's radical supporters. But the nine republics obtained implicit acceptance of the Baltic and Caucasian republics' right to secede; the transfer of significant economic and administrative power from the center to the remaining republics; and a promise of a new constitution and genuinely democratic elections throughout the Union by 1992. Yeltsin then persuaded the miners to return to work in exchange for shifting mine ownership to the Russian Republic, with a pledge to allow the miners to privatize their enterprises as joint ventures working for the market, not the Plan, thereby asserting that local control meant economic transformation. Finally, in unpublished protocols to the April 23 agreement, Yeltsin won two further victories: independent television for his republic and a partly separate KGB. Although the term "Round Table" was not used formally, it was used privately by Yeltsin's advisers. And the agreement was in fact the first session of a negotiated transfer of real power in the USSR, though many further sessions will be required to complete the process.

The Transfer of Power

The demonstration of March 28 and the agreement of April 23 produced a new surge to the left in Russia, which culminated in the democratic breakthrough of the June 12 elections. The right, discredited by its failed winter coup, now appeared as a paper tiger inspiring more contempt than fear. And Gorbachev, in another display of his capacity for creative adaption to defeat, became once again a "reformer" and an ally of Yeltsin. In return, Yeltsin ceased his populist attacks on the diminished president and assumed a statesmanlike willingness to cooperate with "the center" to overcome the national crisis.

Thus Russia, two years after the Polish revolution, found itself with its first non-communist government, but obliged to coexist with the still-standing communist regime. Such dual power obviously cannot last, any more than it did in Poland—or in Russia in 1917. One or the other party will eventually have to go; and the preservation of communist authority is incompatible with constitutionalism, private property, and the market.

The Fall of the Berlin Wall

Timothy Garton Ash

The Berlin Wall was built in 1961 to stem the flood of
Germans in the Communist east trying to escape to the
democratic West Germany. The wall became the symbol
of the cold war between the Soviet Union and the West.

There were two events that precipitated the 1989 revolution in East Germany and the tearing down of the wall,
argues Timothy Garton Ash in the following selection.
The first, according to Ash, was the preceding revolutions
in Poland and Hungary. After Hungary broke with Communist rule and Soviet domination, it opened its borders
to the West, allowing East Germans to once again flee to
West Germany. But the more important event, in Ash's
opinion, was Mikhail Gorbachev's withdrawal of Soviet
support for the East German Communist regime.

Timothy Garton Ash is a fellow of St. Antony's College, Oxford, England. He is the author of *The Magic
Lantern* and *The File: A Personal History*.

Everyone has seen the pictures of joyful celebration in West
Berlin, the vast crowds stopping the traffic on the Kurfürs-
tendamm, *Sekt* corks popping, perfect strangers tearfully
embracing—the greatest street party in the history of the
world. Yes, it was like that. But it was not only like that, nor
was that, for me, the most moving part. Most of the estimated two million East Germans who flooded into West
Berlin over the weekend just walked the streets in quiet family groups, often with small children in strollers. They
queued up at a bank to collect the DM100 "greeting money"

Reprinted from Timothy Garton Ash, "The German Revolution," *The New York
Review of Books*, December 21, 1989, with permission from *The New York Review of
Books*. Copyright © 1989 NYREV, Inc.

(about $55) which has long been offered to visiting East Germans by the West German government, and then they went, very cautiously, shopping. Generally they bought one or two small items, perhaps some fresh fruit, a Western newspaper, and toys for the children. Then, clasping their shopping bags, they walked quietly back through the Wall, through the gray, deserted streets of East Berlin, home.

East Berliners Visit the West

It is very difficult to describe the quality of this experience because what they actually did was so stunningly ordinary. In effect, they just took a bus from Hackney or Dagenham to Piccadilly Circus, and went shopping in the West End. Berliners walked the streets of Berlin. What could be more normal? And yet, what could be more fantastic! "Twenty-eight years and ninety-one days," said one man in his late thirties, walking back up Friedrichstrasse. Twenty-eight years and ninety-one days since the building of the Wall. On that day, in August 1961, his parents had wanted to go to a late-night Western in a West Berlin cinema. But their eleven-year-old son had been too tired. In the early hours they woke to the sound of tanks. He had never been to West Berlin from that day to this. A taxi driver asked me, with a sly smile, "How much is the ferry to England?" The day before yesterday the question would have been unthinkable.

Everyone, but everyone, on the streets of East Berlin has just been, or is just going, to West Berlin. A breathless, denim-jacketed couple stop me to ask, "Is this the way out?" They have come hotfoot from Leipzig. "Our hearts are going pitter-pat," they say, in broad Saxon dialect. People look the same as they make their way home—except for the tell-tale Western shopping bag. But everyone is inwardly changed, changed utterly. "Now people are standing up straight," says a hotel porter. "They are speaking their minds. Even work is more fun. I think the sick will get up from their hospital beds." And it was in East rather than West Berlin that this weekend had the magic, Pentecostal quality which I last experienced in Poland in autumn 1980. Ordinary men and women find their voice and their courage—*Lebensmut*, as the porter puts it. These are moments when you feel that somewhere an angel has opened his wings.

Ordinary people doing very ordinary things (shopping!), the Berliners nonetheless immediately grasped the historical dimensions of the event. "Of course the real villain was Hitler," said one. A note stuck to a remnant of the Wall read "Stalin is dead, Europe lives." And the man who counted twenty-eight years and ninety-one days told me he had been most moved by an improvised poster saying "ONLY TODAY IS THE WAR REALLY OVER."

West Germany's mass-circulation *Bild* newspaper carried, under a black, red, and gold banner headline declaring "Good Morning, Germany," an effusive thank-you letter from the editors to Mikhail Gorbachev. The East Germans also feel grateful to Gorbachev. But more important, they feel they have won this opening for themselves. For it was only the pressure of their huge, peaceful demonstrations that compelled the Party leadership to take this step. "You see, it shows Lenin was wrong," observed one worker. "Lenin said a revolution could only succeed with violence. But this was a peaceful revolution." And even the Communist party's Central Committee acknowledged at the beginning of its hastily drafted Action Program that "a revolutionary people's movement has set in motion a process of profound upheavals."

Gorbachev's Role

Why did it happen? And why so quickly? No one had predicted it. I talked to opposition leaders in East Berlin in early July, and they were still pessimistic. With hindsight—and a little help from Alexis de Tocqueville—we may perhaps be a little wiser. At the very least, one can list in order some factors that brought the cup of discontent to overflowing. In the beginning was not, as most commentators suggest, Gorbachev. In the beginning was the Wall itself: the Wall and the system it both represented and preserved. Geographically, the Wall did not run around East Germany, it was at its very center. Psychologically, it ran through every heart. It is difficult even for people from other East European countries to appreciate the full psychological burden it imposed. An East Berlin doctor wrote a book describing the real sicknesses—and of course the suicides—that resulted. He called it *The Wall Sickness*. There was thus always, even at the beginning of the 1980s, when I lived in East Berlin, a large shot of special bitterness at the bottom of the cup. In a sense, the mystery was always why the people of East Germany did not revolt.

The second causal factor, both in time and importance, was Gorbachev. The "Gorbachev effect" was stronger in East Germany than anywhere else in Eastern Europe because the East German state was more strongly oriented toward—and ultimately dependent on—the Soviet Union than any other. It is not for nothing that a 1974 amendment to the constitution proclaimed "The German Democratic Republic is forever and irrevocably allied with the Union of Soviet Socialist Republics." East Germany's young people had for years been told that "to learn from the Soviet Union is to learn how to win" (*Von der Sowjetunion lernen heisst siegen lernen*). So they did! For several years now we have seen East Germans turning the name of Gorbachev, and the Soviet example, against their rulers.

And then, of course, Gorbachev personally gave the last push—during his visit to mark the fortieth anniversary of the GDR on October 7—with his carefully calculated utterance that "life itself punishes those who delay," the leaked news that he had told [Erich] Honecker Soviet troops would not be used for internal repression, and (according to well-informed West German sources) gave his direct encouragement to younger Party leaders like Egon Krenz and Günter Schabowski, to move to depose Honecker.

Hungary Opens the Border to the West

By comparison with the Soviet example and direct influence, the Polish and Hungarian examples were of secondary importance for the East Germans. To be sure, everyone learned about them, in great detail, from the West German television they watch nightly. To be sure, Hungary and Poland demonstrated that such changes were possible. But the old German contempt for *Polnische Wirtschaft* is so widespread in the GDR that, except for a few Church and opposition intellectuals, the economic misery in Poland more than cancelled out the political example. Hungary—a favored holiday place for East Germans, with a better economic situation and a history (and, dare one say, national character) less fatefully at odds with Germany's—Hungary perhaps had a greater impact. Yet the crucial Hungarian contribution was not the example of its internal reforms, but the opening of its frontier to Austria.

As soon as the Hungarians started cutting the barbed wire of the "iron curtain," in May, East Germans began fleeing across it. As the numbers grew, and East Germans gathered in refugee camps in Budapest, the Hungarian authorities decided, in early September, to let them go officially (suspending their bilateral consular agreement with the GDR). The trickle turned into a flood: some fifteen thousand in the first three days. Others sought an exit route via the West German embassies in Prague and Warsaw. This hemorrhage was the final catalyst for internal change in East Germany.

Church-protected opposition activity had been slowly growing throughout the summer. There had been independent monitoring of the local elections in May, which clearly demonstrated that they had been rigged—under Egon Krenz's supervision. The East German authorities' emphatic endorsement of the repression in China brought another wave of protests.

It is important to recall that right up to, and during, the fortieth anniversary celebrations on October 7, the police—under Egon Krenz—used force and, indeed, gratuitous brutality, to disperse these protests and intimidate anyone who might think of joining in. Young men were dragged along the cobbled streets by their hair, women and children thrown into prison, innocent bystanders beaten.

The Start of Demonstrations

If one can identify a turning point it was perhaps Monday, October 9, the day after Gorbachev left. A large opposition demonstration was planned on Karl Marx Square in Leipzig. But riot police, state security forces, and members of the paramilitary factory "combat groups" stood ready to clear East Germany's Tiananmen Square with truncheons and, it was subsequently reported, live ammunition. An article by the commander of one of these groups in the local paper on October 6 said they were prepared to defend socialism "if need be, with weapon in hand." But in the event some seventy thousand people came out to make their peaceful protest, and this time, suddenly, force was not used to disperse them. (The figure of seventy thousand, like all the other crowd figures, can only be taken as a very crude estimate, at best an order of magnitude.) It was subsequently claimed by sources close to Egon Krenz that he, being in overall political control of internal security, had taken the brave, Gorbachevian decision not to use force. It was even claimed that he had personally gone to Leipzig to prevent bloodshed.

Subsequent accounts by those actually involved in Leipzig, however, give a rather different picture. By these accounts, the crucial action was taken by the famous Leipzig conductor, Kurt Masur, together with a well-known cabaret artist, Bernd Lutz Lange, and a priest, Peter Zimmermann. They managed to persuade three local Party leaders to join them in a dramatic, last minute appeal for nonviolence, which was read in the churches and broadcast over loudspeakers. This, and the sheer number of demonstrators, made the difference between triumph and disaster.

It was, it seems, only later in the evening, when the demonstration was already peacefully on its way, that Krenz telephoned from Berlin to give his belated approval to this courageous local initiative. (The possible role of the National People's Army whether—as reported—Erich Honecker actually signed an order for it to shoot; and whether—as also reported—Soviet commanders intervened to restrain the East German army: all this remains, as I write, speculation.) The moment was, nonetheless, decisive for Krenz's own bid for power. Nine days later he replaced Honecker as Party leader. But in those nine days, the revolution had begun.

The Demonstrations Grow

To say the growth of popular protest was "exponential" would be an understatement. It was a nonviolent explosion. Those extraordinary, peaceful, determined Monday evening demonstrations in Leipzig—starting with "peace prayers" in the churches—grew week by week, from a guesstimated seventy thousand, to double that, to three hundred thousand, to perhaps half a million (who knows?). Virtually the whole of East Germany suddenly went into labor, an old world—to recall Karl Marx's image—pregnant with the new. From that time forward the people acted and the Party reacted. Power came from the streets, where the same slogans and demands were heard again and again. "Freedom!" demanded the Leipzig demonstrators, and Krenz announced a new travel law. "Without a visa from Berlin to Pisa," said the crowds, and Krenz reopened the frontier to Czechoslovakia. "A suggestion for May Day: let the leadership parade past the people," said a banner, quoted by the writer Christa Wolf in the huge demonstration in East Berlin on November 4. And the leaders began to fall. "Free elections!" demanded the people, and the Council of Ministers resigned en masse. "We are the people!" they chanted—and the Wall was open.

The cup of bitterness was already full to the brim. The years of Wall Sickness, the lies, the stagnation, the Soviet and Hungarian examples, the rigged elections, the police violence—all added their dose. The moment that the lid of repression was lifted, the cup simply overflowed. And then, with amazing speed, the East Germans discovered what the Poles had discovered ten years before, during the Pope's visit in 1979. They discovered that they all felt and thought the same, and that together they could be strong. They discovered their solidarity.

There is, perhaps, one other special reason why things went so fast. Nowhere in Eastern Europe are people better informed—watching West German television every night, receiving thousands of West German visitors, and, in recent years, being allowed to travel a little more freely themselves. Nowhere has the private disillusionment been more extensive or articulate—even among Party members. So when people at last took to the streets, they instantly discovered that they wanted the same things. The learning had been done already—in private.

And one last element. In a classic pre-revolutionary situation, we are told, the ruled lose their fear while the rulers lose their will to rule. Was that to some extent true of the Socialist Unity party? In the long gerontocratic twilight of the Honecker regime, and under the slow, steady influence of contacts with West Germany, did not the next generation of leaders begin to lose its conviction that it had the right to rule? And above all, the right to rule by force, here, in the center of Europe, at the end of the twentieth century? Listening to Honecker's successors one feels that they have no inner conviction of their right to be there. Tocqueville would have recognized the signs.

"Long live the October Revolution of 1989," said another banner on the Alexanderplatz. And so it was, and at the time of writing still is: the first peaceful revolution in German history.

Chapter 4

Collapse of the Union

Turning Points

IN WORLD HISTORY

The August 1991 Coup

Michael Mandelbaum

On August 19, 1991, Mikhail Gorbachev, president of the Soviet Union and general secretary of the Communist Party (CPSU), was placed under arrest at his vacation house in the Crimea. The arrest was ordered by the State Committee on the Emergency Situation, a small group of hard-line Soviet officials who sought to reestablish authoritarian central control of the country. Their attempt to seize power lasted only three days, during which time Boris Yeltsin, the recently elected president of Russia, emerged as a leader of the growing resistance to continued Communist rule.

Writing in early 1992 following the official end of the Soviet Union, Michael Mandelbaum argues in the following article that the August coup failed, in part because Gorbachev's policy of economic restructuring brought about an economic crisis. In addition, democratization in the political sphere led to severe criticism of Communist rule, which undermined the Soviet government's legitimacy and power, he contends.

Michael Mandelbaum is the Christian Herter Professor of American Foreign Policy at the Paul H. Nitze School of Advanced International Studies at Johns Hopkins University. He is the author and editor of many books, including *The Rise of Nations in the Soviet Union*.

On August 24, 1991, three days after the collapse of an attempted coup by a group of high Soviet officials in Moscow, Marshal Sergei Akhromeyev killed himself in his Kremlin

Reprinted from Michael Mandelbaum, "Coup de Grace: The End of the Soviet Union," *Foreign Affairs*, vol. 71, no. 1, 1992, by permission of *Foreign Affairs*. Copyright 1992 by the Council on Foreign Relations.

office. Mikhail Gorbachev's special adviser on military affairs left a suicide note: "Everything I have worked for is being destroyed."

Akhromeyev had devoted his life to three institutions: the Soviet army, in whose service he had been wounded at Leningrad in 1941 and through whose ranks he had risen to the position of chief of the General Staff (1984–88); the Communist Party, which he had joined at 20 and on whose Central Committee he had served since 1983; and the Union of Soviet Socialist Republics itself, officially founded a year before his birth in 1923. In the wake of the failed coup all three were disintegrating.

The Disintegration of the Soviet Union

The armed forces were divided and disgraced. Entire units had refused to take part in the coup. A number of the troops sent to besiege the Russian parliament building—where a crowd that ultimately numbered 100,000 had gathered to defend the Russian president, Boris Yeltsin, and his government—defected to Yeltsin's side. After the coup had failed Defense Minister Dimitri Yazov and his deputy, Valentin Varennikov, were arrested. Yevgeny I. Shaposhnikov, the newly appointed minister, announced that 80 percent of the army's officers would be replaced because they were politically suspect.

The Communist Party was shattered. As jubilant crowds cheered, statues of communist heroes were pulled down all over Moscow. Gorbachev, shortly after his return from his ordeal in the Crimea, resigned as leader of the party, dissolved the Central Committee, ordered an end to party activity in the military, the security apparatus and the government, and told local party organizations that they would have to fend for themselves.

The union of 15 republics was itself dissolving. In Moscow people began to wave the blue, white and red flag of prerevolutionary Russia. The republics scrambled to declare their independence, the Ukrainian parliament voting for full independence by 321 to 1. For 75 years the vast stretch of Eurasia that was the Soviet Union had been tightly, often brutally controlled from Moscow, which had come to be known as "the center." The president of Armenia, Levon Ter-Petrossian, declared that "the center has committed suicide."

The Failure of the Coup

The coup might have been expected to succeed. The ranks of the eight-man junta that on August 19, 1991, announced it was assuming power, proclaiming a state of emergency, banning demonstrations, closing newspapers and outlawing political parties, included the leaders of the most powerful institutions of the Soviet Union: the government, the security apparatus and the military-industrial complex.[1] Yet they failed completely. Two minor episodes during the three dramatic days of August 19–21 exemplify the reasons for their failure.

On August 20 Yeltsin dispatched his foreign minister, Andrei Kozyrev, to Paris to prepare a government-in-exile should that become necessary. The junta learned of the trip and sent word to Moscow's Sheremetyevo Airport to detain Kozyrev. He succeeded in leaving, however, because the order to stop him went to the airport's VIP lounge while Kozyrev simply stood in the departure lines with ordinary passengers. It apparently did not occur to the plotters that a high official would fail to take advantage of the privileges available to him.

In short, the men who launched the coup were incompetent. They did not send troops and tanks into the streets of Moscow until a full six hours after declaring the state of emergency. They neglected to seize Yeltsin immediately, thus making it possible for him to become the focal point of resistance. They failed to cut the Russian parliament's communications with the rest of the world.

It was, to use a phrase familiar under the old regime, "no

1. The members of the "State Committee on the Emergency Situation" included: Gennadi Yanaev, Gorbachev's vice president who announced he was assuming the presidency; Vladimir Kryuchkov, chairman of the KGB; Yazov, the defense minister; Valentin Pavlov, prime minister; Boris Pugo, interior minister; Oleg Baklanov, first deputy chairman of the Defense Council; Vasily Starodubtsev, chairman of the Farmer's Union; and Aleksandr Tizyakov, president of the Association of State Enterprises.

accident" that the coup-plotters bungled so badly. The people at the top of the communist system were not the best and the brightest of the society they governed. That system did not encourage or reward initiative, imagination or decisiveness. It valued, instead, dull conformity and slavish obedience to authority. Several members of the junta were later reported to have spent most of the 72 hours of the coup drunk.

The other exemplary episode took place on Monday afternoon, August 19, the first day of the coup. The junta called a press conference. Gennadi Yanaev, the vice president who had assumed Gorbachev's duties because, he said, the president was "ill," made a statement and fielded questions. One journalist asked whether he had sought "any suggestion or any advice through General Pinochet." The question evoked laughter. It was meant to be sarcastic and belittling by associating the coup-plotters with the conservative Chilean dictator who had overthrown Marxist President Salvador Allende in 1974 and had thus been routinely reviled by Soviet propaganda.

The event, the question and the response were all telling. When Lenin seized power in Petrograd in November 1917 he did not feel it necessary to call a press conference to explain and justify what he had done. Nor were his successors in the habit of entertaining questions from the press. And when they did offer their thoughts in public, no one had ever dared to mock them. In Stalin's day failing to applaud the leader vigorously enough was cause for being sent to prison—or worse.

Since Stalin's day, however, things had changed. The Soviet Union in which Yanaev was attempting to seize power was a very different country from the one that Lenin and Stalin, indeed that Khrushchev and even Brezhnev had ruled. So different was it, in fact, that each of the three great institutions to which Marshal Akhromeyev had devoted his life was already in an advanced state of decay by August 19.

The Disgraced Military and the Shattered Party

Well before it balked at the junta's orders the army had been severely battered. In 1988 it had withdrawn from Afghanistan after nine years and 15,000 deaths without having pacified the country. The next year the revolutions in Poland, Hungary, East Germany and Czechoslovakia ended the Cold War, depriving the Soviet armed forces of what had been, for four decades, their central mission. Troops stationed in those countries had to leave; many had no homes to which to return.

Draft evasion became rampant, especially outside Russia. The army was divided politically by rank, age, region and ethnic group. Junior officers began criticizing their superiors; several were elected to all-union and republican parliaments, where they expressed dissenting views on military questions. The political leadership committed itself to substantial reductions in military spending, and proposals were floated to abolish conscription and rely instead on volunteers to fill the army's ranks.

In all, the military suffered from a severe loss of status. In the Brezhnev era, in particular, official propaganda had glorified the mighty Soviet army as the stalwart defender of socialism. By 1991 it was despised outside Russia as an agent of imperial oppression and had come to be seen in the Russian heartland as a self-serving bureaucracy whose endless appetite for resources was bankrupting the country.

The Communist Party was similarly reeling from blows to its privileged standing before Gorbachev effectively closed it down. It was subject for the first time in six decades to open criticism, which turned into an avalanche of denunciation. Far from being the champion of the toiling masses and the vanguard of the just society, as it had always portrayed itself, the party came to be seen as a criminal conspiracy dedicated to preserving its own position. The elections of 1989 and 1990 to the national and republican supreme soviets humiliated the party, as people voted in droves against communist officeholders even when there was no opposing candidate.

Members deserted the party in enormous numbers. By one estimate four million people, fully 20 percent of the membership, had quit the party in the year immediately preceding the coup. In some places the local party apparatus simply disintegrated. Gorbachev renounced the long-standing and fundamental communist claim to a monopoly of power, and the month before the coup he pushed through a party charter that virtually abandoned the formerly sacred precepts of Marxism-Leninism. After his election as Russian president, Yeltsin ordered party cells in workplaces throughout Russia dissolved, challenging the basis of the communist grip on the everyday lives of the people of the Soviet Union.

Dissolving the Union

As for the union itself, it was well on the way to becoming a hollow shell even before the republics began to declare independence in the coup's wake. The republican elections had brought to power governments determined not simply to take orders from Moscow, as had been the rule in Soviet politics for decades. Each of the 15 republics had proclaimed itself "sovereign," meaning that its own laws took precedence over those of the center. Ukraine, the second most important of them after Russia, was moving to recruit its own armed forces and issue its own currency.

On the eve of the coup nine republics were preparing to sign a new union treaty, which would have deprived Moscow of virtually all economic power and left the republics with the right both to challenge any powers the center retained and to secede if they were dissatisfied with the new arrangements. [Six of the 15 Soviet republics—Lithuania, Latvia, Estonia, Moldova, Armenia and Georgia—refused even to take part in the negotiations, in a kind of de facto secession from the Soviet Union.] The prospect of this new union treaty probably triggered the coup attempt, for it would have eliminated most of the functions of precisely those organizations that the plotters headed. The coup was a last-ditch attempt to preserve their own power. But that power had already been severely eroded. As the political scientist William Taubman put it at the time: "The coup occurred because of all the changes that have taken place, and it failed because of all the changes that have taken place." The coup-plotters struck to restore the old order; the result of their failure was to put it out of its misery. What began as a coup d'état to preserve it turned out to be the coup de grace for the Soviet Union.

The Failure of Gorbachev's Glasnost

How did all this come about? How did it happen that a mighty imperial state, troubled but stable only a few years before, had come to the brink of collapse in 1991? Who and what were responsible?

The chief architect of the Soviet collapse was Mikhail Gorbachev himself. During the coup, as a prisoner of the junta in his Crimean villa, he was the object of a struggle between the partisans of the old order and the champions of liberal values. But it was Gorbachev who had, in the period between his coming to power in 1985 and the fateful days of August 1991, created the conditions that had touched off this struggle.

The Soviet leader had created them unintentionally. His aim had been to strengthen the political and economic systems that he inherited, to strip away their Stalinist accretions and make the Soviet Union a modern dynamic state. Instead he had fatally weakened it. Intending to reform Soviet communism he had, rather, destroyed it. The three major policies that he had launched to fashion a more efficient and humane form of socialism—glasnost, democratization and perestroika—had in the end subverted, discredited and all but done away with the network of political and economic institutions that his Communist Party had constructed in Russia and surrounding countries since 1917.

The policy of glasnost relaxed bureaucratic controls on information, broadened the parameters of permitted discussion and thereby enabled the people of the Soviet Union to say more, hear more and learn more about their past and present. Gorbachev's purpose had been to enlist the intelligentsia in his campaign to revitalize the country and to generate popular pressure on the party apparatus, which had resisted the changes he was trying to make. He plainly wanted to encourage criticism of his predecessor, Leonid Brezhnev, and to resume the campaign against Stalin that Khrushchev had launched but that Brezhnev had ended.

Glasnost, however, did not stop there. The sainted Lenin, and even Gorbachev himself, came in for critical attention. Gorbachev wanted to foster a reassessment of some selected features of Soviet life. Instead glasnost called all of it into question, including, ultimately, the role of the general secretary of the Communist Party.

Glasnost Undermines Party Authority

More broadly, the people of the Soviet Union were able for the first time to speak the truth about their history and their lives. That meant that they could learn the truth and could acknowledge it to one another. The effect was cathartic, and the catharsis had a profound, indeed a revolutionary, impact on Soviet politics. It began to undo the enduring effects of the terror that the Communist Party had routinely practiced during its first three decades in power. Of the first wave of that terror, imposed not by Stalin in the 1930s but by Lenin during the civil war, the historian Richard Pipes has written:

> The Red Terror gave the population to understand that under a regime that felt no hesitation in executing innocents, innocence was no guarantee of survival. The best hope of surviving lay in making oneself as inconspicuous as possible, which meant abandoning any thought of independent public activity, indeed any concern with public affairs, and withdrawing into one's private world. Once society disintegrated into an agglomeration of human atoms, each fearful of being noticed and concerned exclusively with physical survival, then it ceased to matter what society thought, for the government had the entire sphere of public activity to itself.

Glasnost enabled the people of the Soviet Union to lay claim to the public sphere after seven decades of exile from it. Through democratization they had the opportunity, for the first time, to act collectively in that sphere. Gorbachev's purpose in permitting elections, again, was to generate popular support for his program. Democratization was to be a political weapon in his battle against the Communist Party apparatus. That apparatus was deeply entrenched, wholly mistrustful of what he was trying to do and generally adept at frustrating his plans. The experiment in democracy that he launched did not demonstrate, as Gorbachev had hoped, that he enjoyed popular support. Rather it showed that two widely held beliefs about the political inclinations of the people of the Soviet Union were wrong.

Elections discredited the official dictum that the Communist Party had earned public gratitude and support for the "noble, far-sighted" leadership it had provided since 1917. They discredited, as well, the view held by many Western students of the Soviet Union that the party did have a measure of legitimacy in the eyes of the population. Its achievements in defeating fascism between 1941 and 1945 and providing a modestly rising living standard thereafter were thought to have earned it a measure of respect, which was reinforced by the political passivity, the resignation to things as they are, that was presumed to be the dominant Russian approach to public life. The elections of 1989 and 1990 showed the people of the Soviet Union to be neither respectful of nor resigned to communist rule.

Democratization also created the opportunity for the beginnings of an alternative to the communist political elite to emerge. In Russia its main orientation was anticommunism, and Boris Yeltsin became its leading figure. Outside Russia the opportunity for political participation revealed that popular political allegiance was not to socialism, or the Soviet Union, or to Mikhail Gorbachev, but rather to nationalism, which was deeply anti-Soviet in character.

The Effect of Economic Stagnation

Glasnost and democratization were, for Gorbachev, means to an end. That end was the improvement of Soviet economic performance. Economic reform was the central feature of this program. When he came to power in 1985 the Soviet elite believed that the regime's principal task was to lift the country out of the economic stagnation into which it had lapsed at the end of the Brezhnev era. Without revived economic growth, they feared, the Soviet Union would fall ever further behind the West in economic and perhaps military terms. Ultimately it risked being overtaken by China, where Deng Xiaoping's market reforms were producing a surge of growth.

Stagnation posed dangers at home as well. Without economic growth the regime would be unable to fulfill its part of the unofficial "social contract," under whose terms the public renounced any say over public affairs in return for a slowly rising standard of living. The revolt of the Polish workers in 1980–81 under the banner of Solidarity served as a cautionary example for the men in the Kremlin.

At first Gorbachev continued the approach that Yuri Andropov had begun in 1982: he tried to impose greater discipline on the work force. The centerpiece of his initial set of economic measures was a highly publicized and intrusive public campaign against the consumption of alcohol. It earned Gorbachev the title of "Mineral Water General Secretary," but did not noticeably reduce Russian drinking. Instead, by forcing people to make their own liquor rather than buying it from the state, the campaign caused shortages of sugar and deprived the government of a large chunk of its income.

This, in turn, contributed to Gorbachev's most enduring and destructive economic legacy: a severe fiscal imbalance. The center's obligations expanded as it poured more and more money into investment and tried to buy public support with generous wage increases. At the same time its income plummeted, as republican governments and enterprises, having gained more power, refused to send revenues to Moscow. In the months before the coup the republics were engaged in what was, in effect, one of the largest tax strikes in history. The fiscal policy of the Brezhnev regime had been relatively strict; Gorbachev's was extremely lax. To cover the widening gap between obligations and income the central government printed rubles at an accelerating pace. By August 1991 the economy was reeling.

Gorbachev's Role

In the great historical drama that is the collapse of the Soviet Union Mikhail Gorbachev was neither a villain nor a fool—although in retrospect some of the things he did came to seem foolish. He was not a Western-style democrat, but it is scarcely conceivable that someone committed to Western political principles could have risen to the top of the Communist Party of the Soviet Union. His view of socialism, however muddled and contradictory, was plainly more humane than the reality of the system for which he inherited responsibility. For most of his time in power, moreover, he had to fight against the conservatism of that system, which expressed itself mainly in inertia but occasionally in active opposition to his designs. If he came increasingly to seem a political maneuverer, it was because he had to maneuver—or believed that he had to maneuver—to survive in power and to protect the liberal measures already taken.

Finally, and most important, Mikhail Gorbachev's character, however flawed, was marked by a basic decency missing in every previous leader of the Soviet Union and indeed in every ruler of imperial Russia before that. He abjured one of the principal methods by which his predecessors had governed. He refused to shoot. He refused—with the exception of several episodes in the Baltics and the Caucasus in which civilians were killed—to countenance the use of violence against the citizens of his country and of eastern Europe, even when what they did dismayed, angered or appalled him. For this alone he deserved the Nobel Peace Prize he received in the fall of 1990 and deserves as well the place of honor he will occupy in the history of the twentieth century.

But after August 21 Gorbachev belonged to history, not to the ongoing political life of what had been the Soviet Union. Although he was rescued from enemies who had only recently been colleagues, the act of rescue swept away the institutional platform on which he had stood. He had made his career as a reformer of communism. In the aftermath of the coup there was nothing left to reform.

A Disillusioned Military

Gabriel Schoenfeld

The August 1991 coup, mounted by hard-line Soviet officials opposed to autonomy in the Soviet republics and
other reforms, failed in part because the Soviet military
refused to support it. Though troops and tanks patrolled
the streets of Moscow during the crisis, the soldiers did
not act to suppress political demonstrations or resistance
to the orders of the State Committee on the State of
Emergency.

Writing shortly after the defeat of the coup, Gabriel
Schoenfeld outlines in the following article the state of the
Soviet armed forces. Violence, particularly interethnic tension, was a problem in the Soviet military, he states, resulting in a large number of homicides and suicides among soldiers. This violence contributed to the problem of draft
dodging among young men, which was at epidemic proportions, according to Schoenfeld. The lack of housing, food,
and money for salaries also contributed to low morale
among the troops, he maintains; the military was in such bad
shape that it could not be counted on to support the coup.

Gabriel Schoenfeld is the editor of *Soviet Prospects.*

The coup, we now know, failed. But is there a reason to believe
it could ever have succeeded? The Soviet armed forces—the
critical instrument of control—were already in acute crisis. The
coup leaders never successfully dispatched the military into the
fray. To launch their desperate plot they surely counted on military support, but their hopes were founded on a delusion.

Reprinted from Gabriel Schoenfeld, "Uniform Failure," *The New Republic*, September 9, 1991, by permission of *The New Republic*; © 1991, The New Republic,
Inc.

Soviet Military Forces

The junta's prime instrument would have been the Internal Troops, controlled by the MVD, the Interior Ministry. Their charge is the preservation of domestic order, but they are not entirely ethnic Russian and their mettle had never been tested in an internal conflict of this type. Although Boris Pugo, the interior minister, sat on the emergency committee, the political allegiance of the troops under his control is still a mystery. And even if they were reliable, their manpower—roughly 300,000—would never have been able to put down an entire empire.

The OMON (Special Mission Militia Detachments) forces, better known as the black berets, also fall under the formal control of the MVD. These crack units were thought to be the most loyal and brutal troops at the new regime's disposal. But there are only thirty-five units of them. Estimates of their total manpower range from 10,000 to 30,000 men. And getting them to do the junta's bidding would have been more complicated than is generally assumed. In the Baltics, where their roving patrols had already left several dead, they were commanded directly by Moscow. But elsewhere they reported to local outposts of the MVD, where loyalties in the post-coup atmosphere were deeply confused. At best, the OMON units would have been able to mount a brutal display of force, which might have galvanized opposition as much as held down revolt.

Like the MVD, the KGB [Soviet secret police] has its own private armies. It has approximately 40,000 special purpose troops—*spetsznaz* forces, as they are called. Their mission is counterinsurgency, counterterrorism, and, in wartime, to wreak havoc behind enemy lines. In the espionage and defector non-fiction genre they are painted as bloodthirsty criminal killers in the service of the state. But the lurid portrait was always probably more fiction than fact, and in any case their ability to hold down mass revolt was extremely dubious. The KGB also has 230,000 border troops, but, stretched along the country's enormous frontier, they were in no shape to come to the junta's aid. Other KGB special units provided secure governmental communications and safeguarded the USSR's nuclear weapons. Useful, no doubt, but not exactly for clinging to power.

The regular army, with 1,473,000 troops, was the junta's weightiest, but dullest, sword. Conscripted from the population, its ethnic composition and the political attitudes of its rank-and-file soldiers mirror the society at large. Although Russians are prone to wild exaggeration, the most recent statements by ranking Soviet military officials and reports in the Soviet press make it clear that these troops were in no state for an operation as massive and as ambitious as a successful coup would have required.

Over the past six years many soldiers have caught the anti-communism disease. Forty percent of servicemen who voted in the Russian republic elections cast their ballots for Boris Yeltsin. Even Defense Minister and coup plotter Dmitri Yazov has been compelled to admit that "the army has sustained considerable losses in the ideological struggle for the minds and hearts of the younger generation." One reason that servicemen think incorrect political thoughts is because life in the Red Army is very harsh. Newly released figures published in the magazine *Kuranty* show that in the past fifteen years 120,000 soldiers died, even without counting casualties from Afghanistan. Suicide accounts for 50 percent of these deaths, with death from "inflicted injuries," a euphemism for homicide, responsible for another 20 percent.

The widespread and intractable practice of hazing is one source of the high morbidity; ethnic conflict is another. An episode in the Carpathian military district is typical. Fighting erupted between Kazakh soldiers and members of another Central Asian national group stationed at the same base. According to the temporarily banned newspaper *Komsomolskaya Pravda*, soldiers at the base regularly "waged implacable 'night-time' battles among themselves" in their barracks and "fights and insults had become a customary occurrence." In a December 1990 skirmish, fifteen soldiers, including the unit's deputy commander for political affairs, were wounded in an exchange of gunfire. "The state of the army reflects the situation in society," commented the prosecutor of the Carpathian military district who investigated the affair.

The Lack of Discipline

The discipline problems spring in part from the trouble in finding a few good men. The pool from which draftees are selected is shrinking. Several factors explain the trend. The number of young men found unfit for service on account of poor health is rising, a reflection of the growing health problems in the society at large. As a result of health and other deferments, only 43 percent of the draft-age population is eligible to serve. As the pool shrinks, the educational level of the troops is experiencing a sharp decline. In 1988 only 2.2 percent of draftees lacked a high school education. By 1990 the number of high school dropouts being asked to serve had increased sixfold. Lieutenant General Ivan Matveyev, who has responsibilities in the manpower area, says that the army's "intellectual standard is falling." What is worse, he told *Izvestia*, of every Soviet draftee one in four has a criminal record. An army populated with hooligans and thieves "has an extremely negative impact on the entire combat readiness of our units," he warned.

Those who are summoned for duty don't always show up. In 1990, 86,000 recruits neglected to report to induction centers. This year the spring recruitment campaign was "much more complex than in the fall of last year," Matveyev says. In Russia, the Ukraine, Belorussia, and Azerbaijan, the plan was fulfilled by 100 percent. But in the remaining eleven republics the results were poor. Some of the soldiers in these areas are said to have been eager to serve. "We have spoken to many of them," says Matveyev. "They repeatedly told us that they would have gone to serve . . . but they were afraid that the local authorities would oppress them for taking such a step." The top-ranking political commissar in the military, General Nikolai Shlyaga, said in a recent *Red Star* interview that the shortfall is "increasing the tension of military service" as well as heightening "physical and moral and psychological fatigue."

The overworked soldiers and officers are underhoused. In Moscow alone, according to the military newspaper *Krasnaya Zvezda*, there are 10,800 officers' families without apartments; 500 of the officers either fought in Afghanistan or were called in to help extinguish the Chernobyl nuclear reactor. Today they are "in the position of refugees." Defense Minister Yazov said recently that providing housing to servicemen and their families is a problem that "continues to remain acute" across the country. In April he said that 192,000 families were without housing. Many husbands are forced to live apart from their wives: one in five among officers' families, one in three among those officers returning from abroad. According to Shlyaga, the military has lost the "source of accommodation acquisition" because an "immense quantity of apartments is being retained by those who are no longer linked with the Ministry of Defense." What is to blame for the shortage of military housing? Shlyaga blames "economic autonomy and the market." It is no accident that the junta immediately said that building more housing was its top economic priority.

As in civilian life, food for the troops is scarce, particularly for soldiers stationed in enemy territory like the Caucasus and the Baltics. The Defense Ministry's recent plan for improving supplies involved taking 9,700 tons of meat and meat products, 49,500 tons of milk and dairy products, 2,900 tons of vegetable oil, and 4,300 tons of sugar out of the USSR government reserve for troops and officers in the rebellious regions. In addition, 13,900 tons of "edible fish products" were to be allocated to the military. These delicacies were to be made available "by means of reducing the market allocation to specific consumers," Sovietese for civilians.

Even before the coup, the military's growing set of domestic functions was causing discontent. Along with corruption and privilege came the new political functions the military was supposed to perform. Military patrols of urban centers to combat crime and the injection of paratroopers and other units into conflicts in the Baltics and the Caucasus were steps that came in for open criticism not simply from civilians but from soldiers and senior officers as well. Demoralized from within, with decreasing levels of physical and political support, the Soviet military had begun to crack long before August 19. No one should be surprised that it proved useless in the execution of the coup.

The Emergence of Boris Yeltsin

Martin Malia

In June 1991, Boris Yeltsin was elected president of the Russian republic (establishing himself as a rival to Gorbachev's leadership) and became one of the leading advocates of radical reform.

In the following selection, written in 1992, shortly after the breakup of the Soviet Union and the establishment of independent governments in Russia and the fourteen other republics, Martin Malia divides the demise of Communist rule in Russia and the Soviet Union into three stages. The first stage was Gorbachev's program of perestroika, which was intended to reform and preserve Communist rule but ultimately undermined it. The second stage was the downfall of the Communist regimes of Eastern Europe, which showed that Soviet power was weakening. The last stage, still ongoing, is the transformation of Russia into a democracy with a capitalist market economy. The success of this final stage, Malia argues, requires the dismantling of every last vestige of Soviet rule, a process that has necessitated separation from the union, radical economic measures, and some seemingly autocratic political maneuvers by Yeltsin.

Martin Malia is professor of Russian history at the University of California, Berkeley. He is the author of *The Soviet Tragedy: A History of Socialism in Russia, 1917–1991*.

It has become clear that the process of communism's disintegration is as revolutionary as the process that established it in power. And this second revolution, a revolution against the

Reprinted from Martin Malia, "The Yeltsin Revolution," *The New Republic*, March 16, 1992, by permission of *The New Republic*; © 1992, The New Republic, Inc.

heritage of the first revolution, has just as clearly not yet run its course. So far this new revolution has known three phases. The first was Gorbachev's perestroika, which one of his idea men, Fedor Burlatsky, now characterizes as "a revolution of the dilettantes," an impossible wager to reform the system without abandoning its socialist foundations. The second was the actual demise of communism, when the wager ended in the total collapse of the system: the fall of Eastern Europe in 1989, which demonstrated that the "conquests of socialism" were reversible, and hence the system everywhere was mortal; then the coup de grace in the heart of the system, Russia, in 1991. At present Boris Yeltsin and the Russian democrats are launching a third phase, that of building a post-Communist order, or as they would put it, of "returning Russia to Europe" by creating a "normal society." The great question now is whether this, too, will turn out to be an impossible wager.

Clearly no one in the West takes Yeltsin for a miracle worker, as some once did Gorbachev, and there is no Western cult of his personality. Quite the contrary, his government is regarded with suspicion, if not hostility. At best he is accorded grudging support in the interests of post-Soviet stability. The lack of a positive Western response to the Yeltsin wager could weigh against its chances of success. This is a government, after all, that aims at integration into the world community.

The Failure of the Soviet System

But the principal factor governing the prospects for Yeltsin's reform is the legacy of Soviet failure, including perestroika. The scope of the Soviet collapse is unprecedented in modern, indeed world, history. This point bears emphasis because mainline American Sovietologists have long misconstrued the Soviet system, making it appear much more of a success than it really was. They argued that the USSR was no longer totalitarian but had developed into an "institutional pluralism," and was thus capable of a "transition" to some sort of social democracy. Their processing of flawed Soviet data through Western models for calculating the GNP [gross national product] produced an economic success story that augured well for an evolution to democracy and that also informed the CIA's absurd belief that the Soviet economy was some 60 percent of the American.

Thus we were presented with a maturing Soviet society quite prepared to make the wager of perestroika a success. And so such authorities as Professors Jerry Hough and Stephen Cohen, for five years, regularly assured us. But the exit from communism, when it came, was not a transition or an evolution. It was a brusque collapse, a total implosion, of a sort unheard of in history: a great state abolished itself utterly—in a matter of weeks—and right from under its president. The reason this happened is that the Soviet Union, *pace* most Western Sovietology, was in fact a total society, with all aspects of life linked in what one scholar called a "mono-organization" whole. At its core was the Party to which all aspects of life were subordinated: the economy, government, culture, private life itself. This total society logically ended in a total collapse of all its interrelated parts at once. Thus we now have in the midst of the resulting rubble a total problem embracing every aspect of life.

Post-Communist Democracy in Russia

What is Yeltsin's program for coping with this universal crisis? Indeed, does Russia's first democratic government have a coherent program at all? And how do its policies relate to Russian nationalism, the matter that seems to worry the West most about post-Sovietism? The bedrock of the Russian democratic program since 1989 is to undo everything that communism has done since 1917, including Gorbachev. As such, the program is truly revolutionary, its notion of "democracy" a post-communist and revolutionary notion. Yeltsin and the democrats have too often been presented in the West simply as populist rivals of Gorbachev, out for power. But all Yeltsin's statements, from his June 1991 presidential campaign through his 1992 New Year's address, show that he seeks to effect the "rebirth of Russia" by "liberating" her from the "destructive disaster of communism." This aim should be taken quite seriously, and literally.

Thus, Russian democracy means, first, refusal of the Communist monopoly of political power, which translates as the principle of a multiparty order. Democracy means, second, refusal of the Communist monopoly of economic power, which translates as the principle of private property. And the rule of law derives logically from the first two principles. Finally, at the end of the process of challenging the Communist order came the challenge to still another Party monopoly of power—that of state authority—which translates as the dissolution of the pseudo-federation, or Union.

The Attempt to Reform Communism

The history of this program's development bears repeating, since it was generated by a series of shocks, of collisions with Party authority. The first came at the Congress of People's Deputies in May–June 1989. Even though Gorbachev had an overwhelming, and in the words of [historian] Yuri Afanasiev, "aggressively submissive" majority, a liberal minority of the Congress spoke out, on national TV, against the appalling ills of the system. The result was a "demystification" of communism from which it never recovered. At the same time these liberals, largely from the *Moscow Tribune* group, became convinced that Gorbachev in no way contemplated power-sharing and must be openly opposed. They formed the Interregional Group of Deputies, under Andrei Sakharov and Yeltsin, which brought together all the future stars of Russian democracy. . . . Russian "civil society," as all groups independent of the state now came to be known, thereby received a political expression; and its program was the end of the Party's "leading role" in all spheres of life.

At first the heretical right to private property was mentioned only sotto voce by the democrats. But with the collapse of Eastern European communism in the fall of 1989 this issue, together with its corollary—the market—now came to the fore. By spring 1990 the example of Poland's "big bang" transition to the market led the Soviet government to draft plans for transition to a "regulated market," another self-defeating half-measure. But they were soon forced to go further when a new front against the Party-state was opened up in June 1990 by the movement for the sovereignty of the Union republics. Launched by Russia, following the Baltic example, this movement by the end of the summer had spread throughout the Union. The very existence of the "center" was now called into question.

Because of this weakening of the center, it became possible for the democrats to force the issue of private property. The result was the "500-Day Plan" associated with Stanislav Shatalin and Grigori Yavlinsky. This plan was not exactly "shock therapy," because the shift to the market was spread over a year and a half, but it had revolutionary implications. A political as much as an economic document, it emanated from a group of younger economists under Yavlinsky who wanted simply to finish with the system. They planned to do this by establishing republic, or local, control in moving to the market, an approach that would automatically undermine the Party-state's "center." Yeltsin quickly espoused this plan, and then prevailed on Gorbachev to accept it also. But in September Gorbachev suddenly drew back, as he and the rest of the establishment realized the political threat this economic program entailed.

The August Coup

From the fall of 1990 to the spring of 1991 Gorbachev moved to the "right," back to the Party, police, army, and military-industrial hierarchies. The Yeltsin democrats, sensing they could soon be eliminated, fought back with demonstrations and strikes. As a result, Gorbachev in April flipped again to the left, giving way to Yeltsin and the republics on most points in a new, more flexible Union treaty. But this capitulation appeared to the old guard as the death sentence of the Party-state. Just before the new treaty's signing on August 19, this group declared their president to be incapacitated and took over, as a prelude to quashing the democrats by force.

Two things about this famous "coup" require emphasis, because both are prudishly ignored in the Western press. First, this "coup" was in fact no coup at all, because the "coup plotters," as they are quaintly called, were none other than the Soviet government: the vice president, the prime minister, the ministers of defense and interior, the head of the KGB, the chairman of the Supreme Soviet, and the chief of staff of Gorbachev's personal Cabinet. They were quite simply the whole Communist establishment; their aim was to depose a chief whose indecision they believed, correctly, was leading the system to catastrophe. If Gorbachev did not know that these close collaborators, all of whom he had appointed, were working toward a state of emergency, then he was incompetent, which is as bad as complicit.

The second notable thing about the August coup is that Yeltsin and the democrats were ready not only to resist it, but also to escalate this resistance into a countercoup against the Party-state. Once the junta's military thrust had been thwarted, Yeltsin suspended the Communist Party, took over the KGB and army command, appointed an economic committee under Yavlinsky, and began measures to decommunize and professionalize public functions. All of this was done by a cascade of decrees previously prepared in the Russian Council of Ministers. Thus, although all constitutional forms were preserved by restoring Gorbachev to power, and indeed using him to validate the new decrees, in fact a countercoup had been carried out disestablishing the Communist system. This behavior was criticized abroad at the time as "autocratic." But there could be no democracy in Russia without first dismantling the Leninist system. It would have been absurd to try to pass Yeltsin's measures through the "due process" of a Communist legislature. The only feasible course was to seize the opportunity provided by the post-coup vacuum and to act swiftly, while the momentum of victory was still strong.

The Democratic Transformation

So began the third and most radical stage of what had become an open revolution against Leninism. And this third stage will be the most difficult in the exit from communism. For getting rid, at last, of the system also means provoking the final collapse of all its components: the economy, the administrative system, the state structure itself. Nor were the democrats ready for these problems. Their clear adversary, the Party, had evaporated. Thrust into power far sooner than they had anticipated, the new government floundered in its first six weeks, eroding the trust of a public bewildered by Yeltsin's lack of follow-through and panicked as full realization of the economic disaster at last hit them. . . .

After August two great issues faced the new government: how to effect the unavoidable shift to the market and private property, and what to do about the "Union." And these two were closely linked: economic reform within the Union as a whole could only be based on compromise and hence would be by steps; economic reform in Russia alone would mean a sharp plunge, and hence meant destroying the Union framework. On both issues the radical option was finally chosen— but only after four months of struggle within the democratic coalition, and between Russia and the other republics.

In August a special committee under the Russian prime minister, Ivan Silayev, and Yavlinsky was put in charge of the economy and made into a Union body. This approach led by October 1 to the signing of an economic Union at a meeting of most of the republics in Alma-Ata. A month after Alma-Ata, however, further talks failed to give life to the new economic Union because of a deep divergence of Russia's interests from the other republics'. The conflict was due above all to the fact that Russia—unlike all the others except the Baltic states and Caucasian republics—had made an anti-Communist revolution. In Ukraine, Belarus, Kazakhstan, and Central Asia, the Party of [Ukraine president] Leonid Kravchuk, [Belarus president] Ivan Shushkevich, and [Kazakhstan president] Nursultan Nazarbayev is still in power. All had behaved ambiguously during the coup. Most were neither ready nor eager for rapid marketization.

Russia Goes Its Own Way

In late October the Yeltsin government therefore opted for a radical "Russia first" program, which the republics could follow as they might. In an address on October 28, Yeltsin announced that most prices would be freed by year's end, without wage indexation; privatization would also begin. He also called for accompanying emergency political measures. First, he had elections suspended for a year. Public opinion surveys made by the government had shown that if elections were held, the democrats would be in trouble. The Russians had also noted that October 1991 elections to the Polish

Sejm had returned a fragmented, unmanageable legislature. Yeltsin thus received power to rule by decree, subject to some parliamentary supervision. Finally, he assumed direct responsibility by taking the post of premier himself. He declared that if his new government did not begin to produce results within a year, he would step down.

When things had shaken down by November, it turned out that the August government of Prime Minister Silayev, and yesteryear's economic innovator, Yavlinsky, who advocated an all-Union, phased approach, had lost out to a more junior group of economists, mostly under 35, led by Yegor Gaidar, who favored a "Russia first" program of shock therapy. It is Gennadi Burbulis, the allegedly benighted professor of scientific communism, who persuaded Yeltsin (obviously no expert in economics) to adopt this radical program, and to form the new ministry around the "Young Turks," or the "Boys in Reeboks," as they are known.

Accordingly, at the end of November Burbulis became first deputy prime minister, Gaidar deputy prime minister for the economy and finances, and Alexander Shokhin deputy prime minister for labor and employment. In the words of Mikhail Berger, the highly regarded economic expert of *Izvestia*, these men and their colleagues are the first group of real economists ever to be put in charge of the Russian economy. Basically pragmatic, they have also worked with the International Monetary Fund and the World Bank to make sure their program meets international standards, and with such Western economists as Jeffrey Sachs of Harvard and Anders Aslund, the Swedish economist and Soviet expert, who have been given offices near the Kremlin and have worked actively in preparing Gaidar's reform.

Radical Economic Reform Measures

This reform proposes the most far-reaching change since Stalin built socialism. In December 1991 the country was opened to almost unrestricted foreign investment, with a right to repatriate profits. On January 2, 1992, came the liberation of prices except for basic food staples, energy, and transportation, where prices are to be increased three- or fourfold. Still to come are control of the budget deficit and inflation, stabilization of the currency, and internal convertibility of the ruble. Privatization of 70 percent of retail commerce and services has been targeted for the end of 1992. At the same time, measures of "social defense" have been adopted by Labor Minister Shokhin to tide the country over what can only be a painful transition for the majority of the population, some 50 percent of which lives below the official poverty line.

In addition, major decisions have at long last been made about agriculture, the greatest scandal of the Soviet economy. At the end of the year Yeltsin decreed that land would be given to peasants as private property, with resale subject only to minimal restrictions. This measure was to take effect immediately to permit results before spring sowing. Moreover, Russia's state and collective farms are to be dissolved. Gorbachev never contemplated anything more than long-term leasing of land to peasants, a precarious tenure they were never willing to accept. Yeltsin's decision is truly revolutionary, the surest sign that the new government is in earnest. Though many criticisms can be made of this program, Russia at last *has* a program, and Yeltsin must act while he still enjoys public confidence. The program is risky, but it is less risky than doing nothing.

This choice of a radical economic program was also a major factor in condemning the Union. Gaidar and his "boys" had always wished to get rid of the dead weight of the republics and their conservatism. When in December 1991 the latter tried to postpone the date of price liberalization from December 15 to late January, Russia unilaterally fixed the date at January 2. Most of the republics followed. If the former empire is to modernize its economy rapidly, clearly Russia will have to be the locomotive of the transformation.

Votes for Independence in the Republics: Ukraine

Robert Cullen

During 1991 the central government and the republics of the Soviet Union were embroiled in a debate over the future of the union. A few republics—notably Estonia and Lithuania—had announced their intention to secede as early as March 1990. The other republics, though, negotiated a draft union treaty that would preserve central political control while allowing the individual republics greater economic autonomy. In the confused aftermath of the August 1991 abortive coup, however, the majority of republics declared independence.

Writing one month after the final dissolution of the Soviet Union, Robert Cullen describes Ukraine's secession. Ukraine's decision to declare independence shattered any hopes for reimplementing the negotiated treaty and preserving the union, he argues; by the time Ukraine held a referendum on independence in December 1991, few Ukrainians supported the preservation of the Soviet Union.

Robert Cullen is a journalist. He is the author of the books *Soviet Sources, Twilight of Empire: Inside the Crumbling Soviet Bloc,* and *Dispatch from a Cold Country.*

Yuri Shcherbak's articles on Chernobyl, which appeared in *Literaturnaya Gazeta* and a magazine called *Yunost,* won him a major journalism prize and made him a leader of the nascent environmental movement in Ukraine. At the end of 1986, he helped found a party called Green World. He told

Reprinted from Robert Cullen, "Report from Ukraine," *The New Yorker,* January 27, 1992, by permission of the author.

me, with some pride, that it was the first non-Communist political party in Ukraine since the K.G.B. wiped out the last of the nationalist guerrillas, in the early nineteen-fifties. In 1989, to his surprise, a group of factory workers nominated him to run for the Congress of People's Deputies, the new Soviet legislature. The elections that year suggested the transitional nature of the era. The Communist Party still dominated most districts in Ukraine and throughout the Soviet Union, but enough insurgents managed to win seats to give the Congress a significant minority of non-Communists. One of them was Yuri Shcherbak.

The Congress of People's Deputies

When Shcherbak arrived in Moscow for the Congress, in May of 1989, he recalled, he still believed in the possibility of reforming and revitalizing the Soviet Union. He helped to organize a group of reform-minded deputies, called the Inter-Regional Group, whose political mentor was Andrei Sakharov. "We adopted a resolution about the union," he told me. "It said that the Stalinist empire was falling apart and could exist no longer, and that the time had come to reëxamine the union treaty and on a new basis create a— well, we didn't call it a union, but that was the sense of it."

As we spoke, more than two years later, the disintegration of the union was almost complete. But Shcherbak believed that parts of it might have been saved if Gorbachev and his people had acted decisively in 1989 to decentralize the government and reform the economy. "We showed them the only path to salvation," he said. "If they had taken it, if they had got out in front of events, they might have done a lot better, although the union was doomed in some parts even then. Armenia and Azerbaijan were already out of control, and the Baltic states would have left in any case. But a new, decentralizing union treaty might have brought forth some moderate national forces. If they had begun a decisive economic reform then, the political energy might have been switched to the economy. They could have saved—" He did not finish the sentence.

Back in 1989, when Shcherbak and his reformist allies showed their ideas to Gorbachev's chief lieutenant in the

Supreme Soviet, Anatoly Lukyanov, he had become angry and replied, "No! No! How could you do this?"

"They didn't pay any attention," Shcherbak recalled. "They played with us like a cat with a mouse. They really didn't want any reforms. Russia always behaves as a messianic great power. The Russians think that the world looks only to them."

The Roots of Ukrainian Secession

In 1989, Shcherbak was not yet a secessionist. By the middle of 1991, he was. I asked him what had caused him to conclude that reform could not salvage the union.

"After I became a member of the Supreme Soviet, I learned about the extent of the financial catastrophe in Moscow," he answered. "I realized that Ryzhkov"—Nikolai Ryzhkov, the former Prime Minister—" was a criminal who ought to be put away. And Valentin Pavlov, his Minister of Finance. They've led us into an enormous financial catastrophe with the amount of money they've printed."

There was another reason for Shcherbak's conclusion. In June, 1991, he said, the chairman of the presidium of the Ukrainian legislature, a Communist named Leonid Kravchuk, decided that he wanted to give the public the impression that things were changing by adding an opposition figure to his Cabinet. Kravchuk invited Shcherbak to become Ukraine's Minister for Environmental Protection, and Shcherbak accepted. Once in office, he began to learn the full dimensions of the environmental damage wrought during seventy-odd years of submission to Moscow. Chernobyl was only one of many dangerous problems. Major cities—among them Sevastopol, home to the Soviet Black Sea fleet—had shortages of drinkable water, because the local water supplies were fouled with toxins. The average Ukrainian's life expectancy was six years shorter than that of the average citizen in the West. "I understood that what happened here happened because the leaders in Moscow behaved as if they were occupiers," he told me. . . .

On August 24, 1991, after the failure of the coup in Moscow—and, not coincidentally, the downfall of the Soviet Communist Party—Leonid Kravchuk suddenly announced his resignation from the Party and his conversion to the cause of Ukrainian independence. Thereupon, with only one dissent, the Ukrainian legislature voted in favor of a declaration of independence, subject to approval in a referendum to be held December 1st.

On August 26th, the Supreme Soviet of the U.S.S.R. convened in Moscow to discuss the coup and its aftermath. Gorbachev sat with the presidium, behind the speaker's lectern, in the well of the vast hall, and he rose to give the first major speech of the session. Even though several republics besides Ukraine had declared independence following the coup, Gorbachev was intent on saving the union, apparently hoping that the republics' declarations were essentially rhetorical. He tried to rally support for his draft union treaty—an agreement that would preserve at least some central control.

Gorbachev Attempts to Preserve the Union

A few hours later, the time came for Ukraine to reply to Gorbachev's appeal, and the task fell to Yuri Shcherbak. Everyone in the Kremlin knew that Ukraine's response was critical. Without Ukraine's farmlands, a union could not hope to feed itself, and without Ukraine's mostly Slavic population, of fifty-two million, the Slavs remaining in a union might soon find themselves outnumbered by Muslims from Central Asia. Yuri Shcherbak hastily translated into Russian the resolution that the Ukrainian legislature had adopted two days before: "The Supreme Soviet of Ukraine solemnly declares the independence of Ukraine and the creation of an independent, Ukrainian state." Then he walked to the well of the hall and read the resolution.

"There was dead silence, a terrible silence," Shcherbak recalled, not without a hint of satisfaction at the memory. "In the middle of my speech, Gorbachev stood up and walked out.". . .

Ukrainian Nationalism

Nationalist politics came later to Ukraine than to some of the non-Slavic Soviet republics. In Armenia and the Baltic states, environmentalists' protests led almost immediately to the formation of popular movements that soon became pro-independence parties. In Ukraine, a couple of years elapsed between the formation of Yuri Shcherbak's Green movement and the creation of a purely political organization. "There were several reasons for that," I was told one day in November by Ivan Drach, a Ukrainian writer. For one thing, Drach explained, the Ukrainian intelligentsia had closer ties to the Russian Communists who launched *perestroika* than the intellectuals in other republics had. Drach's career provided a good example. He got part of his higher education in Moscow during the thaw of the Khrushchev years, and worked as an organizer for the Communist Youth League while attending the university. He joined the Party and waited for the day when it would adopt the reforms that Khrushchev had bumblingly initiated. But the Party in Ukraine proved highly resistant to reform. Gorbachev did not get around to dismissing [Ukrainian Communist Party leader Vladimir] Shcherbitsky until late in 1989. "Shcherbitsky was useful to Gorbachev in Ukraine, because he knew how to keep control of things, and he didn't allow liberal democratic movements," Drach said.

By 1989, though, Shcherbitsky and the local Party no longer had complete control. An amnesty had recently released a number of prisoners whom Shcherbitsky's regime had long since packed off to Siberia for nationalist agitation. Two of them were Vyacheslav Chornovil and Levko Lukyanenko, who had spent fifteen and twenty-seven years, respectively, in Soviet prisons, and these two joined forces with some Kiev intellectuals—including Drach, who was by then a leader of the Ukrainian Writers' Union—to form Rukh (Ukrainian for "the movement"). The organization held its founding congress in September. Drach recalled, "Representatives of the K.G.B. came up to us and said, 'Look around. You have three thousand delegates. We have fifteen thousand people surrounding you.' And, in fact, there were paddy wagons all around." But the movement was by then too big to stop, and the Rukh congress proceeded. Drach became its chairman.

The Referendum on the Soviet Union

The Ukrainian Communist Party did not crumble in the face of this opposition, as the Parties in republics like Lithuania and

Armenia had done. Instead, it began to advocate political sovereignty for Ukraine—a muddled concept that tried to straddle the nationalists' call for independence and Moscow's demand for preservation of the union. In a reasonably open and competitive election in March, 1990, the Party won three-fourths of the seats in the republic's legislature. A year later, in a union-wide referendum on the future status of the Soviet Union, the Party's position again prevailed. More than seventy per cent of the Ukrainian voters responded favorably to a question posed at Gorbachev's initiative: "Do you consider necessary the preservation of the Union of Soviet Socialist Republics as a renewed federation of equal, sovereign republics, in which the rights and freedoms of an individual of any nationality will be fully guaranteed?" The Ukrainian legislature, at the suggestion of the Communist leadership, added a second question: "Do you agree that Ukraine should be part of a Union of Soviet Sovereign Republics on the basis of the declaration on the state sovereignty of Ukraine?" More than eighty per cent of the voters said yes to that question—a result that muddied whatever meaning the referendum might have had.

The Party had by that time produced a new leader for Ukraine—Leonid Kravchuk, the chairman of the presidium of the legislature. Kravchuk, who is now fifty-seven, has carefully barbered silver hair and the jowly, florid face of a man who for a long time has not had to stand in line for meat. He likes to wear double-breasted suits, which give him the look of a Chicago politico of the thirties. Kravchuk spent the Brezhnev years and the first four Gorbachev years as a functionary in the Ideology Department of the Communist Party in Kiev. He was the man, Yuri Shcherbak recalled, who telephoned newspaper editors to berate them if the portrait of Brezhnev they printed on their front pages was too small. Vitaly Korotich, who, in the pre-*glasnost* era, was the editor of a Ukrainian magazine devoted to translations of foreign literature, remembers Kravchuk as the man who handed down the list of acceptable and unacceptable foreign writers. The list, Korotich recalled, banned Saul Bellow ("a Zionist") but approved of E.L. Doctorow (on the grounds that he portrayed the struggle of the working class).

The Emergence of Leonid Kravchuk

Kravchuk inherited the leadership after Gorbachev oversaw the removal of Shcherbitsky and then called Shcherbitsky's successor, Vladimir Ivashko, to serve in Moscow. Once in power, Kravchuk continued the Party's policy of straddling the independence issue: he talked of sovereignty to appease the nationalists, and he talked of staying in some form of union to appease Moscow. He managed to stay astride the fence until August 19, 1991, the first day of Moscow's aborted coup.

The leaders of some of the republics immediately and unequivocally condemned the coup. Kravchuk held a wet finger up to the wind and all but endorsed it. Speaking to Moscow television, he said, "What happened was bound to happen. . . . The situation could not remain as it was—a situation without power, when the center was in no condition to rule." He noted with satisfaction that Ukrainian workers were continuing to do their jobs. Only when the coup unravelled, and it became clear that Communists everywhere were in jeopardy, did Kravchuk turn against the plotters. On August 24th, he declared that he had renounced his Party positions on August 19th—something he had not chosen to reveal when the coup still looked as if it might succeed. Also on August 24th, while crowds outside the legislature chanted, "Shame on Kravchuk!" he and his Communist allies experienced a battlefield conversion to the cause of secession. By the end of the day, the legislature had voted overwhelmingly for independence, passing the resolution that Yuri Shcherbak read in front of Gorbachev. The declaration had one condition: approval in the referendum on December 1st. The legislature added another item to that ballot: the direct election of a President. Kravchuk immediately became the leading candidate.

The Question of Borders for Independent Republics

In Moscow, Boris Yeltsin's Russian government inadvertently helped persuade many Ukrainians that independence was the right choice. On August 26th, Yeltsin's press secretary said that if Ukraine wished to become independent Russia reserved the right to discuss a revision of borders. Everyone in both republics understood the reference at once. The present territory of Ukraine, particularly along the border with Russia, includes a number of areas where Russians, or Russian speakers, are the majority. In the days when all policy emanated from Moscow, this situation made little difference. But now, with power shifting to local and republic governments, it might make a considerable difference to, say, Russian coal miners in the Donbas region of Ukraine whether that region belonged to Ukraine or to Russia. The statement issued in Yeltsin's name raised the possibility of conflicts analogous to the nasty war being fought by Serbs and Croatians in Yugoslavia.

The next day, Yeltsin's government revoked the statement, calling it a mistake. Yeltsin sent a delegation led by his vice-president, Aleksandr Rutskoy, to Kiev to assure Kravchuk that Russia had no intention of claiming any Ukrainian territory. (The confusion arose, a well-placed member of the Russian government told me afterward, because of a debate among Yeltsin's advisers over how to respond to Ukraine's declaration of independence. Some advisers had indeed wanted to raise the issue of border adjustments, and the press secretary mistakenly thought that their views had prevailed.) The meeting between Kravchuk and Rutskoy defused the situation for the time being, but the episode served to remind everyone in Ukraine that before the Russians were Communists they had been imperialists, and that, despite Yeltsin's protestations, they might become imperialists again.

By September, no one of prominence in Ukraine was arguing the case for remaining in a union with a central government in Moscow. Once Kravchuk and the Party apparatus decided on independence, the Ukrainian media began promoting the new line as assiduously as they had once promoted the unbreakable fraternity of the Soviet peoples. A Ukrainian-American organization arranged for an American television-production crew to come to Ukraine and film a series of commercials designed to sell the idea of independence to Russians in Ukraine. Ukrainian television accepted the commercials and promised to play them often, at no charge. No one made commercials promoting the alternative. Seven candidates were on the Presidential ballot (each had collected a hundred thousand signatures on nominating petitions), and they all advocated independence. The debate in the campaign focussed on finer points. Kravchuk, who before August had suggested that Ukraine should sign some kind of loose union treaty, now took the position that the union-treaty effort was doomed, because it envisioned placing a state structure over the republics. The only union he would consider, he pledged, would be an economic union along the lines of the European Community. He might also, he added, support a collective-security arrangement with the erstwhile Soviet republics, with joint control of nuclear weapons, but he insisted on Ukraine's right to its own army. Supporters of Vyacheslav Chornovil, the Rukh candidate, and Levko Lukyanenko, who ran as the candidate of the Ukrainian Republican Party, complained, with some justification, that Kravchuk had preëmpted their platform.

The Ukrainian Presidential Campaign

Kravchuk accomplished this pirouette almost blithely. On an afternoon in late November, I went to hear him speak at Kiev's baroque state opera house on the occasion of the hundred-and-twenty-fifth birthday of Mykhailo Hrushevsky. Back in 1906, Hrushevsky, a historian, had first challenged the imperial Russian view of a shared past of the Ukrainians and the Russians, putting forward the idea that the Ukrainians were a distinct nation. In the chaotic months after the Russian Revolution, he had served, briefly, as President of Ukraine. Once the Bolsheviks came to power, he went into exile. He returned to Ukraine in 1924, but his works and ideas were banned, and he died in political disgrace in 1934. With the turn of events since August, however, Hrushevsky was back in style. His portrait, framed in bunting of pale blue and yellow—the colors of the Ukrainian flag—hung over the stage of the opera house much as Lenin's portrait would have hung amid red bunting in Communist days. At the appointed hour, Kravchuk and his

Cabinet strode onstage and took their seats, facing the audience. There was polite applause. Kravchuk then rose to deliver his speech from a lectern, in much the same way that I had seen Soviet speakers rise to deliver speeches in honor of Lenin's birthday or International Women's Day, or any of the other holidays of the old order.

"The dramatic history of our nation, like every nation, has giants whose names will never be forgotten," Kravchuk said, speaking in a flat, droning voice. "One of them is Hrushevsky." He went on at length about the historian, his ideas, and the repression of those ideas. "We were told he was a reactionary. I myself witnessed how Hrushevsky's works were burned," he said.

I found it remarkable that Kravchuk could deliver this speech without once referring to, explaining, or apologizing for his own long service in the agency directly responsible for banning Hrushevsky and his ideas. Some of my Ukrainian acquaintances saw the irony, but they were prepared, a little cynically, to overlook it, given their concern for the future. "If we refused to vote for hypocrites, we couldn't elect a government, because we don't have enough people who sat in jails," I was later told by Natalia Yakovenko, a historian. "For the time being, we have no choice but to believe that, yes, these people"—former Communists, like Kravchuk—"have changed. And it seems to me that in this transition period Kravchuk and his people are better than the other choices. They know their opposition—other ex-Communists, like Yeltsin—very well. They know their way of thinking and acting. And I think we need a very careful leadership. Given how we are armed, any little spark of conflict could start us on a bloody course. So let them run the government for two or three years. I suspect that for the moment that serves the interest of Ukraine. The next time, we just won't elect them.". . .

Election Results

More than eighty per cent of the voters had approved Ukrainian independence. (In Crimea, the figure was only fifty-four per cent, he said. Since it could be assumed that the Ukrainians and the Tatars voted heavily for independence, the figure suggested that the majority of the Russians in Crimea voted against it.) Leonid Kravchuk had received about fifty-six per cent of the votes and would become President without a runoff.

These results, combined with Kravchuk's stated determination not to sign a union treaty, put an end to Gorbachev's wan final efforts to preserve the Soviet Union. During November, Yeltsin had participated in a series of meetings, organized by Gorbachev, that had reached a vague, tentative agreement on what a new union might look like. But after the Ukrainian vote Yeltsin stated publicly that he could not sign a union treaty that did not include Ukraine. On December 8th, he, Kravchuk, and the Byelarussian leader Stanislav Shushkevich, meeting in a hunting lodge near Brest, quickly reached agreement to form a Commonwealth of Independent States, which would try to get along without a central government. It was not necessarily what Yeltsin had wanted, and it was certainly not what Gorbachev had wanted, but it was all that Ukraine would agree to—and Ukraine, for the first time in several centuries, was in a position to impose its views on Russia. By the end of the month, all the former Soviet republics except Lithuania, Latvia, Estonia, and Georgia had agreed to join the commonwealth. Although the agreement left a lot of unanswered questions, such as the disposition of the Soviet Navy's Black Sea fleet, the republics entered into it voluntarily, rather than submitting to a plan from the center, and that fact gave it, I thought, at least a chance of survival. On Christmas Day, Mikhail Gorbachev resigned the Presidency of a Soviet Union that, except for his presence in the Kremlin, had effectively ceased to exist.

Chapter 5

Strife in the Former Union

Turning | Points
IN WORLD HISTORY

War in Nagorno-Karabakh: Armenia Versus Azerbaijan

Arif Yunusov

Glasnost (openness) unleashed many ethnic disputes and hostilities between the various constituent nationalities of the Soviet Union. One of the most serious conflicts developed over Nagorno-Karabakh, a semiautonomous enclave of Armenians located within the borders of Azerbaijan. Fighting erupted between informal militias of Armenians and Azerbaijanis in 1987, as Armenia petitioned the central government for control over the region. The Soviet military was unable to control the conflict, and the fighting quickly grew into a full-scale war between the two Soviet republics. Armenian forces eventually gained control over the enclave and over a corridor of territory connecting Nagorno-Karabakh to the Armenian border. In May 1994 the now-independent states of Armenia and Azerbaijan signed a cease-fire agreement, but the dispute remains unresolved.

In the following viewpoint, written in 1997, Arif Yunusov examines the aftermath of this conflict. As Soviet republics, he points out, Armenia and Azerbaijan had developed ethnically diverse populations. The war, however, through so-called ethnic cleansing has created a large number of refugees in Azerbaijan, adding to Azerbaijan's economic troubles as an independent state, he argues.

Arif Yunusov is a historian in Baku, Azerbaijan.

Reprinted with permission, from Arif Yunusov, "Demographic Disaster," *Index on Censorship*, no. 4, July 1997. This article was originally published in *Index on Censorship 6/77*. For more information contact: <contact@indexoncensorship.org>; fax: 011-44-171-278 1878, or visit http://www.oneworld.org/index_oc.

Azerbaijan was the first post-Soviet republic to face a refugee problem. Meetings and demonstrations began in neighbouring Armenia in autumn 1987 demanding the transfer of the mainly Armenian-populated enclave of Nagorno-Karabakh from Azerbaijani to Armenian jurisdiction. Clashes between Armenians and Azerbaijanis in many areas of Armenia led to the exodus of the first hundreds of Azerbaijanis from Armenia. By the end of January 1988, this figure had reached more than 4,000. This was the first time there had been refugees on Soviet territory since the end of World War II, but the Soviet leadership was quick to ban any mention of the subject, and quickly settled the refugees in and around the Azerbaijani city of Sumgait.

War and Ethnic Cleansing

The situation worsened rapidly when full-scale war between Armenia and Azerbaijan broke out in February 1988. By the beginning of 1990, all Azerbaijanis, as well as Muslim Kurds—some 186,000 people—had been forced from Armenia into Azerbaijan. The entry of Soviet forces into Azerbaijan's capital, Baku, in January 1990, and the bloody aftermath, saw a new wave of migration. More than 100,000 Russians, mostly families of soldiers, left Azerbaijan. In turn, 279,000 Armenians had fled Azerbaijan for Armenia; a further 44,000 headed for Russia.

At about the same time, in June 1989, over 50,000 Meskhetian Turks, fleeing potential massacre in Uzbekistan, also sought refuge in Azerbaijan.

The collapse of the Soviet Union, and the resulting independence for Azerbaijan and Armenia in 1991, turned the Karabakh conflict into an international affair. In autumn 1991, with Russian help, the Karabakh-Armenian forces began an offensive and by the following summer had driven the entire local Azerbaijani and Kurdish population from Nagorno-Karabakh and from the Lachin region wedged between Karabakh and the Armenian border. Those driven from their homes, officially known as internally displaced persons (IDPs), swelled the number of refugees. The resulting counter-attack by the Azerbaijani army drove the Armenian population from the Shaumyan region to the north of Karabakh.

By the end of 1993, political chaos in Azerbaijan and the power vacuum in the capital enabled Armenia to occupy six districts of Azerbaijan outside Nagorno-Karabakh. The flood of refugees from these regions became so intense that it jeopardised the social and economic stability of Azerbaijan. Fearing social revolt, the Azerbaijani authorities closed all the roads from the conflict zone to Baku and other major towns in summer 1993. Refugee camps mushroomed along these roads.

The signing of the Karabakh ceasefire agreement in May 1994 allowed the authorities to stabilise the situation in Azerbaijan and to get a grip on the problem of the IDPs. The continuous movement of the IDPs and their simultaneous registration in several locations created some confusion over numbers. In December 1993 the government announced a figure of 780,000 refugees. Together with the earlier refugees from Armenia and Uzbekistan, there were over one million refugees and IDPs on Azeri soil.

However, by 1 January 1997, revised figures put their combined number at 843,000, some 11 per cent of Azerbaijan's population. Independent experts put the figure nearer 750,000.

Refugees Change Azerbaijan's Population

Regardless of precise numbers, the seven-year conflict has brought about vast changes in the demographic and religious make-up of Azerbaijan. Before the conflict began, Azerbaijan had a population of just over 7 million, of whom 83 per cent were Azerbaijanis; 87 per cent of the population were Muslim, 12.5 per cent Christian and 0.5 per cent Jewish.

The Slav population, mostly Russian, was also heavily affected. Official figures show that after 1989, some 169,000 Russians, 15,000 Ukrainians and 3,000 Belarusians emigrated (the Russians claim that as many as 220,000 Russians departed, leaving around 180,000). Most left between 1990 and 1992, worried by the political instability; for those who left later, the primary motivation was economic.

In all, more than 600,000 non-Azeris left the republic

after 1988, most of them Christians: 323,000 of the 390,000 Armenians living in Azerbaijan fled; those that remained were in Armenian-controlled Karabakh. By 1 January 1997, with the total population around 7.5 million, Azeris made up 90 per cent of the population; Christians had fallen to only four per cent of the population. The Muslims' share of the total had risen to 95 per cent.

Behind these dry statistics lie the pain and suffering of huge numbers of the population, regardless of nationality, faith or current location. Refugees are the most vulnerable sector of the population. Over and above the problems afflicting the whole population—the severe economic crisis, the fall in production and unemployment—refugees face their own specific problems. Almost all are victims or witnesses of violence inflicted during military operations or were forced to flee their homes under fear of death. Many have developed psychiatric problems or have needed medical treatment.

The refugees also face serious psychological difficulties in their new places of residence. Most are from small villages and those who settled in towns have taken some time to adapt. There have been cases of conflict with local residents. Today the refugees face new and paradoxical dangers. When the Karabakh ceasefire halted military operations in May 1994 the refugees hoped their lot would soon improve. But negotiations have dragged on and the refugees have had to find ways of surviving, always in competition with the local population. If the talks drag on too long and the economic situation gets worse, there could be serious tensions, above all in the large cities.

Refugee Camps

Refugees still living in camps face another set of problems. While they do at least receive aid supplies, any hint that aid might be cut off causes an outbreak of panic which could lead to uprisings. The first signs of this were evident at the end of 1996 when a number of aid agencies halted their work in Azerbaijan.

Life in a camp is unnatural and unsettled. Camps are often built without regard for the mentality and previous way of life of the refugees. People of different levels of education, profession and traditions are lumped together. Where the refugees depend totally on outside help, this has led to numerous arguments and conflicts of interest. Life is particularly hard for women and girls, as neither the state agencies nor aid organisations bear in mind their particular needs when building the camps or distributing the aid.

These difficulties have led to severe crises within many refugee families. Men seek fruitlessly for work, many women secretly turn to prostitution as a means of survival and many children cannot go to school as the uniforms and books are too expensive. This environment is also a breeding ground for crime.

Migration did not cease when the fighting came to a stop. On the contrary, the most active refugees, above all the young, migrate to neighbouring countries. Unable to find work in Azerbaijan, they have gone to Russia, Turkey and Iran. In Turkey and Iran they work mainly on building sites, as labourers or as shepherds, earning some US$100–150 per month, plus board and lodging.

But Russia is still the most common destination. The Azerbaijani press reckons that more than 1.5 million left for Russia between 1993 and 1996 and that the number of Azerbaijani citizens now working there is between 2 and 3 million, some 30 per cent of Azerbaijan's total population.

The Russian press has reported that the Azerbaijani community, among which there is an increasing number of refugees, is a significant force in business, including criminal business. About one million of this community live in Moscow and the surrounding region. A significant number of refugees in the 20–40 age range, while officially registered in Azerbaijan, find illegal trading jobs lasting several months in Moscow and other major cities across Russia.

The exodus of such a large proportion of the population, even if only temporary, will also cause problems for the nation itself. Most of those leaving Azerbaijan are men, the overwhelming majority of them unmarried. The ratio of the sexes has thus been unbalanced. Given the significant number of those killed, wounded or crippled, many women are doomed to remain single.

Independence for Russian Minorities: War in Chechnya

Vera Tolz

In the midst of the disintegration of the Soviet Union in 1991, as the fifteen constituent republics were establishing their independence, the autonomous region of Chechnya declared its secession from the Russian republic. The move highlighted the fact that Russia is a federation of ethnically diverse autonomous and semiautonomous regions. In late 1994, as Chechnya stridently asserted its independence, Russian president Boris Yeltsin ordered troops to quell the Chechen rebellion. By 1996, Russian troops had defeated the Chechen forces and reasserted control over the capital, but fighting continued.

Writing in late 1996, Vera Tolz argues in the following article that the nationalist independence movements of the former Soviet republics instilled the leaders of the newly independent Russia with a fear of nationalist movements among the federation's own ethnic minority constituents. The forceful repression of Chechnya's bid for independence, she contends, bodes ill for Russia's ability to peacefully forge a democratic union out of its ethnically diverse population.

Vera Tolz is a lecturer in Russian history at the University of Salford near Manchester, England. She is the author of *The USSR's Emerging Multiparty System* and *Russian Academicians and the Revolution* and the editor of *The Demise of the USSR: From Communism to Independence.*

Reprinted, with permission, from Vera Tolz, "The War in Chechnya," *Current History*, October 1996; © 1996, Current History, Inc.

On August 23, 1996—20 months after Russian President Boris Yeltsin ordered a full-scale military intervention in the breakaway republic of Chechnya—*Izvestia* compared Russia's war in Chechnya with America's war in Vietnam. The comparison was not in Russia's favor; the newspaper argued that while the United States eventually learned from its Vietnam experience, Russia has yet to learn anything from the Chechen war. Indeed, almost two years after the war began, the solution to the Chechen conflict is still not in sight.

The war in Chechnya raises a number of questions about the methods the Russian government uses to solve political problems; about Russia's attitude toward its former colonies (including the newly independent states of the former Soviet Union); and about the state of the Russian armed forces and President Boris Yeltsin's ability to exercise control over them. More specifically, the war raises doubts about the ability of all subjects of the Russian Federation to become full-fledged citizens of one nation. Even if Moscow manages to sign a bilateral treaty with Chechnya stipulating that the republic remain part of Russia, would the Chechen people ever regard themselves as voluntarily belonging to the community of citizens of the Russian state? And if not, can Russian democratization succeed without national unity?

A History of Animosity

In a detailed analysis of the Chechen crisis, Yeltsin's adviser on nationalities problems, Emil Pain, and political scientist Arkadi Popov attribute Chechnya's drive for independence to the fact that the Chechen-Ingush autonomous republic had always ranked near the bottom of economic and social indicators in Russia. It is significant that their analysis completely omits the history of Chechen-Russian relations. This history was apparently also ignored by those politicians who, in late 1994, decided to begin military operations against the secessionist republic. But the fact that the Chechens had been at the forefront of the fierce resistance to Russian rule in the Caucasus in the prerevolutionary period and that they were among the most persecuted ethnic groups in the Soviet period are crucial to understanding the origins of the current conflict.

The Russians first attempted to establish their influence over the North Caucasus in the sixteenth century. At the final stage of this process, in the nineteenth century, it took the Russian army over five decades to put down the resistance of the "Mountaineers." The Caucasian War, which ended in 1859, was arguably the most brutal of all Russia's colonial campaigns. Even after its conquest, the North Caucasus was hardly integrated into the Russian empire, with the Chechens and other Mountaineers passively resisting Russian domination until 1917. During the civil war following the October Revolution, the Mountaineers made an unsuccessful attempt to assert their independence. In 1944, another tragedy befell the Chechens when Stalin ordered their deportation to Kazakhstan on trumped-up charges of mass collaboration with the Germans.

Russian military journalist Pavel Felgengauer argues that this history fell victim to Stalin's myth that all non-Russians joined the Russian empire voluntarily. "As a result, Russians have for all practical purposes forgotten the Great Caucasian War. . . . But the Chechens forgot nothing. Neither the war itself, nor the gallantry of Imam Shamil's men, nor the savageness of the fighting and the scorched-land tactics of General Aleksei Ermolov and other Caucasian viceroys. Nor, of course, the brutal 1944 deportation of their entire nation by Russian [Soviet] troops." The emergence of a separatist movement among the Chechens during Soviet President Mikhail Gorbachev's political liberalization program thus comes as no surprise.

From Burr to Thorn

In the summer of 1991, the All-National Congress of Chechen People (ANCC) announced that the Chechen part of the Russian Federation's Autonomous Republic of Checheno-Ingushetia would secede from the Soviet Union and the Russian Federation. The congress made the newly formed Executive Committee of the ANCC the highest body of political power in the republic, with retired Soviet army General Dzhokhar Dudayev chairman of the committee. At the time, Moscow paid little attention to this declaration.

On October 27,1991, presidential elections were held in Chechnya. Dudayev won, becoming the first popularly elected president in Chechen history. President Dudayev confirmed the earlier proclamation of independence. The Russian Congress of People's Deputies refused to recognize the legitimacy of the Chechen elections, noting that 6 of 14 districts in the Chechen-Ingush republic had refused to take part in the vote.

A November 7, 1991, decree by Yeltsin introducing emergency rule in Chechnya in reaction to its declaration of independence merely contributed to the growth of anti-Moscow sentiments and increased Dudayev's prestige in the republic. It was only in December 1992 that the Russian parliament recognized the division of the Chechen-Ingush republic into two parts, with Ingushetia firmly remaining part of the Russian Federation. Chechnya's independence, however, remains unrecognized by Russia or the international community.

Between 1992 and 1994, the Chechen leadership arranged the withdrawal of Russian troops from the republic. Neither federal nor local authorities were in control of Chechnya in the early 1990s. There was no police, no parliament, and no unified financial system in this self-proclaimed independent republic. Even the borders were not firmly established. The vagueness of Chechnya's political status led to the creation of the biggest market for arms and drugs in the Commonwealth of Independent States. According to some observers, this benefited groups not only in Chechnya but also in Moscow.

Russia made some attempts to conduct negotiations with various political forces in the rebel republic. In January 1993, a delegation of Russian parliamentarians visited Grozny and signed a protocol on the preparation of a treaty on the delimitation of powers between Moscow and Chechnya. Dudayev was excluded from these negotiations, however, and strongly opposed the talks as long as Moscow continued to refuse to recognize Chechnya's independence. Instead of meeting with Dudayev, Russia's representatives dealt with members of the Chechen parliament—a body that played virtually no role in the republic's politics.

Hopes for a Treaty

New hopes for an agreement with Chechnya emerged following the successful signing of a bilateral treaty between Moscow and Tatarstan in February 1994. This treaty granted Tatarstan a wide range of political and economic powers in exchange for its agreement to remain part of the Russian Federation. That April, Yeltsin instructed his government to draft a treaty between Moscow and Chechnya using the Tatarstan agreement as a model. The deputy prime minister responsible for nationalities policies, Sergei Shakhrai, was put in charge of the process.

The attempt was doomed from the start. Shakhrai, who was a key proponent of excluding Dudayev from the negotiation process, was unacceptable to the Chechen leadership. Yeltsin also rejected advice that any meaningful negotiations with Grozny should involve Dudayev. Those favoring Dudayev's participation argued that Dudayev's involvement in negotiations would degrade his heroic image. Under these circumstances, Moscow could hope that when new presidential elections were held in Chechnya in 1995, Dudayev would be voted out of office.

It is hard to say how realistic this scenario was. In any event, Yeltsin embarked on another path, and decided to rely on the fragile and disunited anti-Dudayev opposition in the predominantly Russian Upper Terek region of Chechnya. Moscow backed the opposition's proclamation of an alternative government and supplied it with military equipment and money. On November 26, 1994, these Chechen opposition forces attempted to take over Grozny. They failed and, after an initial denial, Moscow had to admit the involvement of Russian security forces in the attack. Two weeks later, Russian troops entered Chechnya and, on December 31, they began to storm Grozny. . . .

A Chronology of the War

There is no legislation in Russia on the use of the army in internal conflicts. In the case of Chechnya, the president, after soliciting the opinions of a few members of the National

Security Council and the power ministries, made the decision virtually on his own. He also failed to inform the parliament of his decision to use force, as required by the constitution. The initial performance of the Russian military in Chechnya was extremely poor. The Russians suffered heavy losses and at several points the military command was on the verge of totally losing control of its troops. The operation was apparently not properly planned, and insufficiently trained young recruits were sent into battle without even having maps of the city of Grozny. The winter weather prevented air support for the ground forces. The Chechen side's readiness for war and popular determination to defend the homeland were underestimated by the Russian side. However, Russian military superiority eventually led to control of Grozny by March 1995 and to the continuation of a Russian offensive that has been accompanied by enormous brutality, high casualties among the civilian population, and devastation of the republic's cities and villages. By the summer of 1995, federal troops had established control over the main strategic points in the Chechen plains and over several important strongholds in the mountains.

It was at this point that the Chechens resorted to terrorism. In June 1995, Chechen military commander Shamyl Basaev led a raid on the Russian republic town of Budyonnovsk that left 120 civilians dead in fighting between Chechen and Russian forces when Basaev's forces took over a hospital and held nearly 2,000 people hostage. In January 1996, Chechen fighters took hostages in the town of Kizlyar in Dagestan. These actions forced the Russian government to negotiate with the Chechens. . . .

The Implications for Russia

Yeltsin justified launching the war against Chechnya by citing the need to preserve the integrity of the Russian Federation. But Moscow's mangled operations in the republic make the possibility of any voluntary Chechen union with Moscow extremely unlikely. Not only is it difficult to imagine the Chechens voluntarily accepting their membership in a new nation forged out of citizens of the Russian Federation, but in the eyes of many Russians, the Chechens are not rightful citizens of the state. Although the Moscow media has been highly critical of Russian military actions in the republic, the image of the Chechens as criminals and terrorists—an image created by the same media between 1992 and 1994—has had a significant impact on Russians. According to a nationwide opinion poll conducted by the Russian Association for the Study of Public Opinion and Market in the spring of 1996, 54 percent of those polled did not want to live next to Chechens.

The war in Chechnya could also have broad implications for the development of Russian federalism. Since 1990, the Russian leadership has been aware of the fragility of ethnic federations. The disintegration of the Soviet Union only exacerbated Moscow's suspicion of ethnic autonomies in the Russian Federation. It has been argued by Western and Russian scholars that the creation by the Bolshevik government of republics named after titular nationalities, and the allotment of privileges to the titular nationalities on the territories of these republics, created an environment highly conducive to nationalism and facilitated the transformation of ethnic groups into full-fledged nations striving for political independence. During the Soviet period, titular nationalities in autonomous republics in the Russian republic enjoyed far fewer privileges than their counterparts in the Union republics and were—and still are—in most cases outnumbered by the Russians in their own regions. Moreover, the majority of Russia's ethnic republics do not have borders with foreign states, but are situated in the Russian heartland. Yet the fear that the Russian Federation might disintegrate along ethnic lines has had a strong impact on the views and policies of the Russian government. The proclamation of independence by Chechnya reinforced this fear.

A Plan to Abolish Russian Republics

It was not ultranationalist leader Vladimir Zhirinovsky, as is often erroneously assumed, but the Russian parliament's constitutional commission that in 1990 for the first time suggested that autonomous republics in the Russian Federation should be abolished. Instead, Russia's internal divisions would be made along economic-territorial lines. In 1992 and 1993, in his struggle against parliament, Yeltsin courted the leaderships of Russia's ethnic republics, trying to draw them to his side; the plans to abolish ethnic republics by incorporating them into neighboring, predominantly Russian, economic-territorial regions were shelved.

In the wake of the Chechen war, the plans to abolish the republics reemerged. In 1995, Deputy Prime Minister Shakhrai, the mayor of St. Petersburg, Anatoly Sobchak, and several other politicians revived plans to redivide the Russian Federation solely along economic and territorial lines. Shakhrai hoped that the plan would be implemented before the June 1996 presidential elections. This, of course, did not happen, and Yeltsin remains unsure whether he can curb the resistance such a move would inevitably provoke in the republics. But would the abolition of the ethnic formations save the Russian Federation from disintegration?

The Russian leadership probably exaggerates the danger of separatism by the majority of ethnic republics. Since most republics are not economically and politically viable on their own, their political elites attempt to strike the most favorable economic and financial deals with Moscow rather than secede from the Russian Federation. Russia's ethnic republics were not even able to present a unified position on the Chechen war. Many leaders had their own agendas, and some did not want to complicate relations with Moscow. Moreover, the war in Chechnya failed to significantly increase public support for nationalist separatist parties in the majority of ethnic republics. Therefore, Moscow's treatment of ethnic republics as hotbeds of separatism and a threat to Russia's unity seems to be a mistake.

If the federal government in Russia remains weak and continues to lack coherent regional and economic policies, disintegration along regional-economic rather than ethno-federal lines will become much more likely. At the same time, the existence of ethnically based constituent units in the federation complicates the process of forging a new nation on the territory of the Russian Federation, viewed as a community of citizens united by common political institutions. Instead, structural divisions along ethnic lines stimulate the development of ethnic nationalism, which, in contrast to civic nationalism, often is an obstacle on the path to democratization. (Ethnic nationalism defines nationhood in terms of lineage, whereas civic nationalism defines it in terms of citizenship and political participation.)

Problematic Republics in the North Caucasus

The conclusion that the majority of ethnic republics do not pose any immediate threat to Russia's territorial integrity does not fully apply to autonomous entities in the North Caucasus, whose situation is different. The North Caucasus is the area with the largest number of territorial disputes and ethnic tensions in the Russian Federation. In contrast to Russia's other ethnic autonomies, titular nationalities in the North Caucasus often constitute a majority in their territories and all but one (Georgia) have a border with a foreign state. This makes their secession from Russia potentially easier.

Moscow has not worked out a clear plan of what to do with the North Caucasus. It has not been successful in helping to solve a territorial dispute between Ingushetia and North Ossetia or easing interethnic tensions in Dagestan, Kabardino-Balkaria, and Karachay-Cherkessia. These republics, especially Ingushetia and Dagestan, have been considerably affected by the war in Chechnya and the popular support for anti-Russian, separatist forces has grown there. Moreover, Moscow's pro-Ossetian position in the territorial dispute between the North Ossetians and the Ingush contributed to the growth of anti-Russian sentiments among the leaders of the main political movement in the North Caucasus, the Confederation of the Mountain Peoples of the Caucasus (as of 1992, the Confederation of Peoples of the Caucasus).

Established in November 1991, the movement strives to represent the political interests of all the Mountaineers. In 1992 it organized elections to a parliament of the Mountaineers in which each ethnic group in the Caucasus was represented by three deputies. Some members of the movement began to call for the creation of a Republic of the Mountaineers, independent of Russia. However, there is no consensus on the creation of such a republic or on other issues among the Mountaineers and their leaders—a lack of unity Russia is using and will continue to use in maintaining its control over the area. Meanwhile, some Moscow politicians argue that it might be best to let troublesome areas in the North Caucasus secede. This view will hardly win the immediate support of the government, but in the future, if the North Caucasus remains unintegrated, it might be the only option left for Moscow if the Russian government takes democratization seriously.

Instability in Georgia

Ken Gluck

Georgia was among the first of the Soviet republics to press for and declare independence from the Soviet Union. It was also the first to hold democratic elections and choose a new government. Zviad Gamsakhurdia, who gained prominence as a dissident under the Soviet regime, was elected president in May 1991. His rule, however, was marked by seemingly odd behavior, including paranoid accusations against leaders of the political opposition. A coup deposing Gamsakhurdia in January 1992 set the tone for Georgian politics to date. The former Soviet foreign minister Eduard Shevardnadze, elected Georgia's president in late 1992, was the target of an assassination attempt in 1995.

In the following selection, written two months after the overthrow of Gamsakhurdia (which occurred within weeks of the formal dissolution of the Soviet Union), Ken Gluck remarks that the coup in Georgia is a sign that democratic development will be difficult in the former Soviet republic. In Gluck's opinion, the violent overthrow of the democratically elected Gamsakhurdia displayed fear and loathing among the new leaders toward the electorate of Georgia.

Ken Gluck is a journalist living in Moscow.

"Democracy has triumphed in Georgia," the victorious soldiers assured people. If so, it will be the second victory in little more than a year for democracy in the former Soviet re-

Reprinted, with permission, from Ken Gluck, "Revolt of the Intelligentsia," *The Nation*, March 2, 1992; © 1992.

public in the Caucasus. The first victory pushed the Communists from power in two sets of elections back before the Soviet Union died its unnatural death. The latest victory pushed elected President Zviad Gamsakhurdia from power in two weeks of gun battles on the streets of Tbilisi, the Georgian capital. The fighting brought several hundred rebel Georgian National Guardsmen and like-minded volunteers into the center of the city with their machine guns, howitzers, tanks and even a few rockets. From just before Catholic Christmas right up until Orthodox Christmas thirteen days later, they blasted away at the monumental beige government complex where Gamsakhurdia reigned with a similar assortment of weaponry.

Civil War in Tbilisi, Georgia

Gamsakhurdia finally gave way to the incessant barrage, fleeing in the middle of the night to neighboring Armenia. With his fall, Georgia erected yet another landmark along the Soviet Union's road to a shining, post-Communist future. In May 1991 Gamsakhurdia became the first democratically elected president in the Soviet Union, beating out Boris Yeltsin by almost three weeks. As he abandoned the city in his armored Mercedes in the early hours of January 6, he became the first elected leader in the former Soviet Union to be violently overthrown.

The "people's insurrection against totalitarianism," as Prime Minister Tengiz Sigua put it, had triumphed. But the people who poured into the streets with the end of the fighting were mostly mourning the 120 dead and the shattered visage of the city. People walked down Rustaveli Prospect staring tearfully at the burned and gutted nineteenth-century buildings that had made Tbilisi one of the most beautiful cities in the Soviet Union. The shock of seeing the destroyed avenue somewhat eased the hatred that had tormented the city for months. But the battle lines remain in people's heads. Some walked in compact groups, holding on to one another tightly and wondering how Gamsakhurdia could have chosen to destroy their city rather than to leave peacefully. Others walked among the ruins, wiping their eyes and asking where the opposition had found the hate to destroy the most cherished part of the city. "It was the most beautiful place in Georgia, even though the Communists built it. Now they have destroyed it."

The First Democratic Elections

The presidential elections in May 1991, which brought Gamsakhurdia to power with 87 percent of the vote, marked the acme of democratic hopes in the republic. Gamsakhurdia, unlike the new leaders of most other republics, was not a recycled bureaucrat with a fresh ideology pinned to his chest. While Yeltsin was serving as an unusually dynamic party hack in Sverdlovsk, Gamsakhurdia worked with the Georgian Helsinki Union. As such he was the first and only former "dissident" to come to power in the former Soviet Union. (Gamsakhurdia's critics, cruelly, emphasize his forced television confession in 1978.)

As Gamsakhurdia's regime began to consolidate power, however, Georgia's spring of democratic hope soon began to freeze over. Paranoia became state policy. Gamsakhurdia's opponents became "dark forces attempting to sabotage Georgia." The spring 1991 earthquake that rocked the northern half of the republic didn't just happen; it was artificially created by the Soviet Defense Ministry. The anti-Gamsakhurdia demonstrators who paralyzed the capital in August and September were "Kremlin agents" working at the behest of a massive conspiracy involving former foreign minister Eduard Shevardnadze, Soviet President Mikhail Gorbachev and even George Bush, who allegedly cut a sinister deal with the Soviets to deny Georgia its independence.

As elsewhere in the former Soviet Union, nationalism in Georgia has aggressively filled the vacuum left by the fall of Communism. And Gamsakhurdia used Georgian chauvinism viciously against the republic's ethnic minorities, who make up 30 percent of the population. Georgia's attempt to crush Ossetian autonomy in the north of the republic led to a slowly boiling war of hit-and-run attacks and hostage taking.

Reforms stalled under the anti-Communist government. Looking for bright spots in the economic picture, Givi Tak-

takashvili, the chairman of the Georgian Parliament's Committee on Economic Reform, was forced to turn to ancient history. "The West will come to Georgia's aid," he explained. "We helped the West during the Crusades. When the Mongols were descending on Europe, we formed a barrier. The West will help. Gentlemen never forget to pay their debts."

Political arrests, which had ceased in the waning months of Communist power, began to make a comeback under Gamsakhurdia. "We have to recognize that right now in Georgia there are more political prisoners than there were under Brezhnev," lamented Heinrich Altunian, a longtime human rights activist who is now a member of the Ukrainian Parliament. In his attacks on political opponents, Gamsakhurdia repeatedly lashed out at "enemies of the people," the rubric under which millions of Soviet citizens were sent to exile or death under Stalin. Georgia under Gamsakhurdia, wrote Nicholai Andreev in a full-page commentary in *Izvestia* in June, recalls the "years of stagnation" under Brezhnev. (Andreev's article was never read in Georgia. Whether by government order or their own feelings of loyalty to Gamsakhurdia, the local printing workers refused to publish that day's *Izvestia*.)

The obvious distinction that Andreev overlooked was that Gamsakhurdia, unlike Brezhnev, was capable of evoking fanatical devotion among a large part of the Georgian population. "He is our lord, our czar. He is a true democrat," one woman assured me after his fall. Over the summer of 1991 the republic became increasingly divided between those who venerated Gamsakhurdia and those who despised him. The veneration was seen mostly among the poor and in rural areas. The hate was concentrated in the capital.

Repression by Gamsakhurdia and Opposition

Opposition to Gamsakhurdia revolved around a collection of small political parties (which more closely resembled political discussion groups than parties) and a loose circle of well-known Georgian cultural and academic figures. Their spirited and nonviolent opposition to Gamsakhurdia was interrupted by August's short-lived right-wing coup attempt. Just before the coup, Prime Minister Sigua quit his post, accusing Gamsakhurdia of stalling on reforms.

Tengiz Kitovani, a longtime Gamsakhurdia associate and the commander of the Georgian National Guard, took a more dangerous step. The Guardsmen had been offended by Gamsakhurdia's alleged agreement to disband the force on orders from the coup leaders in Moscow. Immediately after the coup Kitovani took his troops to Shavnabada, a military base on the outskirts of Tbilisi, and stopped taking orders from the President. "The Guard," he promised, "will side with the people." A few weeks later the rebel troops moved into the city to join the opposition takeover of the television studios. For the first time since the Soviet Army smashed a demonstration in April 1989, leaving twenty dead, military hardware returned to the streets of Tbilisi.

Most of the civilian opposition cheered as the soldiers came over to their side. In the late 1960s and 1970s many young Soviet intellectuals, like their Western counterparts, became enamored with the myth of the Third World revolutionary. The young bearded Che's of Latin America had attractively little in common with the pallor and slurred speech of the seemingly eternal Brezhnev, in spite of the shared rhetoric of Communism. The Georgian intellectuals who joined the National Guardsmen in their armed "liberation" of Tbilisi were susceptible to their own romantic insurrectionary dreams and seemed unaware of the obvious perils of the civil war they were fearlessly approaching. Once the shooting started, however, power and control inevitably shifted to the ones with the guns.

Fighting Erupts

On December 22 shooting erupted at an opposition demonstration at the government headquarters. For the military wing of the opposition, this was the moment they had been waiting for, and possibly hoping for. The next day the rebel troops moved their heavy guns, tanks and soldiers into the city center to begin their assault on the government headquarters. In the street fighting that followed, Rustaveli

Prospect was turned into a tangled mass of charred trucks and fallen trees. One by one, the buildings surrounding the government complex caught fire and burned, and stores were looted.

Just hours after Gamsakhurdia fled, accompanied by the remnants of his government and his defenders, the rebels slowly worked their way through the thick columns at the front of the government complex. Several of the columns hung uselessly from the roof of the building, their bases shot away during the fighting. The soldiers panicked at the popping noises coming from inside the complex and unleashed one last barrage of automatic-weapons fire into the courtyard. But the noises were only from the fire that raged on the right wing of the complex. The fighting was over.

That evening in the cold and dimly lit Hotel Iveria, the rebels celebrated their victory with a hoard of champagne, brandy and wine rescued from the destroyed government complex. As the rest of the city's occupants crawled out of their hiding places and bunkers and returned to the food lines that had only worsened during the conflict, the victorious fighters saw little hope in their future. Most likely they will go back to using the Kalashnikov rifles that lay alongside them as they drank, and the pastel-green hand grenades that hung from their chests. "Maybe Gamsakhurdia will start something in the west, and we'll be needed there. Maybe we'll go back to Ossetia to fight."

What to Do After the Overthrow?

For all of Gamsakhurdia's bumbling authoritarianism and venomous paranoia, nothing he did seems to justify the little-thought-out decision to take up arms against him. None of his crimes seem to justify the death and destruction of Tbilisi's two-week civil war. Gamsakhurdia's muzzling of the press was halfhearted and ineffective. The politically motivated arrests came, for the most part, only after the opposition did its utmost to provoke the government into taking repressive measures. Even before the military campaign to oust him began, Gamsakhurdia's control over his own government was withering. Neither the government nor the opposition ever found the political will to lower the heat of the rhetoric and the level of violence. Some opposition leaders now mimic Gamsakhurdia's aggressive Georgian nationalism. A good number of the fighters who ousted him had first sharpened their skills in the bitter and bloody repression of Ossetian autonomy.

The rebels waged their war in the name of democracy, but new elections are not in Georgia's immediate future. "The people are still not ready," says Prime Minister Sigua (who has been reinstated). Elections were temporarily scheduled for May, but some of the opposition parties are calling for them to be further postponed until the fall. Georgian television is replete with the lurid details of the torture, beatings and theft that allegedly took place in Gamsakhurdia's headquarters during the fighting. "After the people hear of all the horrible crimes he committed, he will be left without any support," Sigua predicted.

Throughout the former Soviet Union, politicians hailed Georgia's new rulers as "the saviors of democracy." The U.S. State Department, like its European counterparts, did not praise Gamsakhurdia's overthrow, but neither was any criticism forthcoming.

The support of Moscow's intellectual elites for the new government is only partly explained by Gamsakhurdia's knack for offending even people and governments that had never heard of him. The Moscow intelligentsia see their political counterparts in the anti-Gamsakhurdia rebellion.

A Legitimate New Government?

Georgia's new government is built on the illegitimacy of its first elected government. But the elections that placed Gamsakhurdia in power were inconveniently clean. In the absence of fraud, the rebels had to bolster their justification for overthrowing the legally elected President by emphasizing the low social origins of his supporters.

The leaders of the opposition never failed to point out that the core of Gamsakhurdia's supporters were uneducated farmers and workers from rural areas. The bullets and rockets that rained down on the government headquarters came from Georgia's enlightened elite, the very group we generally associate with progress in the former Soviet Union. And this elite, by its account, takes precedence over the poorer and less educated citizens who voted Gamsakhurdia into office ten months ago. Such logic is shared by the new rulers and reformers throughout Russia and the other republics. They fear the same populist, anti-intellectual wave that emerged in Georgia. This fear overrides all their eloquent talk of elections and the rule of law. The new elites are hoping to save their "fragile democracy" from the "lumpenized masses." Freed from the Communist sham of a government of workers and peasants, the new elites are now loath to let workers and peasants elect their leaders. In Georgia the argument took its next logical step: demonizing the poor and hapless supporters of the elected President. "Gamsakhurdia's supporters are people with a base mentality. They are a dark and wanton mass," explained well-known film director Georgi Shengalaya, a close adviser to the Military Council, which now holds power.

If the new government does manage to wrest control from the Military Council, it will likely be an improvement on the quirky and incompetent regime that preceded it. But the tragedy of elections leading nowhere and of military force as the ultimate political arbiter has been firmly established as the foundation of Georgian post-Communism. Born in bloodshed, the new government will not easily overcome its disdain for Gamsakhurdia's followers.

On January 7—Christmas Day for Georgians and other Orthodox Christians—a march of 4,000 Gamsakhurdia supporters wound through the streets of the capital, mourning the fall of their leader. As they walked, endlessly chanting, "Zviadi, Zviadi," soldiers from the Military Council began shooting—some into the air and others into the crowd. As the marchers scattered, the soldiers, their faces hidden in scarves, chased them down the avenue, firing into the courtyards and alleyways where people tried to hide. It was the Military Council's first day in complete control of the city.

Russia and the Former Republics

Robert Cullen

Throughout the seventy-odd years of the Soviet Union's existence, Russians immigrated to the smaller republics to work as scientists, factory managers, and political administrators. By 1990, Russians made up as much as half the population of a few republics. When these republics gained independence at the end of 1991, the native populations sometimes sought to deny citizenship to the Russians living among them.

In the following viewpoint, Robert Cullen describes the tense relationship existing between Russia and the former republics two years after the collapse of the Soviet Union. Anti-Russian bias among the republic populaces is just one of the problems, he asserts. Russian troops are involved in ethnic skirmishes in many former republics, he reports. And ethnic minorities within Russia are clamoring for independence, following the example of the republics.

Robert Cullen is a journalist. He is the author of the books *Soviet Sources, Twilight of Empire: Inside the Crumbling Soviet Bloc,* and *Dispatch from a Cold Country.*

Shortly after the June elections in Latvia, a satisfied nationalist named Alexanders Kirsteins offered an interviewer his prognosis for the next phase in the history of the former Soviet republic. Phase 1 had been accomplished much as Kirsteins, leader of the Latvian National Independence Movement, had advocated. After gaining independence,

Reprinted, with permission, from Robert Cullen, "Russia Confronts Its 'Near Abroad,'" *The Nation,* September 20, 1993; © 1993.

Latvia disfranchised roughly half its Russian-speaking population by offering the right to vote primarily to citizens of pre-1940 Latvia and their descendants. That move, predictably, led to this past summer's election results, in which Latvia's ethnic minorities, principally Russians, Ukrainians and Jews, won only a handful of seats in the new Parliament, even though they make up 48 percent of the population. The next step advocated by Kirsteins's party, which finished second in the balloting behind a party called Latvian Way, would be legislation denying unemployment benefits to noncitizens. That done, Kirsteins predicted, a decade of emigration would follow. Hundreds of thousands of people would leave Latvia. It went without saying that those leaving would be Russians.

Anti-Russian Politics

So goes the development of freedom and democracy in one republic two years after the breakup of the U.S.S.R. Events have not moved in the hopeful direction envisioned by those who ringed Russia's White House and faced down the tanks of the Communist Party during the August 1991 *putsch*. Rather quickly, Russians are coming to grips with the fact that they still have national interests in the erstwhile dominions, starting with the Pan-Russian diaspora living in these lands, and that no one is going to look out for those interests if they do not do so themselves. . . .

The precarious situation in the former Soviet Union stems directly from the peculiar way in which the union fell apart in 1991. The immediate trigger for the August *putsch* was Mikhail Gorbachev's plan to sign a new treaty with the republics that would have led to a radically decentralized Soviet Union, albeit one that was still intact. The leaders of the Moscow bureaucracies perceived, correctly, that the treaty was a grave threat to their interests because it would have transferred most budget and administrative power from the center to the republic level. So, intent on preserving the centralized union, they attempted to seize power.

But while the coup plotters saw their action as an effort to save the union, many Russians saw it differently. The people who gathered around the Russian White House thought the *putsch* was an attempt to reimpose all the most hated features of the old regime: the Communist Party's monopoly on power, police terror, phony elections, travel restrictions and censorship. They came out to defend Boris Yeltsin because he symbolized the end of all those things.

When the coup failed, the entire Soviet leadership had been discredited. Only Yeltsin had any claim to political legitimacy. But Yeltsin led the Russian Republic, not the Soviet Union, and he was committed to the devolution of power to the republics' governments. He saw the destruction of the Soviet Union as the only way he could consolidate his own authority. So he invited the presidents of Ukraine and Belarus to a meeting in a hunting lodge. And there, with no public debate or discussion, they agreed to abolish the union. The Congress of People's Deputies of Russia, Ukraine and Belarus voted their approval. The stunned remnants of the Soviet political establishment had no means with which to oppose them. The popular resistance to the *putsch* may have emanated from a desire to defend democracy and individual liberty, but its result was the dissolution of an empire that Russia has been assembling for more than 500 years.

Democratic Development After the Coup

There was not, at the time, a great deal of popular concern about this. The Russian deputies who voted to dissolve the union did so on the basis of two or three rather naïve assumptions. They believed that the governments of the republics, given their independence, would uniformly support a generous code of human rights; they were democrats, after all. They assumed as well that the Western European trend toward unification (which looked much more certain in 1991 than it does in 1993) would quickly take effect in the old Soviet sphere and that within a reasonably short time, Russia and the former republics would reassemble in some sort of voluntary confederation, not unlike the European Community, with Russia as the senior partner.

Of course, nothing of the sort has occurred, and the Russian people are rapidly coming to realize what they lost, as well as what they gained, in August 1991. The dissolution of the old union has produced little but pain, humiliation and bloodshed.

In Central Asia, Russian troops are becoming ensnared in a violent and intractable conflict involving the remnants of Tajikistan's old Communist elite, Islamic fundamentalists and Tajiks living in Afghanistan. The Russians are rather awkwardly trying to defend Tajikistan's border (which is also the border of the Commonwealth of Independent States) against attacks by some of the same Muslims who waged the war against the Soviet Army in Afghanistan; those *muja-hedeen* have support and weapons from Iran and other Islamic sources. Yeltsin is trying, without success, to persuade the Tajik government to negotiate a settlement with the rebels. He is trying to persuade other Central Asian governments to offer more help in defending the border. As he does so, Russian casualties are beginning to mount. Twenty-five Russian soldiers died in a battle in July.

Ethnic Conflict in the Former Republics

The Transcaucasus has no fewer than three wars in progress: Armenians against Azerbaijanis for control of Nagorno-Karabakh; Georgians against Ossetians over the latter's desire to break away from Georgia; and Georgians against Abkhazians for the same reason. All three of these conflicts have the potential to involve outsiders. Turkey and Iran are, by blood and tradition, linked to Azerbaijan, which is currently getting the worst of it in the fight against Armenia. Russian Army units, as well as Cossack freelancers from the Don area, have been engaged against the Georgians, not because they support the Muslim Abkhaz but because they loathe Eduard Shevardnadze, the Georgian President. It was on Shevardnadze's watch at the Soviet Foreign Ministry that the empire started to disintegrate.

In the Trans-Dniestr region of Moldova, Russians and Ukrainians, with the open help of the Russian Army, are waging a separatist war; it is still not clear whether the army got involved in this conflict on orders from its putative civilian masters or of its own volition. Russian speakers in Crimea, which Nikita Khrushchev gave to Ukraine in 1954, are talking of separating and once again becoming a part of Russia. All of these conflicts produce refugees. No reliable statistics exist on the number of Russians who have fled the conflict areas and now seek housing and employment in a homeland where both are in desperately short supply. But estimates range from several hundred thousand to several million. And with some 25 million Russians living in the former Soviet republics, the potential refugee problem is enormous and frightening.

The situation in Latvia and Estonia is particularly galling for the Russians. In Riga nowadays, Latvian soldiers, wearing helmets modeled on the ones worn by the Wehrmacht in World War II, guard the Freedom Monument downtown. In front of the monument, during good weather, Latvians gather with placards like the one on display recently: "May God grant that China does to Russia what Russia did to Latvia." Other placards simply demand that the Russians go home. Latvia's Parliament paused one day in March to honor the memory of the day the S.S.'s Latvian legion first engaged the Soviet Army during World War II. And though the winners in June's election publicly took a fairly moderate line on national issues, the events of the past five years suggest that in Latvian politics, today's extremist nationalist position will be tomorrow's consensus. If that trend holds, the result will be a kind of nonviolent ethnic cleansing, designed to push Russian speakers out of the Baltic and back to an ancestral homeland that has neither jobs nor housing for them.

Ethnic Conflict Within Russia

Even more ominous, from the Russian standpoint, the kind of centrifugal forces that brought about the collapse of the Soviet Union are now at work in Russia itself. Various minority nationalities are declaring their autonomy or refusing to accept laws promulgated in Moscow that do not suit their leaders. Chechnia, a small autonomous republic in the Caucasus, has declared its independence. The integrity and survival of Russia itself are by no means guaranteed.

Understandably, Russians want to see their government play a more assertive role in dealing with the former Soviet republics. According to a national survey taken last October, the Russian leader—either Yeltsin or a future rival—who makes nationalism his issue will mine a rich lode of support. Asked whether Russia should play the role of guarantor of peace and stability in the republics of the old U.S.S.R., 65 percent of the respondents said yes, and only 10 percent said no. That question may have been worded poorly—who could be against peace and stability?—but a question asked earlier, in March 1992, found an identical 65 percent saying they regretted the collapse of the Soviet Union. This consensus does not extend to the use of force to settle conflicts in the old Soviet domain. The October poll found only 17 percent of the respondents ready to endorse sending Russian troops abroad to impose peace.

Already, Yeltsin has begun trying to find a policy more in tune with the new Russian nationalism. He has slowed or suspended (the policy seems to change from week to week) troop withdrawals from Latvia and Estonia in a protest over the disfranchisement of Russians living in those republics. In June, he temporarily halted gas shipments to Estonia. Earlier this year, Yeltsin floated the idea of special powers for Russia in the former republics. His exact words, in fact, suggested that he had been reading the polling data from the Russian Center for Public Opinion Research, because he repeated the language used in the poll. "I think the moment has come," Yeltsin said, "when responsible international organizations, including the United Nations, should grant Russia special powers as a guarantor of peace and stability in the region of the former union."

A few weeks later, Andranik Migranyan, a member of President Yeltsin's advisory council, expanded on this theme at a conference in Washington. "We were shortsighted in our early doctrine, thinking that Russia could rely on international organizations like the Conference on Security and Cooperation in Europe to protect Russian interests," Migranyan said. "This is being replaced by a doctrine that the former Soviet Union is a sphere of vital interests for Russia, where Russia will rely on its own economic, political and military strength."

It would be a mistake to exaggerate the import of these statements. Moscow no longer has a messianic, universalist ideology to impel intervention in far-flung areas of the world. Nor does it have the resources or the appetite to play the kind of global role that the Soviet Union aspired to under Stalin, Khrushchev and Brezhnev. But it does have interests in what Russians call "the near abroad," and among those interests are the well-being of ethnic Russians living in the peripheral republics, stability in those republics and the prevention of incursions into the area by other powers, such as Iran, Turkey, China and the West. No great power—and the Russians see themselves as a once-and-future great power—is likely to tolerate for long the kinds of harassing situations Russia has on its borders. Inevitably, pressure will grow in Russia for a foreign policy that addresses them. No democratic leader will be able to ignore it.

Appendix

Excerpts from Original Documents Pertaining to the Collapse of the Soviet Union

Document 1: Arms Control Cooperation Between the Superpowers

In remarks given at the end of the first summit meeting between the leaders of the two superpowers in Geneva, Switzerland, in November 1985, Gorbachev proposes money-saving cuts in military spending while Reagan pressures for democratic change.

Gorbachev's Remarks

The President and I have done a huge amount of work. We've gone into great detail; we've really done it in depth. And we've done it totally openly and frankly.

We've discussed several most important issues. The relations between our two countries and the situations in the world in general today—these are issues and problems the solving of which in the most concrete way is of concern both to our countries and to the peoples of other countries in the world.

We discussed these issues basing our discussions on both sides' determination to improve relations between the Soviet Union and the United States of America. We decided that we must help to decrease the threat of nuclear war. We must not allow the arms race to move off into space, and we must cut it down on earth.

It goes without saying that discussions of these sort we consider to be very useful, and in its results you find a clear reflection of what the two sides have agreed together. We have to be realistic and straightforward, and therefore the solving of the most important problems concerning the arms race and increasing hopes of peace we didn't succeed in reaching at this meeting.

So of course there are important disagreements on matters of principle that remain between us. However, the President and I have agreed that this work of seeking mutually acceptable decisions for these questions will be continued here in Geneva by our representatives. . . .

But the significance of everything which we have agreed with the President can only, of course, be reflected if we carry it on into concrete measures. If we really want to succeed in something, then both sides are going to have to do an awful lot of work in the spirit of the joint commission—of the joint statement which we have put out.

And in this connection, I would like to announce that the Soviet Union, for its part, will do all it can in this cooperation with the United States of America in order to achieve practical results to cut down the arms race, to cut down the arsenals which we've piled up and give—produce the conditions which will be necessary for peace on earth and in space.

We make this announcement perfectly aware of our responsibility both to our own people and to the other peoples of the earth. And we would very much hope that we can have the same approach from the Administration of the United States of America. If that can be so, then the work that has been done in these days in Geneva will not have been done in vain.

Reagan's Remarks

We've packed a lot into the last two days. I came to Geneva to seek a fresh start in relations between the United States and the Soviet Union and we have done this.

General Secretary Gorbachev and I have held comprehensive discussions covering all elements of our relationship. I'm convinced that we are heading in the right direction. We've reached some useful interim results which are described in the joint statement that is being issued this morning. . . .

Before coming to Geneva, I spoke often of the need to build confidence in our dealings with each other. Frank and forthright conversation at the summit are part of this process. But I'm certain General Secretary Gorbachev would agree that real confidence in each other must be built on deeds, not simply words. This is the thought that ties together all the proposals that the United States has put on the table in the past, and this is the criteria by which our meetings will be judged in the future.

The real report card on Geneva will not come in for months or even years. But we know the questions that must be answered.

Will we join together in sharply reducing offensive nuclear arms and moving to nonnuclear defensive strengths for systems to make this a safer world? Will we join together to help bring about a peaceful resolution of conflicts in Asia, Africa and Central America so that the peoples there can freely determine their own destiny without outside interference? Will the cause of liberty be advanced, and will the treaties and agreements signed—past and future—be fulfilled?

The people of America, the Soviet Union and throughout the world are ready to answer yes.

I leave Geneva today and our fireside summit determined to pursue every opportunity to build a safer world of peace and freedom. There's hard work ahead, but we're ready for it. General Secretary Gorbachev, we ask you to join us in getting the job done, as I'm sure you will.

Mikhail Gorbachev and Ronald Reagan, "Comments by 2 Leaders: 'Cooperation' for 'Hard Work Ahead,'" *New York Times*, November 22, 1985.

Document 2: Mikhail Gorbachev's Statement on Chernobyl

The Soviet government's initial statements on the April 26, 1986, accident at the Chernobyl nuclear power plant gave few details about the extent of the disaster. In a May 15, 1986, Soviet television address, Mikhail Gorbachev downplays both the numbers of people killed and injured in the accident and the scores of citizens evacuated from contaminated areas surrounding the facility.

Good evening, Comrades. As you all know, a misfortune has befallen us—the accident at the Chernobyl Nuclear Power Plant. It has painfully affected Soviet people and caused the anxiety of the international public. For the very first time we have encountered in reality such a sinister force as nuclear energy that has escaped control. . . .

As specialists report, the reactor's capacity suddenly increased during a scheduled shut-down of the fourth unit. The considerable emission of steam and subsequent reaction resulted in the formation of hydrogen, its explosion, damage to the reactor and the associated radioactive release.

It is still too early to pass final judgment on the causes of the accident. All aspects of the problem—design, projecting, technical and operational—are under the close scrutiny of the government commission.

It goes without saying that when the investigation of the causes of the accident is completed, all the necessary conclusions will be drawn and measures will be taken to rule out a repetition of anything of the sort.

As I have said already, it is the first time that we have encountered such an emergency, when it was necessary to quickly curb the dangerous force of the atom that had escaped from under control and to keep the scale of the accident to the minimum.

The seriousness of the situation was obvious. It was necessary to evaluate it urgently and competently. And as soon as we received reliable initial information, we made it available to the Soviet people and sent it through diplomatic channels to the governments of foreign countries.

On the basis of this information, practical work was launched to liquidate the accident and to limit its grave aftermath.

In the situation that had taken shape, we considered it a duty of highest priority to us, a duty of special importance, to ensure the safety of the population and to provide effective assistance to those who had been affected by the accident.

The inhabitants of the settlement near the station were evacuated within a matter of hours. Then, when it had become clear that there was a potential threat to the health of people in the adjoining zone, they also were moved to safe areas.

All this complex work required the utmost speed, organization and precision.

Nevertheless the measures that were taken failed to protect many people. Two died at the time of the accident—Vladimir Nikolayevich Shashenok, an adjuster of automatic systems, and Valery Ivanovich Khodemchuk, an operator of the nuclear power plant. As of today 299 people were in the hospital, diagnosed as having radiation disease of varying degrees of gravity. Seven of them have died. Every possible treatment is being given to the rest. The best scientific and medical specialists of the country, from specialized clinics in Moscow and other cities, are taking part in treating them. They have at their disposal the most modern means of medicine.

On behalf of the CPSU Central Committee and the Soviet Government, I express profound condolences to the families and relatives of the deceased, to the work collectives, to all who have suffered from this misfortune, who have suffered personal loss. The Soviet Government will take care of the families of those who died and who suffered.

Mikhail Gorbachev, "The Chernobyl Accident," *Vital Speeches of the Day*, June 15, 1986.

Document 3: The Need for Economic Reform

After two years of calling for increased worker discipline to revive the Soviet economy, Gorbachev began to attempt serious economic reform by holding Party officials accountable for economic performance. In a June 1987 report to the Communist Party Central Committee, titled "On the Party's Tasks in Fundamentally Restructuring Management of the Economy," he outlines his plans.

Let us begin with the development of the national economy. The political bureau had drawn attention in due time to the complexity and responsibility of this year's tasks. It would seem that this was understandable to all. But serious miscalculations were made already in the first months of the year, leading to malfunction in many sectors of the economy. Both the political bureau and the Government had to take urgent measures to righten the situation, and although it is normalizing, considerable losses have been sustained.

But what had happened at the beginning of the year could have been foreseen and prevented. But this was not done, and those primarily responsible for this are the U.S.S.R. State Planning Committee (Comrade N.V. Talyzin) and the U.S.S.R. State Committee for Material and Technical Supply (Comrade L.A. Voronin).

It is a fact that in many places the enthusiasm has flagged, and work is being conducted in an extremely languid manner. Instances of drunkenness have become frequent again. Loafers, spongers, and pilferers—people who live at the expense of others—again feel at ease.

The causes as a rule turn out to be the same: lack of discipline, negligence, mismanagement and irresponsibility. The same is also evidenced by the violation of Soviet airspace by the West German sports plane and its landing in Moscow. This is an unprecedented occurrence from all points of view.

Some ministries treat the manufacture of consumer goods formally as a secondary matter. In some places it is viewed only as a burden.

We cannot put up with the lag in community and consumer services, with an unsatisfactory situation in passenger, transport, communications, tourism, physical training and sport. Can the situation be considered normal when repairs of housing, household appliances, the making of footwear and clothes both in the city and countryside become a great problem.

It is not accidental that a "shadow economy" of sorts has emerged in that sphere. Consider the following figure: Decisions of the Central Statistical Administration report that, according to their estimates, the population annually pays for these services about 1.5 billion rubles to private individuals.

It is essential to change over from predominantly administrative to predominantly economic methods of management at every level, to broad democratization in administration and to activating the human factor in every way.

This changeover involves:

Firstly, a drastic extension of the margins of independence for amalgamations and factories, their conversion to full-scale profit-and-loss accounting and self-financing, increased responsibility for achieving the highest end results, fulfillment of obligations to clients, a direct linkage of the collective's income level to its work performance and extensive use of the team contract in labor relations.

Secondly, radically transforming centralized economic management, raising its qualitative level and focusing it on the main issues determining the strategy, quality, pace and proportion of development of the national economy as a whole and its balance, while at the same time decisively relieving the center of interference in the day-to-day activities of subordinate economic bodies.

Thirdly, a cardinal reform in planning, pricing, financing and crediting, transition to wholesale trade in productive goods and re-organized management of scientific and technological progress, foreign economic activities, labor and social processes.

Fifthly, going over from the excessively centralized command system of management to a democratic one, promoting self-administration, creating a mechanism for activating the individual's potential, clearly delineating the functions and fundamentally changing the style and methods of work, of party, local government and economic bodies.

Mikhail Gorbachev, "Excerpts from Gorbachev's Report on Restructuring the Soviet Economy," *New York Times*, June 26, 1987.

Document 4: *Perestroika*

Mikhail Gorbachev's 1987 publication of Perestroika *was an attempt to explain, primarily to Westerners, his rationale for embarking on his program of reform within the Soviet Union. In the book, Gorbachev frankly analyzes the problems and failures of the Soviet economy. He also calls for an end to the arms race so that the Soviet Union can focus on its economic problems.*

The adoption of fundamental principles for a radical change in economic management was a big step forward in the program of perestroika. Now perestroika concerns virtually every main aspect of public life. Of course, our notions about the contents, methods and forms of perestroika will be developed, clarified and corrected later on. This is inevitable and natural. This is a living process. No doubt, changes will pose new major problems which will require unorthodox solutions. But the overall concept, and the overall plan of perestroika, not only from the point of view of substance, but also of its component parts, are clear to us.

Perestroika means overcoming the stagnation process, breaking down the braking mechanism, creating a dependable and effective mechanism for the acceleration of social and economic progress and giving it greater dynamism.

Perestroika means mass initiative. It is the comprehensive development of democracy, socialist self-government, encouragement of initiative and creative endeavor, improved order and discipline, more glasnost, criticism and self-criticism in all spheres of our society. It is utmost respect for the individual and consideration for personal indignity.

Perestroika is the all-round intensification of the Soviet economy, the revival and development of the principles of democratic centralism in running the national economy, the universal introduction of economic methods, the renunciation of management by injunction and by administrative methods, and the overall encouragement of innovation and socialist enterprise.

Perestroika means a resolute shift to scientific methods, an ability to provide a solid scientific basis for every new initiative. It means the combination of the achievements of the scientific and technological revolution with a planned economy.

Perestroika means priority development of the social sphere aimed at ever better satisfaction of the Soviet people's requirements for good living and working conditions, for good rest and recreation, education and health care. It means unceasing concern for cultural and spiritual wealth, for the culture of every individual and society as a whole.

Perestroika means the elimination from society of the distortions of socialist ethics, the consistent implementation of the principles of social justice. It means the unity of words and deeds, rights and duties. It is the elevation of honest, highly-qualified labor, the overcoming of leveling tendencies in pay and consumerism.

This is how we see perestroika today. This is how we see our tasks, and the substance and content of our work for the forthcoming period. It is difficult now to say how long that period will take. Of course, it will be much more than two or three years. We are ready for serious, strenuous and tedious work to ensure that our country reaches new heights by the end of the twentieth century.

Mikhail Gorbachev, *Perestroika: New Thinking for Our Country and the World*. New York: Harper & Row, 1987.

Document 5: Establishing the Congress of People's Deputies

Throughout the first years of his reform program, Gorbachev encountered resistance from middle-level managers within the Communist Party. To overcome this opposition, in a June 1988 speech to the Communist Party Central Committee he proposes forming a Congress of People's Deputies and a presidency as counterweights to the Party.

The C.P.S.U. Central Committee is submitting the following proposals for consideration by the conference.

First, that representation of the working people in the top echelon of government be extended considerably.

With this end in view, direct representation of the civic organizations incorporated into our political system should be added to the currently existing territorial representation of the entire population on the Soviet Union and the representation of our nations and nationalities on the Soviet of nationalities. Thus 1,500 deputies would be elected, as they are now, from the territorial and national districts, and approximately another 750 deputies would be elected at the congresses or at plenary sessions of the governing bodies of party, trade union, cooperative, youth, women's, veterans', academic, artistic and other organizations. . . .

All these deputies, elected for a five-year term, would comprise a new representative supreme government body—the Congress of the U.S.S.R. People's Deputies. It would be convened annually to decide on the country's more important constitutional, political and socio-economic issues.

The congress of people's deputies would elect from among its members a relatively small (say 400- to 450-strong) bicameral U.S.S.R. Supreme Soviet which would consider and decide all legislative, administrative and monitoring questions and direct the activities of the bodies accountable to it and of the lower-level soviets. It would be a standing supreme government body reporting to the congress of people's deputies. . . .

Second, the work of the chambers of the U.S.S.R. Supreme Soviet should be stepped up and their current functional anonymity ended. . . . At the same time, the Soviet of Nationalities, which represents all of the country's national entities . . . could consider issues of their economic and social development, interethnic relations, observance of relevant legislation, monitoring the activities performed by U.S.S.R. ministries and agencies and affecting the interests of republics or autonomous entities, etc.

Mikhail Gorbachev, "Key Sections of Gorbachev Speech Given to Party Conference," *New York Times*, June 29, 1988.

Document 6: Ethnic Tensions

At the end of his third year of leadership, Gorbachev faced challenges to his authority from the republics. Armenia and Azerbaijan were at war over the enclave of Nagorno-Karabakh, and the Baltic republics (Latvia, Lithuania, and Estonia) were moving toward secession. In a November

27, 1988, speech to the Presidium of the USSR Supreme Soviet, Gorbachev condemns the secessionist declarations of Estonia.

We are discussing today at the meeting of the Presidium of the U.S.S.R. Supreme Soviet the problem that affects the basic interests of our multi-ethnic state.

At first I shall make some general observations. The Communist Party Central Committee and its Politburo continually emphasize that we live in a multi-ethnic state, that the Soviet Union is our common home. When drawing up and putting into practice plans of revolutionary perestroika, we should proceed from the assumption that we cannot count on success if the work for the transformation of society does not take into consideration the interests of all the nations inhabiting our vast country.

Speaking about the new vast opportunities connected with the democratization of the life of Soviet society, we should not disregard the fact that if they are used not very skillfully, to put it mildly, and without a proper degree of responsibility, it is possible to make serious mistakes that would have negative consequences.

Comrades, it would be disastrous, it would put in jeopardy our perestroika. Let us state it point-blank here, at the meeting of the Presidium, and in front of the country. Some people regard the country and the world in general from their individualistic viewpoint. This is unacceptable. We must not permit a situation which would hamper perestroika and would even make some people think that it is, perhaps, perestroika that is to blame for all that.

This conclusion would be a serious mistake. . . .

To begin with, we are all concerned over what took place in Estonia. Working people all over the country are worried over the developments in Azerbaijan and Armenia, and now in some other republics. The working class expresses its anxiety, and it is understandable.

Now we feel the concern of workers over the state of things in our union. We have come across a situation when resolutions of the supreme body of power of one of the republics run counter to the U.S.S.R. Constitution, and not on minor details, but on problems that affect the destiny of the whole of our union. This is why they should be recognized as erroneous and invalid. . . .

Now we should analyze the essence of the matter to get out of this crisis (I shall call things by their proper names) with a feeling of confidence that we are on the right path and that our union will gain in strength within the framework of perestroika.

Take, for instance, the problem of property. The amendments

adopted by the Supreme Soviet of the republic say that Estonia's land, its mineral resources, the atmospheric air, inland and territorial waters, the shelf, forests and other natural resources are its exclusive property. According to the amendments, transport and communication facilities, state banks, trade, communal and other enterprises organized by the state, the available housing of the cities, as well as other facilities needed for the fulfillment of tasks by the republic of Estonia, also belong to it.

This is a principled deviation from the existing Constitution.

There is only one aim, comrades. We are one family, we have a common home, and we have accomplished much thanks to concerted effort. Some people omit that now, or even try to idealize the bourgeois period in the development of the Baltic republics or the past of other regions. But we know how backward Lithuania was, or when the greatest number of people left Estonia because life there was impossible.

Our future is not in weakening ties among the republics, but in strengthening them, in broadening cooperation. And this does not rule out the notion that those areas where people work better should get more.

Mikhail Gorbachev, "Gorbachev's Address: 'We Are One Family,'" *New York Times*, November 28, 1988.

Document 7: Reformers Within the Congress of People's Deputies

Though 1989 elections to the Congress of People's Deputies were rigged to ensure that the Communist Party would hold a majority, a number of reformers, including longtime dissident Andrei Sakharov, managed to win seats. In a June 9, 1989, statement to the congress's charter session, Sakharov warns that the broad powers granted to Mikhail Gorbachev could possibly lead to dictatorship. He calls for abolishing the Communist Party's monopoly on power and for establishing economic autonomy for the republics.

I should first explain why I voted against the Congress's concluding document. It contains many theses that are correct and important, many ideas that are original and progressive, but, in my opinion, the Congress failed to address the key political task facing it, the need to give substance to the slogan "All Power to the Soviets." The Congress refused to consider a Decree on Power, although a host of urgent economic, social, ethnic, and ecological problems cannot be successfully solved until the question of power is decided. The Congress elected a chairman of the USSR Supreme Soviet [Mikhail

Gorbachev] on its very first day, without a broad political discussion and without even a token alternative candidate. In my opinion, the Congress committed a serious blunder that will significantly reduce its ability to influence national policy and that will prove to be a disservice to our chairman-elect as well.

The constitution now in force assigns absolute and virtually unlimited power to the chairman of the USSR Supreme Soviet. The concentration of that much power in the hands of one man is extremely dangerous even if he is the author of perestroika. In particular, it opens the gate to behind-the-scenes influence. And what happens when someone else fills this post? . . .

We are in the throes of spreading economic catastrophe and a tragic worsening of interethnic relations; one aspect of the powerful and dangerous processes at work has been a general crisis of confidence in the nation's leadership. If we simply float with the current, hoping that things will gradually get better in the distant future, then the accumulating tensions could explode, with dire consequences for our society.

Comrade deputies, at this moment in history, an enormous responsibility has fallen to you. Political decisions are needed in order to strengthen the local Soviet organs and resolve our economic, social, ecological, and ethnic problems. If the Congress of People's Deputies cannot take power into its hands, then there is not the slightest hope that the soviets of Union Republics [the USSR is a federation of fifteen Union Republics], regions, districts, and villages will do so. But without strong local soviets, it won't be possible to implement land reform or any agrarian policy other than nonsensical attempts to resuscitate uneconomic collective farms. Without a strong Congress and strong and independent soviets, it won't be possible to overcome the dictates of the bureaucracy, to work out and implement new laws on commercial enterprises, to fight against ecological folly.

The Congress is called upon to defend the democratic principles of popular government and thereby the irreversibility of perestroika and the harmonious development of our country.

Once again I appeal to the Congress to adopt the following Decree on Power:

Proceeding from the principles of popular government, the Congress of People's Deputies proclaims:

Article 6 of the USSR Constitution is repealed. [Article 6 states that the Communist party is "the leading and guiding force of Soviet society and the nucleus of its political system. . . ."]

The adoption of all-Union laws is the exclusive right of the Congress of People's Deputies. All-Union laws enter into force on the territory of a Union Republic after they have been confirmed by the Union Republic's highest legislative body. . . .

Commissions and committees charged with drafting fiscal and other legislation and with responsibility for permanent oversight of state agencies and of the country's economic, social, and ecological situation will be formed by the Congress and the Supreme Soviet on the basis of equal representation and will be responsible to the Congress.

The Congress shall have the exclusive right to elect and recall the top officials of the USSR, i.e., the chairman of the USSR Supreme Soviet [the head of state], the deputy chairman, the chairman of the USSR Council of Ministers [the head of government], the chairman and members of the Committee for Oversight of the Constitution, the chairman of the USSR Supreme Court, the procurator-general, the head of the State Arbitration Board, the chairman of the Central Bank, and also the chairman of the KGB, the chairman of the State Committee on Television and Radio, and the editor in chief of *Izvestia*. The officials named above are accountable to the Congress and not subject to decisions of the Communist party.

Andrei Sakharov, "A Speech to the People's Congress," *New York Review of Books*, August 17, 1989.

Document 8: The Failures of Perestroika

After more than four years of ruling the Soviet Union, Mikhail Gorbachev was forced to admit that his program of perestroika has failed to revive the Soviet economy and that ethnic conflicts are growing out of control. In a September 11, 1989, television address to the nation, he declares that he is facing a backlash against his leadership by conservative forces within the Communist Party.

Good evening, comrades, I am here to talk to you about our current affairs. The situation in the country is not simple. We all know and feel this. Everything has become entangled in a tight knot: scarcity on the consumer goods market, conflicts in ethnic relations, and difficult and sometimes painful processes in the public consciousness, resulting from the overcoming of distortions and from the renewal of socialism. People are trying to understand where we have found ourselves at the moment, evaluating the pluses and minuses of the path we have covered during the last four-plus years, the development of democracy and the pace of the economic and political reforms.

It is only natural that people want to know the real causes of our weaknesses and failures in carrying out specific programs for perestroika and in tackling urgent problems and to find out why the situation in some areas has deteriorated rather than improved. In short, political life today is characterized by intense debate. But the main thing I want to emphasize is that the mass of people have become involved in this movement and they play an ever growing role in discussing and accomplishing social, economic, and political tasks.

Comrades, this is a fact of fundamental importance because it gives perestroika the elements of constructive and businesslike effort and helps overcome people's alienation from power.

Yet one cannot fail to see a different trend. Against the background of heated debate and a rapid succession of events things are happening that must not be ignored or left unaccounted for. Efforts are being made to discredit perestroika from conservative, leftist and sometimes unmistakably anti-socialist positions. One can hear in this discordant choir voices predicting an imminent chaos and speculation about the threat of a coup and even civil war. It is a fact that some people would like to create an atmosphere of anxiety, despair and uncertainty in society.

It is difficult to avoid the impression that someone stands to gain from the fact that certain forces would like to lead people astray and to make them commit ill-conceived actions.

In effect, the conservative forces are trying to impose on us such evaluations of the situation that would provoke resistance to perestroika and mold in people's mind the view that the process of change begun in society should be halted or at least slowed down; these forces demand that the old command methods of government should be restored. Otherwise, they say, chaos will set in. Meanwhile, the leftist elements suggest tackling extremely difficult problems in one go, without taking into account our actual possibilities or the interests of society. Such demands are presented as concern for the people and its well-being.

Recommendations have also been made lately from which one can assume that our only "salvation" is renouncing the values of socialism and conducting perestroika in the capitalist manner. Such views do exist.

Needless to say, such ideas go against the grain of perestroika, which implies socialist renewal of society.

Mikhail Gorbachev, "Perestroika," *Vital Speeches of the Day*, October 15, 1989.

Document 9: State of Emergency in Armenia and Azerbaijan

The hostile situation in Nagorno-Karabakh became an open conflict in early 1990, prompting Gorbachev to declare a state of emergency and send Soviet troops to Azerbaijan. In a January 20, 1990, television address to the USSR, Gorbachev describes the measures he has taken.

Comrades, we all are witnessing a protracted inter-ethnic conflict between Azerbaijan and Armenia. We all are seriously concerned over the fact that the tension that arose there not only fails to subside, but becomes aggravated from time to time, leading to serious consequences every time.

Over the past two years central authorities have sought to act, for their part, patiently and in thoughtful manner, trying to solve difficult problems exclusively by peaceful, political means.

A comradely dialogue, discussions in the Supreme Soviet, the Central Committee of the party, in the Government, through visits by Soviet people's deputies and repeated meetings in Moscow with the leadership of the two republics and with deputies—all have been used, with the sole aim of achieving harmony, and restoring good-neighborly and simply human relations to find a way out of the dead end, and, in the final analysis, to normalize the situation concerning Nagorno-Karabakh.

By acting in this way, we proceeded from the conviction that violence, enmity and continuation of the conflict would not result in anything good but would only poison the atmosphere still further and lead to still greater loss of life and breed more violence. . . .

Neither side listened to the voice of reason conveyed with particular forcefulness from the rostrum of the second Congress of People's Deputies.

The situation was made use of by antisocial, antipopular elements for further stirring up enmity and exacerbation of the conflict. Armed clashes began, particularly in border areas and in places where Armenians and Azerbaijanis lived side by side.

On Jan. 15 this year, the Presidium of the Supreme Soviet had to adopt a decree introducing a state of emergency in the Nagorno-Karabakh Autonomous Region and in some other areas of Azerbaijan and Armenia. . . .

Soviet people demanded from the country's leadership resolute measures to restore law and order, to ensure safety for people.

You already know that the decree of the Presidium of the U.S.S.R. Supreme Soviet has imposed a state of emergency in Baku, that units of the Interior Ministry and the Soviet Army have moved into the city.

They occupied key objects and took under control Government buildings. Resolute measures are taken against ransackers, organizers and instigators of disturbances. Firearms and ammunition are seized from criminal elements.

To our deep regret there are victims. Military units were met by fire from terrorists in some places and had to use weapons in response.

Grief came today into some houses. I convey to these families my most sincere condolences.

The tragic events in Baku, the border areas of Azerbaijan and Armenia, other regions of the Caucasus have laid bare the price of nationalist rampage, speculation on sacred national feelings. It is a crime to push people to blind enmity, to the madness of fratricidal war.

The state is duty-bound to put an end to lawlessness and inhumanity, to resolutely curb criminal actions of extremists, who have lost human face, who are prepared to take other people's lives for the sake of personal ambitions, selfish interests and power.

The state is duty-bound to return peace and security to people and the possibility to develop in a free and democratic way, to work normally, live peacefully, to raise and upbring children to the peoples of the two republics.

Soldiers and officers of the Soviet Army and Interior troops are fulfilling their duty in defending the Soviet Constitution and law.

Mikhail Gorbachev, "Soviet Chief's Address on Azerbaijan Fighting," *New York Times*, January 21, 1990.

Document 10: The Communist Party Relinquishes Its Monopoly on Power

As the Soviet political split between hard-line conservatives and radical reformers widened, the Communist Party of the Soviet Union was forced to legalize the formation of opposition parties. In a platform adopted in February 1990, it abdicates its constitutional monopoly on power.

The party's policy proceeds from the recognition of the sovereign will of the people as the only source of power. The rule-of-law state of the whole people has no room for dictatorship by any class, and even less so for the power of a management bureaucracy. . . .

The electoral system should be brought in line with the principles of universal, equal, direct suffrage. We wish elections to become an honest competition between representatives of all the sections of society, of individuals and ideas submitted to the judgment of voters by the party, public organizations and movements and individual candidates.

The development of society does not preclude the possibility of forming parties. The procedure for their formation will be established by law and reflected in the Constitution of the U.S.S.R.

The formation and activity of organizations and movements that expound violence and interethnic strife and that pursue extremist, unconstitutional aims should be prohibited by law.

The Soviet Communist Party does not claim a monopoly and is prepared for a political dialogue and cooperation with everyone who favors the renewal of socialist society.

The Soviet Communist Party holds that the separation of legislative, executive and judiciary powers is fundamentally important to the Government's efficiency. In Lenin's words, we should combine the advantages of the Soviet system with the advantages of parliamentarism.

"Party's Agenda: Liberty and Justice," *New York Times*, February 14, 1990.

Document 11: Lithuania Secedes from the Soviet Union

The Baltic republics, which were annexed to the Soviet Union during World War II, were the first to seek independence. In response to this March 12, 1990, statement by Lithuania's parliament, Gorbachev imposed an economic blockade on the republic and eventually forced Lithuania's leaders to withdraw the declaration. Gorbachev later dispatched Soviet troops to quell the nationalist movements in the Baltics.

Expressing the will of the people, the Supreme Soviet of the Lithuanian Republic declares and solemnly proclaims the restoration of the exercise of sovereign powers of the Lithuanian state, which were annulled by an alien power in 1940. From now on, Lithuania is once again an independent state.

The Feb. 16, 1918, Act of Independence of the Supreme Council of Lithuania and the May 15, 1920, Constituent Assembly Resolution on the restoration of a democratic Lithuanian state have never lost their legal force and are the constitutional foundation of the Lithuanian state.

The territory of Lithuania is integral and indivisible, and the constitution of any other state has no jurisdiction within it.

The Lithuanian state emphasizes its adherence to universally recognized principles of international law, recognizes the principles of the inviolability of borders as formulated in Helsinki in 1975 in the Final Act of the Conference on Security and Cooperation in Europe, and guarantees rights of individuals, citizens and ethnic communities.

The Supreme Council of the Republic of Lithuania, expressing sovereign power, by this act begins to achieve the state's full sovereignty.

"Lithuania's Declaration," *New York Times*, March 13, 1990.

Document 12: Gorbachev Shies Away from Radical Reform

Maneuvering between conservative hard-line Communists on one side and radical economic and political reformers and republican nationalists on the other, Gorbachev abandoned plans for a rapid change to a market economy in the Soviet Union. In this October 19, 1990, speech to the USSR Supreme Soviet, Gorbachev introduces a conservative plan for limited economic reform.

You have received the 'Main Directions in Stabilization of the National Economy and the Transition to a Market Economy.'. . .

I would like to spell out why we declined a detailed elaboration of the program, and presented only guidelines. . . . It is better to formulate the general principles and create conditions for broad initiative in the republics and localities in considering their specifics. Where federal leadership is required—monetary, fiscal, credit, currency policy, basic social guarantees for citizens, structural policy, reorganization of administration at the union level—the line must be simple, exact and clear. . . .

To establish a full-blooded market mechanism, we will need a number of years. The document solves the most difficult task of stabilizing the economy and creating the main instruments of the market. . . . The most important thing is in one and one half to two years, maximum, to radically improve the state of finances, stabilize the monetary system and to strengthen the ruble, and on this basis to provide control over inflation, control over the liberation of prices, over the creation of conditions for economic incentives, activating the mechanisms of market self-regulation.

We lost control over the financial situation in the country. This was our most serious mistake in the years of perestroika. The crisis of the consumer market cannot be eliminated until the machines that produce shoes, fabrics and other goods begin working faster than the mint. Achieving a balanced budget today is the No. 1 task, and the most important one. . . . Enterprises in all industries will be put under strict financial conditions. They will have to abandon the thought that the budget or the bank will always come to help them in the end, and that they can count on free credit. . . . But we have to be realistic. This problem cannot be solved in a few months. So in the nearest future, in order to not allow a drastic drop in production, we will have to maintain economic ties by administrative methods.

In the transition period, the state will do everything possible to restrain the growth of retail prices on essential goods. There will be fixed state prices on a number of essential goods. When prices change, pensions, stipends, scholarships, fixed incomes, including doctors, teachers, military servicemen, workers at state offices will be indexed. That is, they will grow along with the growth of prices on goods in the consumer basket.

Mikhail Gorbachev, "Excerpts from Gorbachev's Speech on His Plan for a Market Economy," *New York Times*, October 20, 1990.

Document 13: The Danger of Dictatorship

Soviet foreign minister Eduard Shevardnadze, a longtime friend and associate of Mikhail Gorbachev, was one of the architects of perestroika. When Gorbachev appointed hard-line Communists to positions of power in 1990, Shevardnadze sided with democratic reformers. In this December 20, 1990, speech to the Congress of People's Deputies, he resigns his position as foreign minister and warns the country that Gorbachev is moving toward dictatorship.

Democrats, I'll put it bluntly: Comrade democrats! In the widest meaning of this word: you have scattered. The reformers have gone into hiding. A dictatorship is approaching—I tell you that with full responsibility. No one knows what this dictatorship will be like, what kind of dictator will come to power and what order will be established.

I want to make the following statement. I am resigning. Let this be—and do not react and do not curse me—let this be my contribution, if you like, my protest against the onset of dictatorship.

I would like to express sincere gratitude to Mikhail Sergeyevich Gorbachev. I am his friend. I am a fellow thinker of his. I have always supported, and will support to the end of my days, the ideas of perestroika, the ideas of renewal, the ideas of democracy, of democratization.

We did great work in international affairs. But I think that it is my duty. As a man, as a citizen, as a Communist I cannot reconcile myself with what is happening in my country and to the trials which await our people.

I nevertheless believe that the dictatorship will not succeed, that the future belongs to democracy and freedom.

Eduard Shevardnadze, "The Onset of Dictatorship," *Vital Speeches of the Day*, January 15, 1991.

Document 14: A Treaty to Reform the Union

In a last-ditch effort to prevent the complete disintegration of the Soviet Union, Mikhail Gorbachev cajoled nine republics to endorse a treaty establishing wide-ranging autonomy for the republics but preserving a weakened federal government. The other six republics had already declared their intentions to secede. In an August 6, 1991, television address to the USSR, he outlines the treaty, which is slated to be signed on August 20.

My address to you today deals with an important event in our country's life. As you know, intensive work has been under way lately on the draft of a new union treaty. Today I have sent letters to the heads of the delegations authorized by the republics' supreme soviets, proposing to begin the signing of the treaty on August 20 this year. . . .

Thus, we are entering a decisive stage in the transformation of our multiethnic state into a democratic federation of equitable Soviet sovereign republics. What does the conclusion of the new union treaty mean for the country's life? First and foremost, it is a manifestation of the people's will, expressed at the March 17 referendum. The treaty envisages the transformation of the union on the basis of continuity and renewal.

Union statehood, the result of the work of many generations and of all the nations of our motherland, will be preserved. At the same time, a new, truly voluntary, association of sovereign states is being created. In this association all nations will manage their affairs on their own and will freely develop their culture, language, and traditions.

This is the essence of the reform of our state system. On the one hand, the independence of the republics is effectively guaranteed. On the other hand, tackling common tasks, which they voluntarily delegate to the federal authorities, to the union, is guaranteed in an equally effective way. Resolving these problems required tremendous effort and a deep feeling of responsibility. The republican and federal parliaments, governments, and public and scientific organizations have worked hard. Numerous proposals of citizens were also analyzed. . . .

In the common interest, the republics delegate to union bodies such important functions as ensuring the country's defense and security. United armed forces and the integrity of security bodies are preserved for that purpose. The coordination of law-enforcement bodies makes it possible to protect citizens' interests and to combat crime.

The solution of many important problems will be ensured

254 The Collapse of the Soviet Union

jointly by the union and the republics. The treaty contains provisions on whose basis mechanisms of coordination will operate. When the treaty goes into effect, there will be major changes in the conditions of economic development. It is extremely important that the separation of powers between the union and the republics that is recorded in the treaty envisages the preservation and all-around development of a full-fledged all-union market, with a single currency, financial and crediting system, customs rules, and coordinated principles of social protection. Enterprises have broad opportunities to tap advantages stemming from the economic reform.

It's hard to imagine how economic independence can be achieved if such a market, if the chief players of the market—enterprises and work collectives—are limited in their possibilities.

It is important to preserve old economic ties. Their rupture has a negative impact on the affairs of work collectives.

At the same time, there is a need to form new ties suggested by the present situation.

There is wide room for interaction among republics and regions within the framework of the common economic space. We know now what the rupture of economic ties means and what barriers on borders between republics and separate regions entail.

This ailment, by the way, has not disappeared; it persists. That is why we need a common, full-fledged market. All peoples, republics, and enterprises need it.

Mikhail Gorbachev, "The New Union Treaty," *Vital Speeches of the Day*, September 1, 1991.

Document 15: The State of Emergency

In this August 19, 1991, declaration, the State Committee for the State of Emergency, made up of hard-line Communists who were high-ranking members of Gorbachev's government, announces the imposition of marshal law and the restoration of centralized control over the collapsing union. The abortive coup failed merely three days later.

At the instruction of the Soviet leadership I hereby notify you that a state of emergency is introduced in individual localities of the Union of Soviet Socialist Republics for a period of six months from August 19, 1991, in keeping with the Constitution and laws of the U.S.S.R.

All power in the country is transferred for this period to the State Committee for the State of Emergency in the U.S.S.R.

The measures that are being adopted are temporary. They in no way mean renunciation of the course toward profound reforms in all spheres of life of the state and society.

These are forced measures, dictated by the vital need to save the economy from ruin and the country from hunger, to prevent the escalation of the threat of a large-scale civil conflict with unpredictable consequences for the peoples of the U.S.S.R. and the entire international community.

The most important objective of the state of emergency is to secure conditions that would guarantee each citizen's personal safety and the safety of his or her property.

It is envisaged to liquidate anticonstitutional, ungovernable, and essentially criminal military formations spreading moral and physical terror in several regions of the U.S.S.R. and serving as a catalyst for disintegration processes.

The entire range of measures adopted is directed at the earliest stabilization of the situation in the U.S.S.R., the normalization of social and economic life, the implementation of necessary transformations, and the creation of conditions for the country's allround development.

Any other way would lead to enhanced confrontation and violence, to the innumerable suffering of our peoples and the creation of a dangerous focus of tension from the viewpoint of international security.

The temporary emergency measures by no means affect international commitments assumed by the Soviet Union under existing treaties and agreements.

The U.S.S.R. is prepared to develop further its relations with all states on the basis of universally recognized principles of goodneighborliness, equality, mutual benefit, and noninterference in internal affairs of each other.

We are convinced that our current difficulties are transitory in character and the Soviet Union's contribution to preserving peace and consolidating international security will remain substantial.

The leadership of the U.S.S.R. hopes that the temporary emergency measures will find proper understanding on the part of the peoples and governments, and the United Nations Organization.

Gennadi Yanayev, "A State of Emergency," *Vital Speeches of the Day*, September 15, 1991.

Document 16: Yeltsin's Defiance of the Coup

As coup leaders ordered troops onto the streets of Moscow, Boris Yeltsin and other officials of the newly elected Russian government barricaded themselves in the Russian parliament building. Standing atop a tank,

Yeltsin delivered this August 19, 1991, speech denouncing the coup as un-constitutional and entreating Russians to resist it.

Citizens of Russia: On the night of 18–19 August 1991, the legally elected President of the country was removed from power.

Regardless of the reasons given for his removal, we are dealing with a rightist, reactionary, anti-constitutional coup. Despite all the difficulties and severe trials being experienced by the people, the democratic process in the country is acquiring an increasingly broad sweep and an irreversible character.

The peoples of Russia are becoming masters of their destiny. The uncontrolled powers of unconstitutional organs have been considerably limited, and this includes party organs.

The leadership of Russia has adopted a resolute position toward the union treaty striving for the unity of the Soviet Union and unity of Russia. Our position on this issue permitted a considerable acceleration of the preparation of this treaty, to coordinate it with all the republics and to determine the date of signing as Aug. 20. Tomorrow's signing has been cancelled.

These developments gave rise to angry reactionary forces, pushed them to irresponsible and adventurist attempts to solve the most complicated political and economic problems by methods of force. Attempts to realize a coup have been tried earlier.

We considered and consider that such methods of force are unacceptable. They discredit the union in the eyes of the whole world, undermine our prestige in the world community, and return us to the cold-war era along with the Soviet Union's isolation in the world community. All of this forces us to proclaim that the so-called committee's ascendancy to power is unlawful.

Accordingly we proclaim all decisions and instructions of this committee to be unlawful.

We are confident that the organs of local power will unswervingly adhere to constitutional laws and decrees of the President of Russia.

We appeal to citizens of Russia to give a fitting rebuff to the putschists and demand a return of the country to normal constitutional development.

Undoubtedly it is essential to give the country's President, Gorbachev, an opportunity to address the people. Today he has been blockaded. I have been denied communications with him. We demand an immediate convocation of an extraordinary Congress of People's Deputies of the Union. We are absolutely confident that our countrymen will not permit the sanctioning of the tyranny and lawlessness of the putschists, who have lost all shame and conscience. We address an appeal to servicemen to manifest lofty civic duty and not take part in the reactionary coup.

Until these demands are met, we appeal for a universal unlimited strike.

Boris Yeltsin, "Yeltsin's Remarks: A 'Reactionary Coup,'" *New York Times*, August 20, 1991.

Document 17: Sovereignty for Russia

In the power vacuum that existed in the wake of the failed coup, Boris Yeltsin declared political and economic independence for Russia. In a series of presidential decrees delivered to the Russian parliament on August 21, 1991, he asserted Russian sovereignty over Soviet property and troops and outlawed the Communist Party of Russia.

This is a bold-faced and unprecedented coup d'etat in a situation where democracy is on the rise, and you see that the people taking part in the coup are on the right. They couldn't find at least a few people, so-called quasi democrats, to join them, although they did attempt to find such people, but the people they approached refused to cooperate with them.

They refused to take part in this unconstitutional plot. Now this is what we have done. . . .

Decree No. 59 proclaimed that the committee was unconstitutional. We have set up Russia's Committee for Defense. We have published a decree stating that the troops of the K.G.B. and the Ministry of the Interior, as well as the army, are placed under the jurisdiction of the President of the Russian Federation, in the absence of the Commander in Chief of the armed forces, and taking into account the fact that the Minister of Defense is a criminal, that meant that we have to assume the responsibility for the armed forces on the territory of the Russian Federation. . . .

As regards the actions of Yanayev, Pavlov, and others, there was a decree on the armed forces. The President of the Russian Federation has assumed the authority over the armed forces. The Tulskaya and the Kantinuyevskaya Divisions, airborne troops, have gone over to the side of the Russian Federation, and they are acting on orders of the President of the Russian Federation.

What are the reasons for the failure of the attempts to intern the leadership of the Russian Federation? The President, the chairman of the Council of Ministers, and the acting chairman of the Supreme Soviet of the Russian Federation. The reasons for that are that the Tulskaya Division, instead of seizing the building of the Russian Federation Parliament, protected the building of the Russian Parliament from attack.

We are grateful to the men of the division and General Lebedev, although he is obviously under stress, but by a decree of the President of the Russian Federation, I have assumed the responsibility for that, and I have assumed the responsibility for any actions taken by the law enforcement agencies and the troops acting on my orders.

I have also signed a decree on the operation of enterprises on the territory of the Russian Federation, a decree on the economic sovereignty of the Russian Federation. Let me elaborate on this.

Taking into account that the union treaty was to be signed on the 20th, we had an agreement with the President of the union, that on the 21st and the 22d we would sign a decree transferring the property and the enterprises on the territory of the Russian Federation to the jurisdiction of the Russian Federation. We wanted to place those enterprises under the jurisdiction of the Russian Federation.

But now that the union treaty was not signed yesterday, because of the actions taken by the unconstitutional group of rebels, and since the President is virtually incommunicado, I have signed a decree providing for the economic sovereignty of the Russian Federation, stating that all property on the territory of the Russian Federation is placed under the jurisdiction of the Russian Federation.

Boris Yeltsin, "A Bold-Faced and Unprecedented Coup d'Etat," *Vital Speeches of the Day*, September 15, 1991.

Document 18: Gorbachev's Resignation as General Secretary

Noting the lack of opposition to the coup among Communist Party members, on August 24, 1991, Gorbachev issued this statement resigning his position as general secretary of the Party, though he remained president of the disintegrating Soviet Union. His stature and authority diminished, Gorbachev was forced to acquiesce to a number of Boris Yeltsin's presidential decrees.

The Secretariat and Politburo of the Central Committee of the Communist Party of the Soviet Union did not come out against the coup d'état.

The C.C. did not manage to take a firm position of condemnation and opposition and did not call on Communists to fight the trampling of constitutional law. Among the conspirators were members of the party leadership. A number of party committees and the mass media supported the actions of the state criminals. This put millions of Communists in a false position. Many members of the party refused to collaborate with the conspirators, condemned the coup and joined the fight against it.

No one has the right to blame wholesale all Communists, and I as President consider it my duty to defend them as citizens from unfounded accusations. In this situation, the C.C. of the C.P.S.U. must make the difficult but honest decision to disband itself.

The fate of republican Communist Parties and local party organizations should be decided by themselves. I consider it no longer possible to continue to carry out my duties as General Secretary of the Central Committee of the Soviet Union and I relinquish corresponding authority.

I believe that democratically minded Communists, who remained faithful to constitutional law and to the course of the renewal of society, will speak up for the creation of a new basis of a party capable, together with all progressive forces, of actively joining in the continuation of fundamental democratic reforms for the sake of working people.

Mikhail Gorbachev, "Gorbachev's Statement on Party," *New York Times*, August 25, 1991.

Document 19: Declarations of Independence: Russia, Ukraine, and Byelorussia

As Mikhail Gorbachev continued to implore the republics to sign the draft union treaty and preserve the remnants of the Soviet Union, the republics resolutely insisted on independence. In December 1991, the leaders of Russia, Ukraine, and Byelorussia (renamed Belarus) separately negotiated an arrangement to form a Commonwealth of Independent States and invited other former Soviet republics to join. On December 9, they issued these declarations of independence.

Preamble

We, the republic of Byelorussia, the Russian Federation and the Ukraine . . . state that the U.S.S.R., as a subject of international law and a geopolitical reality, is ceasing its existence.

With the aim of developing equal and mutually beneficial cooperation of the peoples and states, it has been decided to conclude special agreements in the spheres of politics, the economy, culture, education, public health, science, trade, the environment and other fields.

The members of the community . . . will strive for elimination of nuclear weapons and for total disarmament under international control. At the same time, the sides will respect each other's desire to achieve the status of nuclear-free zone and neutral state. It has been decided to preserve unified command of a common military-strategic space and united control over nuclear weapons.

From the moment of the conclusion of the agreement, the application of the norms of third countries, including the former U.S.S.R., on the territory of the states which have signed it, is not permitted, and the activity of bodies of the former union ceases.

STANISLAV SHUSHKEVICH AND VYACHESLAV KEBICH,
Republic of Byelorussia

BORIS YELTSIN AND GENNADI BURBULIS,
Russian Federated Republic

LEONID KRAVCHUK AND VITOLD FOKIN,
Ukraine

Political Pact

We, the heads of state of Byelorussia, Russia and Ukraine:

NOTING that talks on the preparation of a new union treaty have reached a dead end and the process of the secession of republics from the U.S.S.R. and forming the independent states has come to reality;

STATING that the shortsighted policy of the center has led to a deep political and economic crisis, to disintegration of the economy and catastrophic decline of the living conditions of practically all the sectors of the population;

TAKING into account growing social tension in many regions of the former U.S.S.R., which have led to ethnic conflicts and resulted in numerous victims;

ACKNOWLEDGING the responsibility before our people and the world community and the growing necessity of practical implementation of political and economic reforms;

HEREBY declare the formation of a Commonwealth of Independent States, about which the parties signed an agreement on Dec. 8, 1991.

STANISLAV SHUSHKEVICH,
Chairman of Parliament,
Byelorussia

BORIS YELTSIN,
President, Russian Federation

LEONID KRAVCHUK
President, Ukraine

Appendix 261

Economic Pact

Preservation and development of the existing close economic ties between our states is vitally necessary for stabilizing the situation in the national economy and creating the foundations for economic revival.

The parties have agreed to the following:

To carry out coordinated radical economic reforms aimed at creating feasible market mechanisms, transformation of property and ensuring the freedom of entrepreneurship;

To abstain from any actions economically harmful to each other;

To develop economic relations and mutual accounts on the basis of the existing currency unit—the ruble. To introduce national currencies on the basis of special agreements which will guarantee the preservation of the economic interests of the parties;

To sign an interbank agreement aimed at curbing monetary emission, providing for the effective control over money supply and forming a system of mutual accounts;

To conduct coordinated policy of reducing the republics' budget deficits;

To conduct coordinated policy of price liberalization and social protection;

To undertake joint efforts aimed at providing for a single economic space.

VYACHESLAV KEBICH,
Prime Minister, Byelorussia

GENNADI BURBULIS
Secretary of State, Russia

VITOLD FOKIN
Prime Minister, Ukraine

"Texts of Declarations by 3 Republic Leaders," *New York Times*, December 9, 1991.

Document 20: America's Reaction to the Collapse

As the Soviet Union disintegrated, the United States joined the rest of the world in extending official diplomatic recognition to the newly independent former republics. In this December 1991 speech, Secretary of State James A. Baker voices concern about control over the former superpower's vast arsenal of nuclear weapons.

Whatever the original intentions of perestroika and glasnost, by early August of this year, the all-powerful Stalinist state was well on its way to dissolution. A new civil society was breaking out across the Soviet Union. Democracy was replacing communism; power was moving from the center to the republics; and the old centrally-planned economy was in the throes of collapse. . . .

The dramatic collapse of communism in Moscow and the unraveling of the centralized Soviet state confront the West with great opportunities as well as ominous dangers. Popularly-elected leaders now run large and strategically-important republics, including Russia, Ukraine, and Kazakhstan. They look to America and the West for guidance and help in launching genuine, far-reaching political and economic reform. If they can succeed, the centuries-old menace posed to the West, first by czarist autocracy and then by Soviet totalitarianism, will have been permanently altered.

The opportunities are historic:

• We have the chance to anchor Russia, Ukraine, and other republics firmly in the Euro-Atlantic community and democratic commonwealth of nations.

• We have the chance to bring democracy to lands that have little knowledge of it, an achievement that can transcend centuries of history.

• We have the chance to help harness the rich human and material resources of those vast lands to the cause of freedom instead of totalitarianism, thereby immeasurably enhancing the security, prosperity, and freedom of America and the world.

Yet the dangers are equal in scale to the opportunities:

• *Economically*, the old Soviet system has collapsed, multiplying every day the threats these reformers face—from social dislocation to political fragmentation to ethnic violence. Reconstructing economies that have been devastated by central planning is even more difficult than reconstructing from the devastation of war.

• *Politically*, the dangers of protracted anarchy and chaos are obvious. Great empires rarely go quietly into extinction. No one can dismiss the possibility that darker political forces lurk in the wings, representing the remnants of Stalinism or the birth of nationalist extremism or even fascism, ready to exploit the frustrations of a proud but exhausted people in their hour of despair.

• *Strategically*, both of these alternatives—anarchy or reaction—could become threats to the West's vital interests when they shake a land that is still home to nearly 30,000 nuclear weapons and the most powerful arsenal of conventional weaponry ever amassed in Europe.

Taken together, these dangers serve as a call to action for America and the West. This historic watershed—the collapse of communist power in Bolshevism's birthplace—marks the challenge history has dealt us: to see the end of the Soviet Empire turned into a beginning for democracy and economic freedom in Russia and Ukraine, in Kazakhstan and Belarus, in Armenia, Kyrgyzstan, and elsewhere across the former Soviet Empire.

James A. Baker, "America and the Collapse of the Soviet Empire: What Has to Be Done," *Vital Speeches of the Day*, January 1, 1992.

Document 21: Gorbachev's Resignation as President of the Union

Rebuffed in his efforts to revive the union treaty and preserve the Soviet Union, Mikhail Gorbachev resigned as president in a speech on Russian television on December 25, 1991. The following day, the Soviet Union formally ceased to exist.

Dear fellow countrymen, compatriots. Due to the situation which has evolved as a result of the formation of the Commonwealth of Independent States, I hereby discontinue my activities at the post of President of the Union of Soviet Socialist Republics.

I am making this decision on considerations of principle. I firmly came out in favor of the independence of nations and sovereignty for the republics. At the same time, I support the preservation of the union state and the integrity of this country.

The developments took a different course. The policy prevailed of dismembering this country and disuniting the state, which is something I cannot subscribe to. . . .

This being my last opportunity to address you as President of the U.S.S.R., I find it necessary to inform you of what I think of the road that has been trodden by us since 1985.

I find it important because there have been a lot of controversial, superficial, and unbiased judgments made on this score. Destiny so ruled that when I found myself at the helm of this state it already was clear that something was wrong in this country.

We had a lot of everything—land, oil and gas, other natural resources—and there was intellect and talent in abundance. However, we were living much worse than people in the industrialized countries were living and we were increasingly lagging behind them. The reasons were obvious even then. This country was suffocating in the shackles of the bureaucratic command system. Doomed to cater to ideology, and suffer and carry the onerous burden of the arms race, it found itself at the breaking point.

All the half-hearted reforms—and there have been a lot of

them—fell through, one after another. This country was going nowhere and we couldn't possibly live the way we did. We had to change everything radically.

It is for this reason that I have never had any regrets—never had any regrets—that I did not use the capacity of General Secretary just to reign in this country for several years. I would have considered it an irresponsible and immoral decision. I was also aware that to embark on reform of this caliber and in a society like ours was an extremely difficult and even risky undertaking. But even now, I am convinced that the democratic reform that we launched in the spring of 1985 was historically correct.

Mikhail Gorbachev, "Resignation of President Mikhail S. Gorbachev," *Vital Speeches of the Day*, January 15, 1992.

Document 22: The Rise of Russian Nationalism

The renewal of political pluralism in Russia brought the rise of far right Russian nationalists such as Pamyat *leader Vladimir Zhirinovsky. A few far right wing Russian nationalists blamed the United States and a Zionist conspiracy for the collapse of the Soviet Union.*

TIME: Do you see America as a permanent enemy of Russia?

ZHIRINOVSKY: I wouldn't say that America is an enemy in the literal sense of the word. There are no straightforward military actions. [But] a secret war has been going on for 50 years now. . . . If your aim was to bring Russia to collapse, [perestroika] was perfectly executed because you could have done nothing better to destroy Russia.

TIME: Why did the Russian ruble drop so dramatically in value last month?

ZHIRINOVSKY: This was the beginning of a scenario. As a result of the financial debacle, Prime Minister Vladimir Chernomyrdin was to resign and Vladimir Shumeiko (Chairman of the upper house of the Russian parliament), who has better relations with certain circles in the West, was to come to power. The next step was to launch an attack against the Army and provoke unrest. The final stage was supposed to be the establishment of a liberal dictatorship next spring.

TIME: Who was directing this scenario?

ZHIRINOVSKY: According to our information, the CIA and Mossad were involved. They want to keep Russia the way it is today, because this is good for the West. . . .

TIME: You speak a lot about the Americans and Zionists. Do you equate America with Zionism?

ZHIRINOVSKY: They are separate forces but they join together, because America gives strong support to Israel and within America itself, the influence of the Jews is very strong. It's well known that finance and the press in America—and also in Western Europe and Russia—are controlled by Jews.

TIME: Why is that harmful for Russia?

ZHIRINOVSKY: The very difficult economic situation in Russia was the result of activities by these forces. There is no such thing as a poor Jew in Russia . . . while the poorest people in Russia are the Russians.

TIME: You have been quoted as saying that the Jewish people caused a lot of trouble for Russia. What do you mean?

ZHIRINOVSKY: This is nothing original to me. I am just passing on propaganda. [But] the fact is that a majority of people who made the [Bolshevik] Revolution possible, as well as perestroika, were of Jewish origin. In fact, the first Soviet government was almost 90% Jewish. Those who first ran the Gulag prison camps were mostly Jewish, although they were later wiped out by Stalin, because they were Jews. . . .

TIME: It's impossible to listen to you without hearing continual allegations of a Jewish conspiracy.

ZHIRINOVSKY: If we were talking about historical events dated some 50 years ago, I would have my doubts. But this is what is happening in Moscow before my very own eyes. You are far away and have a different civilization. It was always difficult for an outsider to understand what is going on in Russia in the right way.

Reprinted from "Plots, Plots, and More Plots," an interview of Vladimir Zhirinovsky by John Kohan, *Time*, November 21, 1994, p. 83, by permission; © 1994 Time Inc.

Document 23: Democratic Reform in Leningrad

In May 1990, in free elections throughout Russia, Leningrad citizens elected democratic reformer Anatoly Sobchak mayor. He joined Boris Yeltsin in implementing radical economic reforms in Russia.

Q: As the new mayor of Leningrad and one of the leading reformers in the Soviet Union today, you have become a symbol of the struggle to change the ossified Soviet system from below. What are the main obstacles you are facing in your efforts to bring about political democracy and a market economy?

A: Though this may sound odd, the greatest obstacle is not opposition from the Communist Party or the hostile bureaucracy but problems within the democratic forces—their general weakness, their inability to unite behind a common platform and their lack of experience. Perhaps the main problem is the absence of organized democratic parties, which leads to a situation in which every deputy speaks on his own behalf.

This is the case also in Leningrad, despite the fact that we have the most democratic City Council in the country and tremendous support from the population. A recent poll showed that only 2.5% of Leningrad's population has any confidence left in the Communist Party, which is less than the number of party members in the city. . . .

Q: There are many in the West who believe that the economic achievements of perestroika have been negligible. Some blame Gorbachev's indecisiveness, perhaps caused by his need to maneuver constantly between the conservatives and the radicals. Yet Gorbachev has now accepted Yeltsin's blueprint for radical economic reform, known as "500 days." Does this mean that the president has finally cast his lot with the radicals?

A: I think that Gorbachev, as a politician, is a realist and will act as the circumstances demand. He now realizes that the economic plans of Ryzhkov and [Leonid I.] Abalkin are not realistic and have been rejected by the people and life itself.

Q: But why has it taken him so long to realize that?

A: It seems to me that he hoped to change the system with the help of the party, and thus assure its staying in power. This is, of course, an illusion, but he did entertain such hopes.

Q: Wouldn't Gorbachev's support for Yeltsin be seen by the conservatives as final proof of his betrayal of socialism and therefore reason to mobilize against the president?

A: Many have believed for a long time that Gorbachev has betrayed socialism, but others still trust him. Gorbachev has been the most important guarantee against a military takeover, though this danger is receding with each passing day. He has also made sure not to alienate important segments of the political spectrum. . . . For instance, the Presidential Council is a representative body on which all the different political opinions are represented and can make their views heard. As an advisory organ, it is not very effective, since Gorbachev is smarter and more knowledgeable than any of his so-called advisers.

Alex Alexiev, "Anatoly Sobchak: Turning Leningrad into a Reform Beacon by the Sea," *Los Angeles Times*, September 9, 1990, p. M3.

Document 24: The Failure of Perestroika

Alexander Yakovlev was a close associate of Mikhail Gorbachev's and an architect of perestroika. The failure of the reform program left the republics reeling.

I always came out for independence of republics and states, and that got me into trouble not just once. I was attacked at [Communist Party] plenums, in the press, and in the Parliament. But my vision of this process was rather different. Whatever form—union, commonwealth or confederation, I was never particular about the terms—I stood for confederation from the beginning. . . . But what is happening now worries me. There is no mechanism cementing this commonwealth. If the economic union or economic community worked on the basis of market economy, it would hold.

Now [we are in] a stage of market economy that is, in fact, not market economy. Independent states freed themselves from the big center only to establish their own economic centers. . . .

Secondly, what worries me about the dissolution is that, Phoenix-like from ashes, old nationalist-communist, Bolshevik regimes start to come to life. There is even [the danger of] dictatorships. It worries me a lot. The West should be watching it very closely.

Q: Where are these Bolshevik, ultranationalist, communist regimes emerging?

A: In Georgia, for example. It is a downright dictatorship—and with racist sentiments, too. There are similar problems in some of the Central Asian republics and elsewhere in the Caucasus. And I am worried very much with the developments in Ukraine. Even in the Baltics, for which I had such serious hopes, legislative acts are adopted that result in the appearance of second-class citizens. For example, yesterday I wrote a personal letter to Latvian Supreme Soviet Chairman Anatoly Gorbunovs to protest against the law on citizenship that provides for virtually dividing citizens into two parts—genuine citizens and non-genuine, second-class citizens. . . .

Q: How do you assess the situation inside Russia? What are the tasks that face Boris Yeltsin and his government?

A: This is the most difficult question.

Firstly, the Russian government is now getting into a very complicated position. If the criticism was divided into two streams before—that directed at the central government and the country's president, Mikhail Gorbachev, and that aimed at Yeltsin, now it is going to take one direction. All the responsibility, all the criticism, will fall on [Yeltsin's] shoulders.

On the whole, I support his economic reforms or, to be more precise, his direction of economic reforms. But I believe not everything is thought out, especially the intention to introduce the so-called free prices. It seems to me that "free prices" cannot be freed without a demonopolized economy. Secondly, prices can be freed only if retail and wholesale trade have been privatized. Thirdly, I believe that when prices are hiked, the market should be flooded not only with manufactured goods . . . but also the means of production—land and housing—so that money can spread through all the markets, from foodstuffs and consumer goods to land and the means of production—everything.

Michael Parks, "Alexander Yakovlev: The Father of Perestroika Surveys Wreckage of Soviet Empire," *Los Angeles Times*, December 29, 1991, p. M3.

Document 25: Ukraine Withdraws Support for the Draft Union Treaty

By mid-1991, Ukraine was evaluating the possibility and consequences of secession from the Soviet Union. Ukraine's refusal to consider Gorbachev's Draft Union Treaty undermined all support for the plan.

Q: What did you stress in your visits with U.S. government officials?

A: In my meetings, I was regrettably surprised that the West, primarily the U.S. government, still hasn't grasped the fact that the Soviet empire is crumbling, and the reasons for this are political, as well as economic. The political ideology on which the empire is based, otherwise defined as communist ideology, is a system of socialist management that has absolutely discredited itself. . . .

Even the military attempts to crush the national spirit of sovereignty in the Baltics and Georgia, to name a few, have not been successful. Controlling the Soviet Union, such a mass territory, from one central point is impossible.

What [U.S. legislators] need to understand is that history cannot be stopped from moving forward. Despite their fears and reservations, the disintegration of the Soviet Union is inevitable. Perhaps it's not a pleasant way to put it, but the failure of our economy and the overall impoverishment in the Soviet Union is propelling democracy and the development of a free-market system.

Q: Until recently, many publications urged policy-makers to support Gorbachev and the union due to fears of economic and military instability. Now, opinion seems to be changing. What are the economic aspects of these arguments?

A: None of these arguments are new to me, and none present justifiable reasons for countries in the West to fear disintegration. If the goal is to maintain a centralized economy, one planned from above or one which is socialistic, then the union is necessary. But if we're talking about a market economy, then what need is there for a union of republics?

People frequently say the republics, if independent, would never survive because the current structure of the Soviet Union is such that each member of the union is economically dependent on the other. . . . If Ukraine becomes independent, it won't break the existing economic ties it has with Russia or any other republic. As an independent nation, we would retain those ties which are advantageous to us and likewise, I'm sure, Russia would maintain those which benefit it. . . .

Q: Is it true that the communists are trying to co-opt the national liberation movements and reimpose a totalitarian system?

A: You have to understand that what the communists are most afraid of is a market economy—that would make some 15 million bureaucrats expendable. Naturally, they don't want to lose their privileges; they are doing everything in their power to impede the march toward such an economy.

. . . Some of the more pragmatic communists are anticipating the future and taking steps to save themselves. Those communists in Western Ukraine who lost their seats in government left the party and became democrats. Now they serve us the same way they once served the party.

Christine Demkowych, "Vyacheslav Chornovil: Why the West Has So Much Stake in the Ukrainian Drama," *Los Angeles Times*, June 30, 1991, p. M3.

Document 26: Lithuania's Drive for Independence

Under intense economic pressure, Lithuania was forced to withdraw its first declaration of secession issued in early 1990. Despite military intervention in January 1991, Lithuania succeeded in its second attempt to gain independence in May 1991.

Q: Recently, Gorbachev has been successful in working out an agreement with the leaders of nine republics, including [Russian President Boris] Yeltsin. Does that leave the Baltic states, Georgia and Armenia, a bit more isolated?

A: It may be that this way he has created a possibility for the Baltic countries to separate, to remain stable, to save face. Now the Soviet Union does as they want. It's one of the possibilities.

Q: If there is a way out, and there is a new union of the nine, what kind of relations would the nine have to the others?

A: These relations would be the same as with foreign countries. It would be normal. But, we don't trust very much. At the same time they [the Kremlin] are continuing the violent actions.

Q: So in a way, this agreement has made it more difficult for you? If, however, there is a new union of the nine, do you envision a situation where Lithuania would have a special relation or would it just be another independent country?

A: It could be either way. It could be that the Soviet Union would like to retaliate and create economic hardships for these republics by this action, forcing them to regret their actions.

Q: Let me ask you about the economic situation. Your former prime minister, Kazimiera Prunskiene, who at the time had high approval ratings, introduced some economic reforms that were unpopular—price increases, so forth. Her argument at the time was that she took the unpopular but necessary step to raise prices and she was not supported by the group you led. She resigned in part over this.

A: The existing prime minister also raised the prices. That is always, in any country, an unpopular step. Her method was different, though. Raising prices without implementing compensation was strange. . . . They knew that the Soviets were preparing for aggression and they wanted to exploit that unrest, because they knew that the price-raising would create a great deal of instability.

Q: She also criticized you for being too hard in negotiating vis-a-vis Gorbachev.

A: Right now, the most difficult and the most responsible steps are being taken and are being made with my personal input. As far as flexibility and negotiating with Gorbachev go, we are frequently confronted with that situation. Their position is that we are a constituent republic and if we want to separate, we must go the way that involves Soviet loyalty. The Soviets feel that annexation obligates us in their constitution. We adopted our own constitution and declarations and believe that no other constitution is valid. I think there seems to be the desire to create the opinion that I am not suitable as a negotiator with Gorbachev—but that is only talk.

Robert Scheer, "Vytautas Landsbergis: Navigating Through Treacherous Shoals for Lithuania's Independence," *Los Angeles Times*, May 26, 1991.

Glossary

ANCC All National Congress of Chechen People, more commonly known as NCCP (National Congress of Chechen People). In 1991, ANCC appointed Dzhakhar Dudayev president of the Chechnya-Ingushetia Autonomous Region and declared sovereignty from Russia.

apparatchik(i) Communist bureaucrats.

CIA Central Intelligence Agency (U.S.).

Congress of People's Deputies Formed in 1988 by Mikhail Gorbachev as an alternate power base to the Communist Party–controlled government institutions. The Congress became the highest ruling authority in the Soviet Union and elected Gorbachev president.

coup d'etat The violent overthrow or alteration of an existing government by a small group.

CPSU Communist Party of the Soviet Union. The CPSU established and maintained the Communist one-party rule in the Soviet Union from 1917 to 1991. The CPSU controlled all aspects of Soviet economic, political, military, and cultural life until the end of the 1980s.

DOD Department of Defense (U.S.).

Duma The elected assembly in tsarist Russia, instituted by Nicholas II in 1906. The Revolution of 1917 dissolved the institution, but it has since been revived and functions as Russia's lower house of parliament today.

GDR German Democratic Republic (East Germany).

glasnost A Soviet policy permitting open discussion of political and social issues and freer dissemination of news and information.

Hind Soviet/Russian helicopter gunship.

IDPs Internally Displaced Persons. People who wish to flee local persecution, war, or human rights abuses but either cannot or do not wish to cross an international border.

INF Intermediate-range Nuclear Forces.

junta A group of persons controlling a government, especially after a revolutionary seizure of power.

KGB The Soviet secret police.

mujahedin An Afghan revolutionary soldier whose goal is to force the Soviet Union out of Afghanistan and establish an Islamic regime.

MVD Soviet Ministry of Internal Affairs. Special forces that patrolled borders to prevent emigration or internal movement of Soviet citizens.

neformaly Informal groups who used glasnost to promote single-issue reforms.

nomenklatura System of patronage used to reward and promote people who have proven to be reliable and/or loyal members of the Party.

NSC National Security Council (U.S.).

OMON Special Mission Militia Detachments. Special forces used by the Interior Ministry during a state of emergency.

perestroika Policy of economic and governmental reform instituted by Gorbachev.

putsch A secretly plotted and suddenly executed attempt to overthrow a government.

SDI Strategic Defense Initiative; a missile defense system.

START Strategic Arms Reduction Treaty. The agreement reached between the United States and the former Soviet Union on July 31, 1991; the treaty established significant reductions and limitations of strategic offensive arms, such as missile launchers, warheads, and heavy bombers.

START II A pact established on January 3, 1993, between the United States and Russia to reduce long-range nuclear arsenals.

SALT Strategic Arms Limitation Treaty.

SALT I An agreement reached on May 26, 1972, between the Soviet Union and the United States to halt testing of nuclear weapons and cap the increase in numbers of weapons.

SALT II An agreement reached on June 18, 1979, between the Soviet Union and the United States to further limit numbers of nuclear weapons and delivery systems.

Discussion Questions

Chapter 1: Prelude to the Collapse

1. Seweryn Bialer argues that Gorbachev's programs of perestroika and glasnost exposed a crisis of leadership in the Soviet system. According to Bialer, how did Communist leaders become entrenched in their positions of power? How did this lead to the downfall of the Soviet system?

2. Richard V. Allen contends that U.S. president Ronald Reagan pursued a military arms buildup to push the Soviet Union into bankruptcy. What specific policies did the Reagan administration implement? What finally caused the collapse of the Soviet Union, according to Allen?

3. Leonard Silk maintains that the need for economic reform was recognized by the time Andropov took power. What were some of the economic problems as described by Silk? And what types of reform did Soviet economists envision?

4. The explosion at Chernobyl in April 1986 was the worst nuclear accident in history. According to Sergei Roy, how did Soviet citizens view their government prior to the accident? How did they view it afterward?

Chapter 2: Attempts at Reforming the Government

1. S. Frederick Starr contends that perestroika was an attempt by the Soviet leadership to co-opt the thriving underground economy. What economic pressures led to the creation of this underground economy, according to Starr? What evidence of economic pressures does he present? Cite the text to support your answer.

2. Perestroika was an attempt at limited liberalization of the totalitarian Soviet society, in Richard Pipes's opinion. What were Gorbachev's reasons for starting his reform programs? And why was the Soviet Union in danger of collapse when the programs failed?

3. According to Stephen Sestanovich, pressure from the West for political reform within the Communist regime contributed to the collapse of the Soviet Union. What demands were placed on the Soviet Union by the United States? What conditions compelled the Soviet Union to accede to the West's demands?

4. The policies of perestroika and glasnost allowed dissidents to express opposition to the Soviet Communist regime. According to Geoffrey Hosking, what issues did the first opposition groups organize around? What events allowed their transformation into opposition parties?

Chapter 3: Disintegration of Empire

1. The Soviet military's failure in Afghanistan undermined citizens' support for the Communist regime, asserts Anthony Arnold. Coit D. Blacker contends that the fall of the Eastern European socialist governments resulted in a loss of international standing for the Soviet Union and undermined citizens' support of Soviet leadership. In what ways are their arguments similar? In what ways are they different? Cite the text to support your argument.

2. Martha Brill Olcott describes the ethnic conflicts that erupted throughout the Soviet Union after Gorbachev introduced perestroika and glasnost. According to Olcott, what conditions prompted the rise of nationalist movements in the republics? What effect did ethnic conflicts have on reform?

3. Just as elections and roundtable negotiations were the beginning of the downfall of the Eastern European regimes, Martin Malia argues, the June 1991 elections in the Russian republic were the start of the collapse of the Soviet Union. What similarities does Malia find between the two situations? Given that he wrote prior to the collapse of the USSR, was he correct or incorrect in his predictions? Provide examples from the text.

4. Timothy Garton Ash describes the events surrounding the fall of the Berlin Wall. What events sparked the downfall of the East German Communist dictatorship? What was the most important event, in Ash's opinion? How did this event result in the overthrow of the regime?

Chapter 4: Collapse of the Union

1. The August 1991 coup failed because the program of glasnost had exposed the illegitimacy of the Soviet regime, according to Michael Mandelbaum. What weaknesses of the Communist regime were revealed by glasnost? How did openness in Soviet society further erode the Communist government's power? Use examples from the text to support your answers.

2. Gabriel Schoenfeld states that the leaders of the August 1991 coup could not rely on support from the Soviet military. What was

the condition of the Soviet army, according to Schoenfeld? What led to the development of this condition?

3. Martin Malia explains that the transformation of the Soviet republics' economies into free markets is the final stage of the collapse of the Soviet regime. In his opinion, why did perestroika fail to revive the Soviet economy? Why was it absolutely imperative to dismantle the socialist system to promote economic reform? Cite the text to support your answer.

4. The Draft Union Treaty, which would have preserved a confederation of the Soviet republics, fell short because Ukraine withdrew from the agreement. According to Robert Cullen, why was Ukraine so important to the treaty? What factors led to the withdrawal of Ukraine's support? Why did Ukrainians repudiate the treaty?

Chapter 5: Strife in the Former Union
1. The war between Armenia and Azerbaijan over the ethnic enclave of Nagorno-Karabakh has produced hundreds of thousands of refugees. According to Arif Yunusov, what percentage of Armenia's population was made up of Azeris before the war? What Soviet policies contributed to the ethnic diversity in the region?

2. Vera Tolz argues that the war in Chechnya bodes ill for the future stability of Russia. Why did the Russian government react so violently to Chechnya's attempted secession from the federation, according to Tolz?

3. The overthrow of Zviad Gamsakhurdia in the republic of Georgia is chronicled by Ken Gluck. What faction was behind the coup d'état? Why did the coup leaders fear the citizens of Georgia?

4. Robert Cullen describes the relationship between Russia and the other former Soviet republics in the wake of the collapse. What were some of the contentious issues between the republics? What was the effect of these tensions on Russians and ethnic minorities within Russia?

Chronology

December 26, 1979
The Soviet military invades neighboring Afghanistan.

November 1982
Leonid Brezhnev dies and is succeeded as general secretary of the Communist Party by Yuri Andropov, former head of the KGB.

February 1984
Yuri Andropov dies unexpectedly, and the aged Konstantin Chernenko is chosen to fill the post of general secretary.

March 1985
Konstantin Chernenko dies, and Mikhail Gorbachev, the youngest member of the Politburo, is quickly appointed general secretary.

April 1985
At a plenum of the Central Committee of the Supreme Soviet, Gorbachev outlines a program of "reform" but gives few specific proposals. Gorbachev also executes a number of changes in the leadership of the Communist Party, bringing younger, like-minded reformers (including Boris Yeltsin) into positions of power.

November 1985
Gorbachev and U.S. president Ronald Reagan meet in Geneva, Switzerland, for an arms control summit. They agree to a series of meetings in the future .

February–March 1986
At the 27th Party Congress in Moscow, Gorbachev calls for radical reform of the Soviet economy. Yeltsin speaks out against the abuse of privilege by Communist *apparatchiks* (bureaucrats), signaling the beginning of political reforms. More changes in the leadership are made.

April 26, 1986
The reactor at the Chernobyl nuclear facility in Ukraine explodes, resulting in the worst nuclear disaster in history. Soviet announcements on the situation downplay the extent of damage, and Gorbachev makes no official statement on the catastrophe until May 14.

October 1986
Gorbachev and Reagan meet in Reykjavik, Iceland, to discuss cuts in conventional and nuclear weapons, but they reach no agreements.

December 1986
Riots break out in Alma Ata, the capital of Kazakhstan, after Gorbachev removes longtime Kazakh Communist Party chief Dinmukhamed Kunaev from his position. Gorbachev invites Andrei Sakharov to return from political exile. Between 1986 and 1988, hundreds of political prisoners are released from prison.

January 1987
At a Central Committee plenum, Gorbachev proposes a series of political reforms, including elections for government posts and the possibility that non-Party members can hold such posts.

June 1987
At meetings of the Central Committee and the Supreme Soviet, Gorbachev and Minister of Finance Nikolai Ryzhkov condemn the Soviet system of central economic planning. A law granting independence to economic enterprises is enacted.

July–November 1987
Gorbachev proposes the elimination of intermediate-range nuclear missiles from the American and Soviet arsenals.

November 1987
Yeltsin is publicly denounced and demoted after he criticizes Gorbachev and other Communist leaders.

December 1987
Gorbachev takes his first trip to America for a third meeting with Reagan. He is greeted with enthusiasm by Americans. The heads of state sign a ban on intermediate-range nuclear missiles.

February 1988
Gorbachev proposes to withdraw all Soviet troops from Afghanistan starting in May 1988. The withdrawal is completed in February 1989.

February–April 1988
Ethnic violence and civil disorder erupt in Nagorno-Karabakh and other areas of Azerbaijan. Armenians within the ethnic enclave want to unify the territory with the Armenian republic.

May 29–June 2, 1988
Reagan arrives in Moscow for a three-day meeting with Gorbachev, the fourth summit between the two leaders.

June 28, 1988
Gorbachev proposes the formation of the Congress of People's Deputies and the election of a Soviet president.

June–July 1988
Tensions increase between Armenia and Azerbaijan over control of the Nagorno-Karabakh region. The Armenian Supreme Soviet votes to annex the area, but both Azerbaijan and the central Soviet government reject this move.

October 1988
Gorbachev is appointed chairman of the Presidium of the USSR Supreme Soviet, consolidating his power as leader of the Soviet Union.

November 1988
Estonia claims the right to overrule laws and decrees passed by the central government.

December 1988
Addressing the United Nations in New York City, Gorbachev announces that the Soviet Union will withdraw a significant number of troops from Eastern Europe.

January 1989
Estonia passes a law making the Estonian language the official language of government affairs and education. By October 1989, half of the republics have adopted corresponding measures.

February 1989
Discussions begin between the Communist Polish government and leaders of the prodemocracy Solidarity movement.

March 1989
Elections are held for the Congress of People's Deputies. Many Communist Party candidates lose, while many republic nationalist leaders and democratic reformers win.

April 1989
Police and soldiers attack a crowd of nationalist demonstrators in Tbilisi, the capital of Georgia. Nineteen people are killed.

May 1989
Estonia and Lithuania declare sovereignty. Latvia, the third Baltic republic, follows in July.

June 1989
Democratic elections in Poland bring an end to Communist rule in that country. In early July, Gorbachev declares that the Eastern European countries are free to decide their own political futures.

July 1989
The Inter-Regional Group is formed within the Congress of People's Deputies. The coalition unites democratic reformers and republic nationalists in opposition to the Communist government.

November 9, 1989
The Berlin Wall is opened. Between October 1989 and January 1990, all of the remaining Communist governments of Eastern Europe (Czechoslovakia, Hungary, East Germany, Romania, and Bulgaria) are toppled.

January 1990
Armenia and Azerbaijan prepare to go to war over Nagorno-Karabakh. Soviet troops are sent to Azerbaijan in response to the state of emergency.

February 1990
Gorbachev proposes that the Communist Party relinquish its monopoly of power. In elections for local offices throughout the union, Communist Party candidates are defeated by republic nationalists and reformers. The Party begins to lose many members.

March 1990
Lithuania declares independence. Soviet tanks are sent into the capital of Vilnius and supplies of oil and food are cut off by the central authorities. After two months of confrontation, Lithuania rescinds its declaration.

April 1990
Gorbachev abandons a radical economic reform plan that would shift the Soviet Union to a free-market economy in five hundred days. Food and other goods become scarce in stores.

May–June 1990
Boris Yeltsin is elected chairman of the Russian parliament. Two weeks later, Russia asserts its right to overrule Soviet laws. By year's end, all of the republics declare their sovereignty.

September 1990
The Supreme Soviet grants Gorbachev the power to rule by presidential decree. In December it grants more far-reaching power. Nevertheless, rumors begin to circulate about a possible coup attempt by conservative Communists who oppose Gorbachev's policies.

November 1990
A draft treaty is negotiated between the central government and the republics to reform but preserve the union.

January 1991
Soviet troops seize newspaper publishers and television stations in the capitals of the Baltic republics of Latvia and Lithuania. Fourteen demonstrators are killed in Vilnius while resisting the troops, and four are killed in Riga.

March 1991
In a unionwide referendum, Soviet citizens are asked if they support preserving the union. Many of the republics also poll their citizens asking whether they support sovereignty. The results of the referendum are thus inconclusive.

June 1991
Yeltsin is elected president of Russia. Many democratic reformers are elected to office throughout Russia.

August 18–21 1991
Gorbachev is placed under house arrest at his vacation dacha in the Crimea. The State Committee for the State of Emergency announces that Vice President Gennadi Yanayev has replaced Gorbachev. Tanks are ordered onto the streets of Moscow, but most Soviet soldiers disobey orders to quell demonstrations. Yeltsin spearheads resistance to the coup d'état, which collapses after three days.

August 24, 1991
Gorbachev resigns as general secretary of the Communist Party.

August–September 1991
One by one, the republics declare independence.

October 1991
Gorbachev and the leaders of nine republics sign a treaty forming an economic community that preserves the remnants of the Soviet Union.

December 1991
Leaders of Russia, Ukraine, and Belarus found the Commonwealth of Independent States and invite the other republics to join, preempting the earlier treaty.

December 25, 1991
Gorbachev resigns as president of the Soviet Union. The following day, the union formally dissolves.

For Further Research

Books

Victoria E. Bonnell, Ann Cooper, and Gregory Freidin, *Russia at the Barricades: Eyewitness Accounts of the August 1991 Coup.* New York: M.E. Sharpe, 1994.

Christian Science Monitor editors, *Chronicles of the Soviet Coup, 1990–1992: A Reader in Soviet Politics.* Madison, WI: Brown & Benchmark, 1992.

Fred Coleman, *The Decline and Fall of the Soviet Empire: Forty Years That Shook the World, from Stalin to Yeltsin.* New York: St. Martin's Press, 1996.

Robert V. Daniels, *Russia's Transformation: Snapshots of a Crumbling System.* Lanham, MD: Rowman & Littlefield, 1997.

Anne De Tinguy, *Fall of the Soviet Empire.* New York: Eastern European Monographs, 1997.

Mikhail Gorbachev, *Memoirs.* New York: Doubleday, 1996.

Anthony Jones, *End of the Union: Social Revolution and the Collapse of Soviet Communism.* Boulder, CO: Westview Press, 1997.

John Keep, *Last of the Empires: A History of the Soviet Union, 1945–1991.* New York: Oxford University Press, 1997.

Ruslan Khasbulatov with Richard Sakwa, ed., *The Struggle for Russia: Power and Change in the Democratic Revolution.* New York: Routledge, 1993.

Joe M. King, *Russian Journal: During the August Coup of '91.* Macon, GA: Mercer University Press, 1992.

William Moskoff, *Hard Times: Impoverishment and Protest in the Perestroika Years: The Soviet Union, 1985–1991.* New York: M.E. Sharpe, 1993.

Laurie Nadel, *The Kremlin Coup.* Brookfield, CT: Millbrook Press, 1992.

George J. Neimanis, *The Collapse of the Soviet Empire: A View from Riga.* Westport, CT: Greenwood, 1997.

Pavel Palazchenko and Don Oberdorfer, *My Years with Gorbachev and Shevardnadze: The Memoir of a Soviet Interpreter.* University Park: Pennsylvania State University Press, 1997.

Boris Pankin, *Last 100 Days of the Soviet Union*. New York: St. Martin's Press, 1996.

David Pryce-Jones, *The Strange Death of the Soviet Empire*. New York: Henry Holt, 1995.

David Satter, *Age of Delirium: The Rise and Fall of the Soviet Union*. New York: Knopf, 1996.

G.R. Urban, *End of Empire: The Demise of the Soviet Union*. Washington, DC: American University Press, 1992.

Rachel Walker, *Six Years That Shook the World: Perestroika—The Impossible Project*. New York: St. Martin's Press, 1993.

Periodicals

George Berkin, "Secession Blues," *National Review*, September 9, 1991.

James H. Billington, "Russia's Fever Break," *Wilson Quarterly*, Autumn 1991.

Abraham Brumberg, "The Road to Minsk," *New York Review of Books*, January 30, 1992.

Vladimir Bukovsky, "Tumbling Back to the Future," *New York Times Magazine*, January 12, 1992.

Massimo Calabresi, "At Yeltsin's Side," *National Review*, September 23, 1991.

————, "Mikhail Gorbachev's Unintended Consequences," *National Review*, January 20, 1992.

Robert Cullen, "The Coup," *New Yorker*, November 4, 1991.

Paul Dukes, "From Soviet to Russian History," *History Today*, August 1993.

Lawrence Elliott and David Satter, "Three Days That Shook the World," *Reader's Digest*, January 1992.

Gregory Freidin, "To the Barricades," *New Republic*, September 30, 1991.

Thomas Goltz, "Chechnya and the Bear's Long Shadow," *Nation*, February 10, 1997.

Mikhail Gorbachev, interviewed by John Kohan and Strobe Talbott, "I Want to Stay the Course," *Time*, December 23, 1991.

Edward A. Hewett, "The New Soviet Plan," *Foreign Affairs*, Winter 1990/1991.

Vitaly Korotich, "The Ukraine Rising," *Foreign Policy*, Winter 1991/1992.

Martin Malia, "The August Revolution," *New York Review of Books*, September 26, 1991.

James A. Nathan, "Boris Yeltsin's Fatal Folly," *USA Today*, July 1996.

Newsweek, "The Year of Yeltsin," December 30, 1991.

Boris Dmitrievich Pankin, "The Dangers of Nationalism," *Vital Speeches of the Day*, October 15, 1991.

Richard Pipes, "Russia's Past, Russia's Future," *Commentary*, June 1996.

Bill Powell, "A Religious War?" *Newsweek*, October 14, 1996.

David E. Powell, "The Revival of Religion," *Current History*, October 1991.

David Remnick, "The Counterrevolutionary," *New York Review of Books*, March 25, 1993.

Harrison Evans Salisbury, "Groping Toward Democracy," *American Heritage*, February/March 1992.

David Satter, "Why Gorbachev Lost," *National Review*, September 23, 1991.

David K. Shipler, "After the Coup," *New Yorker*, November 11, 1991.

Dimitri K. Simes, "Russia Reborn," *Foreign Policy*, Winter 1991/1992.

Andrew Solomon, "Three Days in August," *New York Times Magazine*, September 29, 1991.

William V. Wallace, "The Democratic Development of the Former Soviet Union," *History Today*, July 1994.

Boris Yeltsin and Catherine A. Fitzpatrick, "Yeltsin," *Newsweek*, May 2, 1994.

Leonid Zagalsky, "Social Realism Bites the Dust," *Bulletin of the Atomic Scientists*, March 1992.

Index